Fritted glazing prototype for the University of Ottawa STEM Complex

Study model for the Federal Justice Complex, Montreal

Sketches for the performance pavilion at Nathan Phillips Square in Toronto

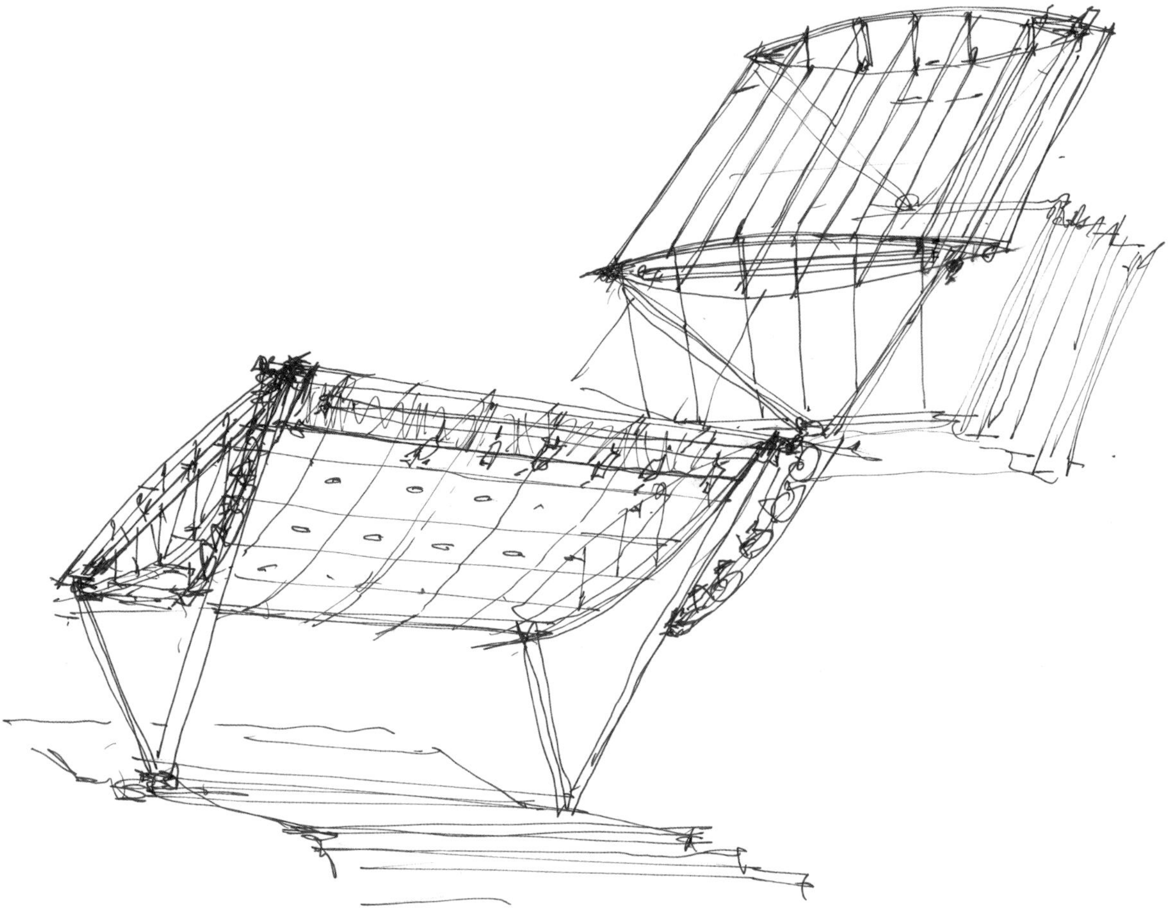

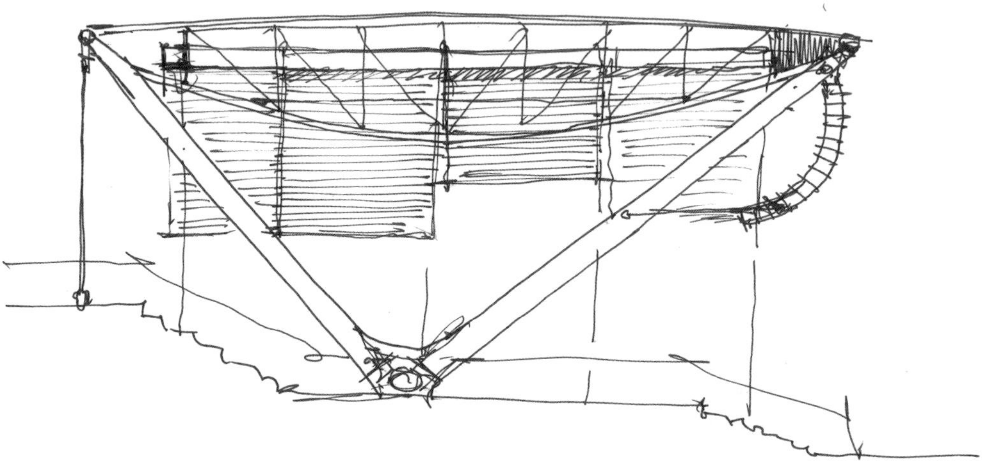

Perkins&Will Toronto's studio at 110 Yonge Street

Surgically replacing the cores in the Bank of Canada

Episodes in Public Architecture

ORO
EDITIONS

Perkins&Will

Episodes in Public Architecture

Andrew Frontini

ORO Editions
Publishers of Architecture, Art, and Design
Gordon Goff: Publisher

www.oroeditions.com
info@oroeditions.com

Published by ORO Editions

Author: Andrew Frontini
Book Design: IN-FO.CO (Adam Michaels and Michael Aberman)
Project Manager: Jake Anderson

10 9 8 7 6 5 4 3 2 1 First Edition

ISBN: 978-1-961856-41-7

Prepress and Print work by ORO Editions Inc
Printed in China

ORO Editions makes a continuous effort to minimize the overall carbon footprint of its publications. As part of this goal, ORO, in association with Global ReLeaf, arranges to plant trees to replace those used in the manufacturing of the paper produced for its books. Global ReLeaf is an international campaign run by American Forests, one of the world's oldest nonprofit conservation organizations. Global ReLeaf is American Forests' education and action program that helps individuals, organizations, agencies, and corporations improve the local and global environment by planting and caring for trees.

Contents

Andrew on bass guitar with Gord Downie (right) of the Slinks, 1982

Introduction

Ian Chodikoff

When Andrew first shared the draft for *Episodes*, it brought into focus memories that inspired me to become an architect, while validating my views on design collaboration and the future potential of architectural practice. Andrew's candid retelling of his experiences in becoming the closest thing to a self-actualized Canadian architect validates several of my personal beliefs in what constitutes a great architect in a world that prioritizes superficial imagery over mutual trust and dialogue.

A few years younger than Andrew, I'm a member of Generation X, an oft-disgruntled and overlooked demographic, but perhaps the first generation to eschew the use of 45-degree angles in architecture (read the chapter on the Meadowvale Community Centre and Library, page 218, to see Andrew's aversion to this set-squared angle of condemnation) and completely transition into the digital era. We are also a generation of architects condemned to practice sandwiched between the unrelenting old workhorses known as the Baby Boomers and our younger Millennial colleagues. Anecdotally speaking, we are also likely to be more cynical about empty formalism and "starchitecture" than Millennials and have likely experienced overt gender and racial discrimination just before the profession woke up to the endemic challenges proactively being dealt with today. It is essential to introduce this context because Andrew had to navigate through it, a zeitgeist moment in time that not only developed his humility and resiliency as an architect, but undoubtedly influenced his lifelong passion for music.

While Douglas Coupland's 1991 novel *Generation X: Tales for an Accelerated Culture* kicked off the angst of the decade as we graduated from architecture school, it was Rem Koolhaas and Bruce Mau's massive *S,M,L,XL* (1995) that broke ground for a new millennium—and a generation of architects. Working as a recent University of British Columbia architecture graduate in Singapore, I bought my 6-pound copy of Koolhaas's architectural rhetoric from a bookseller who pulled the brown-paper-wrapped treatise out from behind the counter. (The government banned the book for criticizing its approach to urban planning and design.) Fast-forward nearly 30 years, and the project credits roll on my computer screen just as Andrew's narrative fades to black in

Singapore, where he and architect Eladia Smoke are about to deliver a presentation at the World Architecture Festival about their respective firms' collaboration for Toronto Public Library's Dawes Road Library—a project representing both "culture as a verb," as Smoke puts it, and an inclusive approach to creating architecture driven by Indigenous principles associated with architecture and community. Projects like these, and the sophisticated authenticity of its architectural process, will undoubtedly signal the need for Andrew's next book.

Much has changed since Andrew described his first real architecture job, at Shore Tilbe Irwin & Partners circa 2000. Our profession has evolved from the theoretical architecture discourse circulating throughout the 1990s to a present-day focus on establishing meaningful relationships and mentorships with consultants, client groups, and diverse public stakeholders. We prioritize performance, inclusion, and engagement, while embracing regenerative design amidst a climate crisis and the reckoning that even the most energy-efficient building somehow contributes to our global climate crisis. We can't hide behind Le Corbusier glasses anymore. Andrew's famously colourful plaid sports jackets and self-deprecating humour are a testament to the leadership required of us when solving our clients' most urgent challenges.

This book showcases 11 significant projects through architectural drawings, photographs, diagrams, and narratives that dive deep into Andrew's experiences, philosophies, and personal growth. His career trajectory embodies his consistent philosophy of infusing cultural meaning and public life into architecture. He began his career by working on small-scale projects and mural paintings. Eventually, he led significant architectural projects, never letting hubris take hold over his desire to remain a lifelong learner inspired by the craft and knowledge of others, while being occasionally humbled through the tumult of creating a building for a client—one of whom, midwife Mary Sharpe, happened to have delivered two of his children.

I first met Andrew in 2005 when, as the editor of *Canadian Architect*, I was reviewing one of his earliest projects, the Whitby Public Library and Civic Square. Touring the building, I remember him pointing out what he considered to be various flaws in the building's design. At multiple points, gesturing to where he wanted "this," but the budget, client, or time frame gave him "that," I was impressed. Working with thousands of architects throughout my career, I seldom hear anyone openly point out aspects of their projects that fell short of their expectations. It is relatively easy for an architect to make a B+ building. But what sets a great architect apart is the continuous refinement achieved through successive projects and a growing body of experience to elevate a building to an A+ level.

Andrew's career is a story of how to complete A-level architecture. Producing award-winning buildings is elusive. Sometimes, you hit the mark. At other times, you are close. But one thing is for sure: You will never get there alone. You need the help and expertise of others. In Andrew's case, they can be far more senior to you, like Dimitri Simos from Thessaloniki. Or they can be younger, like Dan McTavish or Jon Loewen, two wunderkinds Andrew mentored before leading them through an innovative design process for the School of Continuing Studies at York University. Acknowledging and respecting other people's superpowers is a good look. At the very least, it will make people want to continue to work with you—and hire you.

A Taste of Public Life

In his fourth-year semester abroad in Rome, Andrew discovered "the potential of urban space to communicate ideas and frame human experience through theatrical means" via Francesco Borromini's Sant'Ivo alla Sapienza. It would be a few years after graduating from the University of Waterloo in 1991, and after he set up a mural painting operation, creating large-scale installations for bars, restaurants, and after-hours drinking establishments, playing guitar and singing in some of those same establishments, that he would work on a project that allowed him to test his ability to design public spaces.

In 2007, and still part of Shore Tilbe Irwin & Partners as the team lead, he was part of a consortium that included artist and academic Adrian Blackwell, architecture and landscape collective PLANT, and landscape architect Peter Schaudt, that won a competition to transform Nathan Phillips Square in front of Toronto City Hall. "In reimagining Nathan Phillips Square," Andrew writes, "we erased hierarchies to create a space of infinite possibility, which appropriately sets the context for civic governance and its relationship to the people."

Designing for Champions

The Hazel McCallion Academic Learning Centre, completed in 2007 at the University of Toronto Mississauga, marked a turning point in Andrew's career. I toured the building with him for a review that would appear in *Canadian Architect*. The library had a clear design concept: a wooden puzzle box representing the process of discovery and access to knowledge. It was also one of the first libraries where books played an overtly secondary role to a contemporary agora where students work on laptops rather than read physical books. Andrew writes, "While the puzzle box may have grown out of a desperate need for a hook at the time, circumstances and a committed client allowed us to deepen the metaphor." Not many architects would admit to developing a "hook" for their designs, even though we all know how vital a convincing narrative is, especially for public projects. Andrew's "hook" was genuine, and the project was better for it. Moreover, Andrew tells us the importance of having a "committed client" willing to trust, collaborate, and push us to do better in ways that I find inspiring. Designing institutional buildings is particularly challenging as they often involve committees and bureaucracies. Andrew was fortunate to have clients who can champion an architect's work just as they invest their careers into completing a building on their campus or in their community.

Having a championing client was the case for two buildings, Engineering 5 and 7, at the University of Waterloo, completed in 2018. The relationship with the university began 10 years prior, when Andrew first met the client team led by Sue Gooding, assistant to engineering dean Adel Sedra, campus architect Daniel Parent, and Ron Venter, who led the academic planning and programming of the new facility and remained Andrew's "greatest resource in translating the dean's vision and the needs of the various users." Meeting the user group, Frontini was "humbled by the depth and diversity of the engineer," admitting that "like many architects, I am prone to hubris." Keeping your ego in check is essential, as is appreciating the diversity of thought across the spectrum of design- and construction-related professionals.

When Andrew and the Perkins&Will team began the project, he had a new client with Pearl Sullivan as the chair of electrical engineering. Sullivan was, in Andrew's words, "tireless in her promotion of women in engineering and would not rest until the field was demographically and culturally transformed." For her, bringing diversity of thought, viewpoint, and capability was the only way to solve the world's most complex problems. She challenged her peers and students to fail publicly. "Not just to experiment, but to take big risks and share the embarrassments and lessons learned... 'Fail Forward' became the motto of her tenure."

It is apparent that Sullivan deeply impacted Andrew, judging by his writings elsewhere in the book. In the fall of 2018, Andrew watched Dean Sullivan preside over the grand-opening reception of the project while in the final stages of her battle with cancer, noting a sense of purpose and accomplishment in all who were present. "The ecstatic crowd was a testimony to the changing face of engineering. They were young, diverse, and dare I say beautiful in the passion and pride on their faces," he writes.

Coming to Terms With Oneself

Standing behind his client, Anne Bailey, the director of branch libraries for Toronto Public Library, in 2015, Andrew was presenting some early renderings for the new Albion Library in Rexdale, an area of Toronto recognized for its lack of social infrastructure and limited access to green spaces and recreation. "The last thing I need is another white, 50-year-old male architect dressed all in black telling me about how the design for our library needs to be all black and white with grey thrown in for a splash of colour," Bailey remarks. The city librarian added, "We've seen this before. It looks suburban." A third member of the client group likened the early design to a highway rest stop. With his tail between his legs, Andrew fully admits to not getting it right the first time, believing in the slow absorption process of knowledge while picking up all the nuances of a design challenge before synthesizing them. In other words, it takes time to get it right. The evolution of design is a conversation. Andrew writes, "Quite often, it is the most difficult conversations that prove to be catalytic, inspiring a new avenue of investigation or a focus of creative energy."

Be honest enough to show your process, even if your applicable project portfolio may not win you the commission–another bit of wisdom Andrew discusses. Sensing that he didn't have what it took to win the Daphne Cockwell Health Sciences Complex at Toronto Metropolitan University (2013-2019), he, along with Max Richter and Ryan Bragg from the Perkins&Will Vancouver studio, converted the firm's Toronto office into a gallery of exhibits for their second interview, summarizing key elements of their architectural approach and building an emotive narrative drawing upon lessons learned and collaborations earned. They won the project, which would have been disastrous without a strong client collaboration. "It is hard to appreciate the value that your client-side champions bring and the degree to which they protect the project from the institution's pathological impulses until they are no longer there," Andrew explains. "Like any large object, [the project] had a gravitational pull that attracted people and ideas to it, like so much space junk falling to earth. All we could do was roll with the punches and filter the constant request for new programs, departments, and 'novel ideas' through our professional gaze."

The Importance of Lifelong Learning

In the last chapter, dedicated to the Dawes Road branch of the Toronto Public Library, Andrew speaks to the need for architects to adapt and conceive of architecture differently, especially in the wake of the 2021 discovery of 215 Indigenous children buried in unmarked graves on the grounds of a residential school on the Tk'emlúps te Secwépemc First Nation in Kamloops, British Columbia, and the subsequent discovery of 182 unmarked graves at the former Kootenay Indian Residential School.

As we work through a new era of architectural thought resulting from the Truth and Reconciliation Commission of Canada, the Dawes Road Library represents an early example of this new paradigm. The project demanded a highly consultative, collaborative, and public design process. The brief also called for the inclusion of an Indigenous architect as an integral part of the team, with Eladia Smoke of Smoke Architecture proving to be an incredible learning partner in connecting an Indigenous worldview with Perkins&Will's Living Design philosophy.

"If the rest of the industry is pushing ahead in a mad rush to the end of civilization, meaningful dialogue can be hard to sustain across all fronts," Andrew writes. From architecture student to mature principal of a significant architectural practice, Andrew presents a solid narrative arc describing how he learns from mentors, mentees, collaborators, craftspeople, and clients who champion visions. Through lifelong learning and humility, he continues to grow through these "episodes" of wisdom, inspiring the rest of us to solidify our purpose while creating greater community and cultural expression.

Blanket study for Dawes Road Library

Touring Whitby Library under construction

Foundations: A Preface by the Author

Andrew Frontini

This book has a dual nature. First, it documents 11 projects, with architectural drawings, colour photographs, and illustrative diagrams on glossy paper, all in typical fashion for an architectural monograph. Second, it presents a set of narratives, each providing a very personal dive into my role and experience in the project's creation and a reflection on how the work has changed me, shaping my professional and private life. The resulting narratives appear in a distinct graphic and material format, inserted like so many pamphlets into the body of the monograph and deliberately interrupting its general flow. The design of the book is meant to be both practical and conceptual. You can look at the pictures and see how my work with the Perkins&Will Toronto and Ottawa studios has evolved over two decades, without getting bogged down in the fine print. If a project piques your interest, you can just as easily dive into the corresponding narrative and read about it at length. Conceptually, the idea of the insertion aligns with the trajectory of my career and its timing. I'm a Gen Xer operating between the more dominant Baby Boomer and Millennial generations, between the Cold War and globalization, between analog tech and AI, and a host of other antithetical paradigms. In an era of massive change, I've nonetheless pursued a consistent philosophy of practice focused on inserting cultural meaning and public life into every project brief.

I chose the 11 projects shown on these pages from the full output of my 30-year career because I felt that the experience of making them was especially worth sharing, and that together they provide insight into the arc that a career in architecture can take. The book is intended as both an instructive reflection and a projection forward. The voice is consistently mine, and it offers just one perspective on how these spaces came to be. My point of view evolves over time—from that of a rebellious young designer wresting control of a project from his boss to that of a seasoned design director in a big firm shaping the space for new voices to emerge. I am all over these projects, but I am by no means the only player. There were many participants, who would tell different and equally interesting stories about the buildings' design and construction. My architectural output has always been highly responsive to physical, cultural, and programmatic context.

The buildings don't all look the same—and they aren't meant to—but I think they do some of the same things, exploring themes that recur through different times and places, and that today, at our 110 Yonge Street studio in Toronto, we continue to build upon.

The Theatre of Life

> *"I am a sort of closet frontiersman. I am conducting a survey at the threshold of another world; a world which lies in the very midst of our busy city. My expeditions are solitary affairs, although there are many like me and I have often seen them. We are a loose association, who, weather permitting, can usually be found during the business lunch hour with our bodies pressed against a plywood hoarding, peering through the wire mesh into the fantastic realm of some great excavation. These excursions remind us all that the bright, new, and unforgivably dull structures that we must inhabit during the workday were once, at some stage in their history, worthy of fascination. They were worlds of curiosity, technical and otherwise, offering something of the spectacular and the sublime."*

The paragraph above comes from the introduction to my 1991 graduating thesis at the University of Waterloo School of Architecture. The thesis marks the emergence of key preoccupations that have informed my practice. My intent was to offer a critique of the architecture and public realm of the North American city (as typified by Toronto) in the late 1980s. The state of affairs—speculative development run wild, planning guidelines without teeth, and an architectural culture confined to little more than the surface of things—sparked the ire of my student-self. With such banality spreading like a cancer through the city, I found a counterpoint in the construction of the selfsame developments. The massive excavations and emerging superstructures were spectacular, texturally rich, and loaded with stories, if you knew how to read them.

Unfettered development was robbing Toronto's urban life of its vitality. Construction sites littered nearly every block. I thought one might recapture a fragment of the dwindling public realm from each by harnessing the spectacle of construction. One element of the thesis, "The Theatre of Demolition," allowed the general public an opportunity to occupy a protected enclosure, an extension of the city sidewalk, that cantilevered into the heart of an active demolition site. The thesis imagines a public realm full of sensory impact and layered narratives, with people, building materials, and construction equipment telling a story of the emerging city. The thesis also posits an architecture that speaks of its own making, rife with material and structural expression. And lastly, the proposal makes spectators and actors of us all, choreographing our movements through public space as a tale of our own civilization. The structures play a part as well—sometimes serving as an auditorium or stage set, and occasionally as protagonists themselves.

These preoccupations began to take shape even earlier, during my fourth-year semester abroad in Rome. There we studied, across many eras, the potential of urban space to communicate ideas and frame human experience through theatrical means. While the city offers numerous examples of how this can occur, two from the baroque era still resonate with me. The first is the Piazza di Sant'Ignazio, a wondrous piece of urban stagecraft by 18th-century architect Filippo Raguzzini. Beginning in 1727, a modest set of five infill buildings with shops in the lower storey and apartments above was erected across from the existing baroque church of Sant'Ignazio di Loyola in Campo Marzio (1650). Raguzzini treated the assemblage as pure poché, and sculpted the piazza into a theatre with multiple entrances and backstage niches where an endless set of plots and subplots can unfold. The church, for all its Counter-Reformation pomp and finery, can never be sure of holding the limelight, as it might be upstaged at any moment by a passing child or street vendor.

The second example is Francesco Borromini's tiny jewel of a chapel, Sant'Ivo alla Sapienza (1660). With its unorthodox helical lantern, Sant'Ivo represents to me the potential for a piece of architecture itself to behave as a protagonist in the drama of the city—its daily life and its evolution over time. Borromini gives us a particular kind of protagonist—complex, enigmatic, and utterly surprising. The subtlety with which Borromini's odd forms emerge from the complex urban fabric, and the notable differences between his design and its peers, must be read as intentional and as propelling a particular narrative about the city, the Catholic Church, and the architectural culture of the day.

Illustrations from an architectural thesis depicting “theatres” of demolition, excavation, and forming

Sketches of Piazza Sant'Ignazio (top) and Sant'Ivo alla Sapienza in Rome

If these two examples provide insight into how a work of architecture might set the stage for an urban experience and appear as protagonist within it, my studies in Rome also fueled an interest in another sort of storytelling. This might be described as architecture's internal narrative—one that has less to do with the way people inhabit space and the way buildings inhabit cities and more to do with how buildings are made, what they are made of, and how this in turn connects us to a time and a place. All cities are dynamic, constantly disintegrating and being rebuilt, as if to impress upon some unseen parental figure that we are in fact evolving, through the constant restructuring of our physical environment.

Rome is famously a city of ruins. The burden of the past is evident at every corner, rendered as a torturous struggle of maintenance and restoration against the forces of entropy and collapse. Progress seems impossible because the energy that might otherwise be directed toward it is consumed in supporting the crumbling edifice. What is gained from the sacrifice of progress is a particular form of beauty—the beauty of decay. Structures half-collapsed, half-rebuilt, and endlessly being restored behind a scrim of tattered scaffolding hold an endless fascination for me. They serve as reminders of society's heroic impulse to edify our dreams and myths, while also assuring us of the futility of the attempt. Rome tells the story of why things are built, when and how they are built, and why they are fated to disappear forever. It is the best built story ever—but that is not to say that its lessons are not transferable to a less storied context.

Setting the Stage

By the time my dissertation came due in August of 1991, the global economy was grinding to a halt and every crane on the Toronto skyline was idle. I graduated into an economy that had little need for inexperienced architects—and even less capacity to dream. There was, however, an informal churn that afforded a kind of living. I worked construction with a crew of other unemployed architects. We converted an ad agency into an auction house and built a laneway tower in Kensington Market. When that work dried up, I set up a mural-painting operation creating immersive, large-scale works in a series of bars, restaurants, and after-hours drinking establishments. In the evenings I would play the guitar and sing in some of those same establishments.

Eventually, I began to enjoy sporadic employment in three small architectural practices. The experiences at each proved to be formative. At Martin Liefhebber Architect, I was fortunate to work on Canada's first off-grid urban residence, the Canada Mortgage and Housing Corporation's model Healthy House. The 1,500-square-foot single-family house generated its own energy, treated its own water, and integrated urban agriculture. This house opened my eyes to the potential for architecture to address environmental issues and provide a revolutionary counterpoint to the waste and excess of consumer culture. At Natale Scott Browne, while designing modest public washrooms for city parks and highway rest stops, I was exposed to a culture of detail and materiality that aspired to create a uniquely Canadian regional modernism. And at Ferguson Ferguson Architects, I learned that architecture can have a very human personality, that it can make you laugh or inspire curiosity at almost any scale. The Fergusons turned simple additions and augmentations of existing buildings, such as new exit stairs or accessibility features, into urban follies full of wit and imagination. The joy of creating was reflected in a studio culture that was improvisational, interdisciplinary, and consistently joyful.

Each studio presented a clear set of values and a culture that supported the work. What they did not present to me was a pathway for bringing those values to society more broadly. Every architect wants to make an impact, but we aren't trained to manage or grow our enterprises as businesspeople. After seven years of schooling and two years of working, I felt that there had to be a better way, a way to think bigger and be paid for the value that we bring to the table as architects. The quest to combine and balance purpose, creativity, and business acumen would ultimately lead me to the global practice of Perkins&Will, where these conditions of practice are maintained in a delicate balance through constant dialogue.

I returned to Rome in the fall of 1993, this time as an adjunct professor for Waterloo's study abroad program. When the semester ended, I stayed on for a year, conducting what turned out to be an informal postgraduate research project. The project consisted of a series of large-format chalk drawings—nocturnal dramas played out against the architectural backdrop of ancient Rome and its modern suburbs. At the time, I viewed these drawings as part of an emerging art practice, divorced from my architectural career even though they revisited several of the key themes in my thesis, most notably the notion of the city as a stage upon which our collective life is played out.

I grew up in a family where everyone had claims to artistry. My father, a metallurgical engineer, painted in a studio on the ground floor of our old limestone house in Kingston, Ontario, and my mother remains active as a professional potter. During my teenage years, corporate pressures and a restless spirit kept my father away from the family home for extended periods. During one of these absences my brother and I took over his studio and established a unique sibling rivalry in drawing and painting. While architecture school interrupted my art practice, my brother went on to complete his MFA at Ohio State and is an established professional artist in the United States.

I returned from Rome to Toronto again in the early spring of 1994, with this small body of artwork and a child on the way. The recession had only deepened in my absence and work in architecture was neither readily available nor particularly appealing. Reflecting on this period, I am struck by how precarious it was and what a blessing that uncertainty turned out to be in the long run. Over a four-year period, I ran a hybrid practice that included exploratory painting and drawing, architectural illustration, mural painting, and music. At first glance, my chosen profession would seem to be the only thing missing. But in fact, it was always there as the underlying preoccupation. I even see it in the improvised instrumental music my friends and I generated as a band called Quadruped, in part because our sessions helped shape my future approaches to collaboration.

Two more bodies of work emerged during this period. The first was a series of chalk-and-pastel drawings I called "Typologies." Based on the Renaissance tradition of the capriccio, these drawings offered fantastic speculations on the construction and occupation of a series of monumental building types. A flying stadium, a floating prison, a subterranean hospital—each was a protagonist in the complex story of a city in the distant future or unrecorded past. The second body of work, which I began in 2000, was a series of larger-format oil paintings entitled "Rituals," which presented an architectural framework for imaginary non-denominational rites that mark major life events, such as birth, sexual initiation, and death.

By this point, the economy had begun to recover and I found full-time employment as an architect. For several years I tried to

Il Messaggero, chalk on paper, 1994

Stadium, chalk on paper, 1994

Prison, chalk on paper, 1995

Baptism, oil on canvas, 2000

balance my artistic practice against working and parenting. I finally let painting go in the early 2000s, as I joined the established Toronto firm of Shore Tilbe Irwin & Partners and gained a steady income—along with a substantial opportunity to shape public life in built form. The transition marked the end of my solitary speculations. While it seems fitting that the crafting of real public space should be a group activity, the isolation and disruption of my early career have never struck me as lost time, but rather as an opportunity to dream, to formulate a position that would fuel my design explorations for decades to come. At Shore Tilbe Irwin, I was fortunate to join an established practice that, while struggling with its identity and design culture, had a deep portfolio of civic and institutional buildings, which would serve as a foundation for a new generation of public architecture. And when Shore Tilbe Irwin merged with Perkins&Will in 2010, we became part of a global community of like-minded peers—people with whom one could really make a difference.

Design Powers Communities

> *"We believe design can be a catalyst for social change. In our work we innovate program and typology to create vibrant public realms that connect people to each other, their shared history, and the world around them. We are equally interested in the performative and poetic potential of our designs, both of which are explored through innovations in materiality, structure, and the building envelope. What our designs do and what they say can strengthen existing cultures and shape new ones."*

I wrote this statement midway through 2020, just as COVID-19 was gaining momentum, in order to capture the core preoccupations of the Toronto and Ottawa studios of Perkins&Will—not just the projects for which I am the lead designer but the broader portfolio for which I provide general oversight. The statement is intended to be specific in its intent but broadly applicable to a wide range of investigations, be they in public architecture, landscape, urban design, or corporate interiors. At the core of each of these disciplines and their projects is a conviction that the public realm must be central to all inhabited space, for it is the stage upon which culture is expressed and developed. I include the above statement in toto to show how my early preoccupation with the theatre of public life evolved over time and through many projects into a living culture of practice for our large creative team. The two projects described below should illustrate our approach and will hopefully contextualize the "insertions" that follow.

The Agora and the Theatre

In 2007, I was part of a consortium that won an international competition to redesign the plaza in front of Toronto's City Hall (1965)—an iconic design by Finnish architect Viljo Revell. The team comprised Shore Tilbe Irwin (led by me); artist, academic, and urban designer Adrian Blackwell; the architecture and landscape collective PLANT; and Chicago-based landscape architect Peter Schaudt. Beating out 47 other entries from around the world, our scheme was selected for its sensitivity and deference to the legacy architecture, its deep green strategy, and its unique proposition to celebrate the theatre of public life in an open democracy. Adrian brought forward philosopher Richard Sennett's *The Spaces of Democracy* (The University of Michigan, 1998) as the conceptual underpinning for our submission. In his telling, two key spaces served the Athenian democracy: the agora, a place of commercial, intellectual, and cultural exchange, and the theatre, the space where democratic government plays out. If we interpret Revell's masterwork in Sennett's terms, the theatre, or council chamber, appears as a sculptural object levitating above the agora, a.k.a. Nathan Phillips Square, a large adjacent plaza that hosts markets, fairs, celebrations, and demonstrations throughout the year. Our design proposal focused on the interchangeability of roles in a democratic space. Who is performing? Who is the spectator? Where is the stage, and where are the balconies? We heightened the connectivity between the various levels of public space in Revell's original design with the deliberate intent of creating ambiguity about the roles that people assume in public life. In reimagining Nathan Phillips Square, we erased hierarchies to create a space of infinite possibility, which appropriately sets the context for civic governance and its relationship to the people.

Revell's architecture resembles a sculpture by Isamu Noguchi, with defined figures interacting on a modernist tableau. Recognizing its near-perfection, we established narrow margins in which our design approach could respectfully manifest itself. Our insertions fell into discrete categories: detailed material overlays that enriched the human experience at the most intimate scale of contact but were digestible by the original construct, landscape elements that should read as both supportive of and separate from Revell's composition, and lastly a singular new protagonist—a permanent stage on the square. The stage captures the essence of our entire proposal. It is an autonomous object that sits in dialogue with Revell's originals, sharing some DNA but obviously of another era. It serves literally as a stage, with a subterranean dressing room, green room, and VIP access. It is also a grandstand for watching events on the square. It is an intimate public space that offers shade and comfort within the massive modernist plaza. And like the grand stair of a beaux-arts opera house, it is a piece of connective infrastructure that puts the audience on centre stage.

One critical lesson for my practice from the revitalization of Nathan Phillips Square is this ability of an architectural element to play multiple, shifting roles in a public space—and in so doing to transform our relationships to one another. Like actors, these catalytic protagonists have something to say, are immediately legible as characters, and have the potential to change the course of events at a variety of scales. The collaboration itself provided a second critical lesson. Our process was energizing, open, and focused on harvesting the combined talents of everyone present to arrive at the best idea. PLANT curated the team and led the competitions strategy. Partner Lisa Rapoport informed me I had been chosen for my approach to drawing, for my "hand," as she put it. Later in the project, we would struggle with the design of the theatre roof. A young intern architect, Lia Maston, came forward to challenge and reset the design trajectory, and I was grateful for her collaboration on the final form of the theatre. While I had been focused on imposing my will on the established culture at Shore Tilbe Irwin, the Nathan Phillips Square competition and its subsequent execution over nearly a decade provided me with many opportunities to reset my ego and tune my ears to what others had to say. In general, I have tried to carry forward the lesson that, on a design team, we all have dual roles to play, one functional and the other creative. Today, my role is often to listen, to look, and to encourage the best ideas, regardless of their source. Perhaps I have evolved from the "hand" to the "watcher of hands."

Competition illustration for the revitalization of Nathan Phillips Square

The theatre in the context of Revell's City Hall

Nathan Phillips Square on New Year's Eve, 2015

The Chain of Public Space

Over a 15-year period, between 2003 and 2018, I was fortunate to oversee the design and construction of four interconnected projects at the University of Toronto Mississauga campus. Together, these projects allowed us to explore an evolving thesis about public space and material expression. The UTM campus began construction in 1969, with a plan for a perimeter road within which academic and residential buildings floated in a bucolic parkland. The oldest permanent building, a brutalist-era "land ark" containing a host of academic, research, and administrative functions, dominated the centre of the composition for decades. In 2000, the university commissioned a new master plan by Sterling Findlayson that accommodated future growth by increasing density within the ring road. The master plan deftly structured open spaces at a more human scale than its predecessor and just as importantly, given the long and harsh Canadian winter, recommended a series of internal connective routes to facilitate movement across the sprawling campus. Inherent in the master plan's recommendations was the notion that each new building project would contribute its share of this indoor street network, similar to the Renaissance-era mandate for buildings in Bologna, Parma, and other Italian cities to incorporate a street-level arcade, forming a continuous network of covered walkways through the urban centre.

Our first two projects at UTM—the Recreation, Athletics, and Wellness Centre, authored by my colleague Duff Balmer; and the Hazel McCallion Academic Learning Centre (a.k.a. the campus library), which I designed—faithfully interpreted the master plan recommendations, creating robust indoor connections to existing campus buildings and the ring road. Shortly after the library opened in 2007, the client began to express concerns about the volume of foot traffic and associated noise in the library. Within weeks, the library began to look like a sit-in, with student bodies draped over every available surface, intolerable noise levels, and CO_2 sensors routinely going off. The library was a victim of its own success, having become the preferred campus hangout overnight, which in turn made it a difficult place to study and conduct research. At the peak of the crisis, daily gate counts reached 12,000 people, the equivalent of the entire campus population passing through the library every day.

After several months of discussions about what might be wrong with the design of the library itself, we convinced our client to look more broadly at the inventory of study and social spaces on campus. Lisa Given, a professor of library and information studies at the University of Alberta and a researcher on the subject of undergraduate learning behavior, was retained to assess the inventory. Her survey revealed a noticeable deficit of spaces for student collaboration and informal interaction as well as poor infrastructure, amenities, and environments in the spaces that did exist. The good intentions of the master plan had in fact exacerbated the problem by providing a warm, dry route directly to the comfortable new building on the north edge of the campus. The library was planned as "a place for people, not books," to quote the chief librarian, and the resulting bright, open nature of the building had allowed it to stand in for the missing indoor public realm on campus. This, however, was not the building's intended purpose, and asking any one building to compensate for a campus-wide deficit was neither practical nor sustainable.

The challenges that UTM faced as it began a new period of rapid growth were by no means unique. Most of Canada's knowledge infrastructure was created during a massive postwar building boom that peaked in the late 1960s. There are many notable works from this period, visionary architecture from an era of unprecedented optimism such as John Andrews' University of Toronto Scarborough campus, Arthur Erickson's master plan and original buildings at Simon Fraser University, and Ronald Thom's designs for Trent University. In each there is a rich imagining of campus life rendered through the brilliant integration of architecture and landscape. Eventually the appetite for innovation and experimentation was lost and replaced with a harsh functionalism that prevailed until quite recently, exacerbated over decades by a tendency to build piecemeal additions within ever-decreasing budgets. By the end of the century, many Canadian campuses had devolved into rabbit warrens of ad hoc space that barely allowed students to find their classes let alone thrive in a supportive campus culture. Given this context, we became preoccupied with resetting the ratio of public space and fostering learning cultures in our subsequent projects at UTM and other campuses across the country.

The unimaginatively named Instructional Centre was the first of three interconnected buildings at UTM that began to define a new campus green. At the outset of this project, we developed a planning diagram that would transform the Toronto Argonauts' practice football field, located directly south of the Instructional Centre site, into a more diversely programmed campus landscape. The landscape would be defined by a circuit of academic buildings facing the campus ring road and the wooded floodplain of the Credit River beyond. With the Instructional Centre, we established a DNA of public space typologies that would provide desperately needed space for social and academic exchange while knitting the expansion into the existing landscape and building fabric. We conceived of a chain of interior public space that would encircle and overlook the new green—a highly transparent architecture at the ground and second floors, punctuated with student amenities. Oriented perpendicular to this chain would be "learning agorae" that connect visually and spatially with the ring road and the forest beyond. The agorae share core guiding principles as theatres of public life on campus, but their realization over a decade, the diverse contexts they address, and the variety of programs they support have resulted in distinct architectural environments.

While Canada's universities may desperately need an indoor public realm, their funding formulas are based on net usable space that can be assigned to a faculty (for research and offices) or to the registrar (for classrooms). Public space is generally derived as a small percentage of an allowable "gross up" that also includes all of the building's mechanical and electrical infrastructure, support spaces like washrooms and loading docks, and wall thicknesses and structures. If you want to build something more, you have to be clever about it. At UTM, Lisa Given's research regarding the public space deficit created a receptive audience regarding the need for an enhanced public realm, but the formulas governing space allocation were still sacrosanct. One could interpret, but not reinvent.

In planning the Instructional Centre, which was programmatically dominated by classrooms, we extracted our public realm from the "crush space" required to support the flow of people in and out of lectures. By organizing the largest lecture halls on the ground floor, we were able to extrude the crush space footprint vertically to create a three-storey atrium which would become the heart of the learning agora. By strategically placing food service outlets and seating at the south end of this new space and an entrance to the ring road and transit stop on the north end, the plan supports a critical convergence of population. Slender stairs and bridges are set against potent material backdrops or silhouetted against window walls overlooking the landscape. What on a program spreadsheet was merely an allocation to provide safe access to

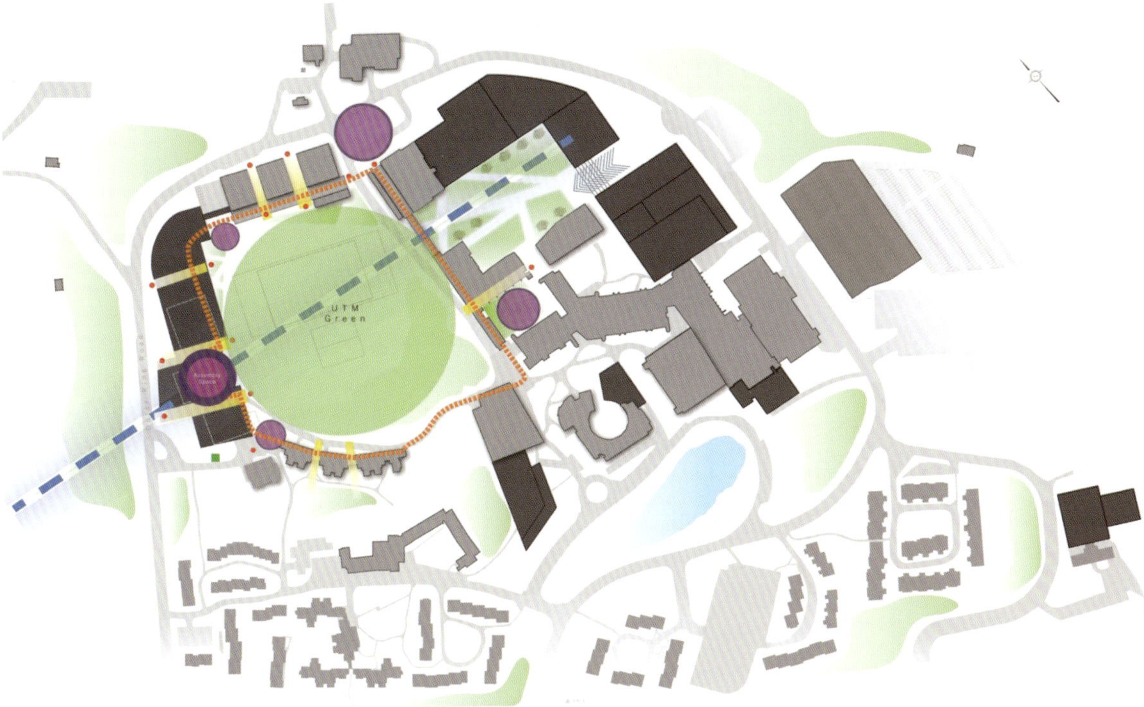

Diagram showing the proposed “chain of public space” at UTM

Sectional model of Maanjiwe nendamowinan

The North Hall at Maanjiwe nendamowinan

and from lecture halls became a place of social and intellectual exchange, celebrating those bursts of movement that punctuate the academic day.

Contextual Amplification

In 2011, two years after the completion of the Instructional Centre, we were awarded the commission to design the first phase of a multiphase replacement of the campus's earliest structure, a low-lying concrete bunker at the north edge of the green. The project would eventually become Deerfield Hall, to which we would add the Maanjiwe nendamowinan complex several years later (2015–2018). We were very slowly drawing a circle around the green and extending the reach of social life on campus. The dialogue between the public space and natural setting establishes the character of life at UTM. One is always moving, studying, conversing, eating, or drinking in relation to the forest or campus green. The architectural amplification, framing, and sequencing of landscape mark episodes of a journey that will set a cultural tone or reveal a shared history.

The material character of these buildings became another area of exploration. In each, a specific material treatment links to the landscape and becomes the dominant identity of both the exterior architecture and the interior public realm: the wood of the forest, the copper ore that lies beneath its surface, or the rich clay soil that has been carved away by the Credit River. The material treatment creates a strong continuity between the exterior and interior, drawing the landscape in and projecting the building's life outward. The notion of an object with a unique and singular material or tectonic language around which public life flows is another consistent theme in many of the projects in this volume.

Thresholds and Proscenium

Our third project of the series, Maanjiwe nendamowinan, takes its name from the Anishinabek expression for a "meeting of minds." From the outset, the project was programmed to house a wide range of academic departments, with spaces for research and teaching but also an event space to serve the entire campus. This major public room gave us an opportunity to craft a dramatic conclusion to UTM's chain of public space and to explore the theatrical potential of the public realm. In the three connected projects at UTM, the interior thresholds become significant as one passes from the space of the agora into the program container, which is more densely occupied and selectively accessed. Interior windows are cut into the containers. Balconies and terraces are carved from them. Bridges penetrate them. The act of moving from the space of a focused task or conversation into the public life of the campus becomes a theatrical act played out against a resonant materiality and the backdrop of nature.

At Maanjiwe nendamowinan, the theatrical potential of the space hearkens back to the Piazza di Sant'Ignazio in Rome, with its multiple entrances drawing people onstage or to become spectators through a set of constantly shifting personal and spatial identities. The potential in this case centres on the building's North Hall–a tiered, divisible space that serves as the social and organizational heart of the building day-to-day and that transforms to support structured events as needed. Amphitheatre seating negotiates the sloping site, connecting the ring road entrance to the campus green, and provides opportunities for casual gatherings and study as well as spectator seating for major occasions such as convocation or student award presentations. A set of three-storey-tall, pivoting partitions marks the threshold between stage and audience, provides a surface for film projections, and allows multiple events to occur simultaneously. Bridges and suspended stairs crisscross the lofty space, linking the two academic blocks and providing opportunities for people to look and interact.

The Story of Making

Maanjiwe nendamowinan communicates the life of a community but also explains the story of its own conception and construction. We intentionally developed an architecture that would evoke the drama of its making. The exposed concrete structure of the building's lower two storeys reference UTM's original brutalist architecture. The two academic blocks are clad in terra-cotta, as containers placed on top of the concrete frame. This is decidedly not how they were built (they are cast-in-place concrete like the rest of the building), but rather a fiction about making things: undergraduate teaching spaces supporting faculty and research, and a new era of academic life rising on the foundations of the old.

Another architectural system celebrates movement between the two worlds of teaching and research: the stairs, landings, and bridges that hang on steel rods from the roof of the North Hall. These elements are designed to evoke the catwalks and scaffolding of a theatre fly tower but, also, in the lightness of their assembly and articulation, invite curiosity and the sort of heightened engagement that comes with stepping onto a bridge suspended in space.

To see and be seen, to animate and contribute to the ebullience of public life—these are the human impulses that shape great cities. The need to affirm and celebrate our collective interdependence drives us to create and inhabit public spaces. To realize the theatrical potential of the city on a suburban campus may seem a strange transposition, but I believe it is what was called for. When UTM's new library became the sole outlet for the social impulse on campus, a space that was categorically not designed as a public theatre appeared besieged when compelled to serve this function. The normal behaviors of conversation and social exchange seemed exaggerated or even perverted in an ill-suited environment. This sense of being out of place, or acting transgressively, then becomes an attractor for truly transgressive behavior. When we don't build for a public life that is inclusive, active, dynamic, and at times theatrical, we thwart human impulse and effectively undermine the enterprise at hand—in this case, the education of young people. In contrast, the acknowledgment of the communal impulse and social behaviors, and the clear delineation of thresholds and gradients of activity, allows people to find space to behave as they must and peacefully coexist around a common enterprise, whether on stage or off.

Dimitri

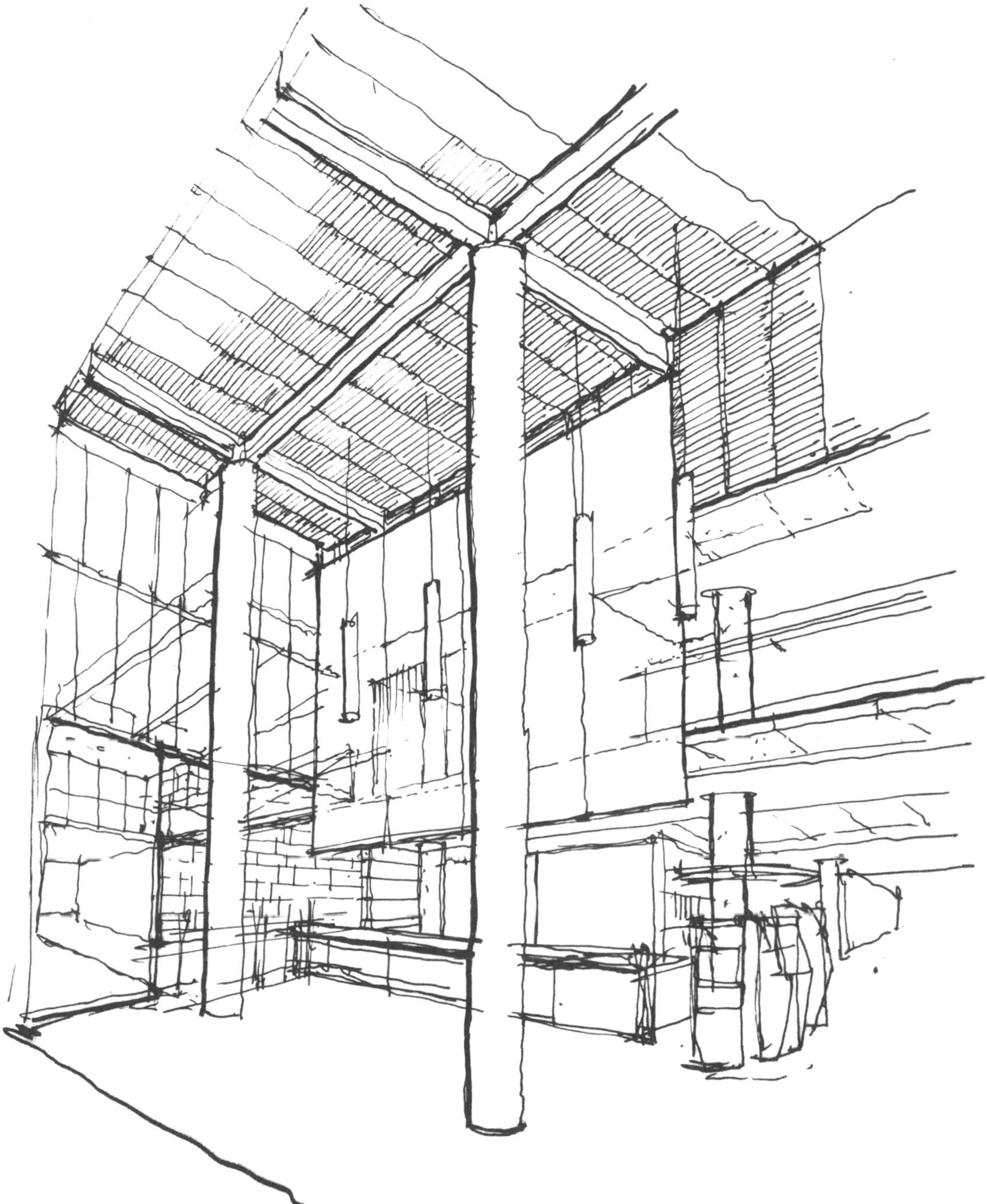

Whitby Public Library and Civic Square

Whitby, Ontario 2002-2005

I had arrived at the offices of Shore Tilbe Irwin & Partners for a job interview. Position: senior designer. Walking off the elevator onto their third-floor lobby with its lush tropical plants and glass reception desk, I felt as though I had traveled in a time machine with a rather short range, of perhaps 10 or 15 years. The office had certain trappings that suggested a creative agency or perhaps a law firm that represents creative types: long skylights above raised planters where rubber plants and *Ficus benjamina* clamored for light; rows of filing cabinets corralled by stepped ziggurats of drywall and glass block; the odd splash of colour (yellow ochre or cadmium red) to terminate a long vista and compensate for a general lack of views to the outside world. It seemed very different than premises of other firms I had visited that week. Those were generally studios. This was an office, and a peculiar one at that.

Located at 19 Duncan Street in Toronto, the premises sprawled across three brick-and-beam Victorian buildings, relics from the heyday of textile manufacturing that the city was once famous for. The occupation of three different buildings with slightly different floor levels gave the office an informal, labyrinthine quality, as one had to navigate up and down, over and around the idiosyncrasies of the historic framework. As if uncomfortable with this lack of order, the firm's partners had sought to neutralize the material character of the old buildings. While other architectural studios in the same district celebrated the rugged expression of bare brick wall, rough-hewn timber, and cast-iron fittings, the partners at STIP had chosen to cover over all traces of it with dropped ceilings, plaster, and carpet in a way that recalled the late '80s and early '90s. The firm's high modernist legacy was suppressed, rather than overtly celebrated. A few worn pieces of furniture by Mies, Saarinen, or Le Corbusier and the dusty print of a heroic brutalist library hanging in a back corridor were the only traces of what had once been a celebrated design practice. I would eventually learn that this aspect of being frozen in time, or between times, lacking the will to revitalize, renew, or even exploit an impressive built legacy was characteristic not just of the office environment but of the firm's culture, which was entirely dominated by four senior partners. I do not mean to unduly dismiss these gentlemen, as they would inadvertently provide me with some of the most potent and enduring lessons of my career.

The man I had come to interview with that fall day in 2000 was D'Arcy Arthurs, who is now my partner and the managing director of Perkins&Will's Ottawa and Toronto studios. D'Arcy was STIP's youngest partner at the time and had taken it upon himself to renew the partnership's flagging design reputation—as much out of a love of architecture as out of a need to ensure his own equity. D'Arcy was and still is utterly candid, affable, and pragmatic. As he toured me around the eerie quiet of STIP's disjointed spaces, he explained in hushed tones the need to quickly evolve, capitalize on the firm's strong legacy, and build a distinct new voice. At that moment in time, STIP was having to joint venture with rising design talents like Kohn Schnier Architects and Stephen Teeple to win new commissions from clients they had served for decades.

D'Arcy found this demoralizing and ultimately challenging from a business perspective. Splitting fees and managing the inevitable friction between the staid executive architect and the ambitious boutique studio was not how he imagined spending his career. D'Arcy had a mission to rebuild from within. The implicit criticism of the status quo was making him unpopular with the senior partners, and he was feeling the strain of being the sole agent for change. He needed allies and, after viewing my portfolio and chatting for the better part of an hour, wondered if I would be up for the challenge. I would not be alone. He had hired one young, talented designer, Duff Balmer, whose then-current design for the Milliken Park Community Recreation Centre showed, in my opinion, the only promise in the large body of work currently underway at STIP. I remember feeling as though I was standing on a precipice. STIP was doing what I desperately wanted to do—building public buildings, the kind of buildings that shape society if you do it right. But they weren't doing it right. And the culture I could intuit from my first visit didn't seem particularly malleable. I had only two things to go on: the obvious commitment of a man I had just met, and Duff's beautifully rendered elevations of a small suburban community centre. I had to answer the question, being armed as I was with scant technical and professional experience: Did I care to join the ranks of this revolution?

I did join STIP, and it proved to be a singular time in my career. I was galvanized by both a clear mandate and a well-defined set of obstacles and opponents in the old guard. When I reflect on those early years at the firm, I am struck by the relentless energy that I poured into transforming the culture, one project and one person at a time. Sometimes diplomatic, sometimes blunt to the point of cruelty, I worked so hard to clear the obstacles and plot the new path forward that when I came out the other side I was perhaps lost. Later in my career I would, having won the battle, struggle to redefine the next campaign. What I learned from the senior partners, which served me in my midlife malaise, is that you'd better keep struggling. If an enemy to your enterprise isn't presented you, perhaps you have to invent one. One could of course opt for a more optimistic set of motivators, but I like energy that comes with conflict and struggle.

It was a lonely endeavour at first, carried out in an almost surreal atmosphere. The convoluted interior of the office seemed to cluster a population of quiet and industrious shadows cranking out the senior design partners' sketches without open discussion or debate. It was only in passing at the plotter or more fully in the safe harbour of a darkened pub that snide and bitter exchanges revealed how people really felt about the work they were doing and the people they were doing it for. But whatever passions and opinions the employees of STIP held for the great art of architecture, they were not openly expressed within the walls of the office. Apart from my allies, D'Arcy and Duff, there seemed to be an entrenched resistance to open discussion about what was good, bad, beautiful, or ugly. There was, however, one exception to this prevailing culture, one that shone in the irreverent and irascible personage of Dimitri Simos. Dimitri was a senior architect entrusted with detailing the most important commissions of the most senior design partner. I had not had the pleasure of working with

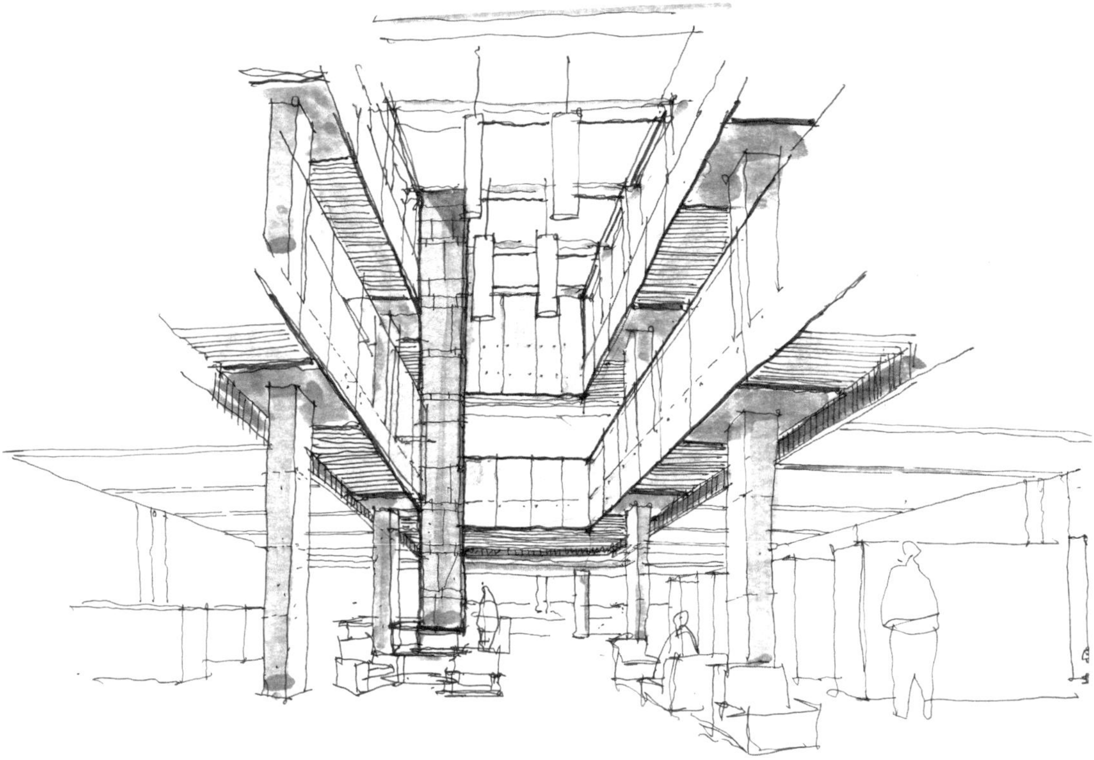

Sketch study for the multistorey light well amid the stacks

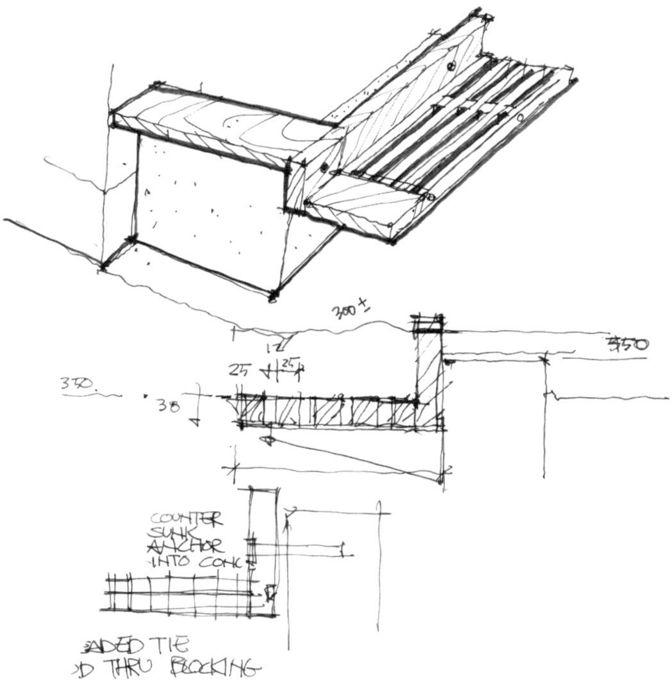

Detail study for a wooden bench

Study for the main lobby, with a security closure, acoustic separation, book drop, and bridge

Sketch of a fireplace nook in the adult reading area

Study for a south-facing seating bay

Dimitri until my third major assignment at STIP, which was the design of the Whitby Public Library and Civic Square. Whitby was never really meant to be mine and in attempting to assume the lead design role, I ruffled a number of feathers. For a while, the fate of the project's design direction hung in the balance, but Dimitri intervened, changing the course of my career, first through his candour and then through his long and patient mentorship.

By the time the proposal call for the Whitby Library and Civic Square came out, I had been with the firm two years and had a small branch library in London and visitor centre for Parks Canada under my belt. I was actively engaged with leading design teams and pursuing commissions. Our senior partner had a keen interest in library design and was a veteran of the typology. While he didn't mind me contributing strategy and writing to the pursuit, he viewed the design commission as his. It was to be a central library for a mid-sized town half an hour west of Toronto, integrating the town archives and a major civic public space. As fate would have it, the weeks we were given to prepare an interview and conceptual proposals coincided with the senior partner's renting of a villa in the Chianti region of Italy. He was not going to reschedule his holiday, but he did leave me with some colour pencil sketches, which he trusted me to develop along with a supporting presentation in his absence.

When our leader returned, I showed him what I had developed, and he wasn't pleased. Working with my young colleague Marc Downing, I had developed a modernist composition with an L-shaped arrangement of library and archives framing a town square in concert with a linear canopy dubbed the "urban filter" and a terraced reflecting pool. The composition was a far cry from the sketch I had been instructed to execute which featured a centrally placed basilica with an octagonal rotunda and barrel-vaulted roof. There was no time to redress the situation, and we went into the interview with as united a front as we could muster. The senior partner would deliver the firm profile and site context, reluctantly ceding the meat of the presentation around our design concepts to me. We had developed an illuminated maquette whose back-projected vitrine expressed the town populace gathered in a grand urban room looking onto the precisely defined civic square. At a critical moment in the last minutes of our presentation, when all of the design drivers had been methodically laid out, I lifted a black cloth off the model to reveal its theatrical abstraction of civic life.

In an act of total insubordination, I had hijacked the design concept, choreographed the entire presentation, relegated my superior to a supporting role, and, adding insult to injury, won the job. That day we beat out three of Toronto's top design firms, two of which STIP recently had been obliged to joint venture with to win commissions. I had made the point that we could do it well and do it on our own. For the senior partners, the win was bittersweet, and the project's success over the following years would continue to drive a wedge between the old guard and the new order.

I must hand it to my senior partner, that in the wake of the winning presentation, he was gracious and complimentary, even if he felt that the design was perhaps missing the mark. For a brief period, he continued to sketch and offer alternate proposals for the library concept and, in a rare act of openness, invited Dimitri, the trusted executor of so many of his designs, to weigh in on a variety of options he was developing. Dimitri recalls that his eyes were immediately drawn to the concept maquette developed for the interview and that everything else he was being shown dropped away. For Dimitri this was the most beautiful thing that had come into the office in a decade. It was alive, it breathed, it was the obvious direction to pursue. The senior partner had at that point gruffly stated:

"Well it's your baby now."

He washed his hands of the entire commission, and assigned Dimitri and me to a collaboration that would reap many benefits over the years. Despite our differences, my superior had stepped aside and given me the best tool in his kit. For this I am indebted and eternally grateful.

When I first met Dimitri, he was in his early 70s, with the eager curiosity and mischievous energy of an eight-year-old boy. His wit was razor sharp, his voice musical, and his love of architecture boundless. He flirted openly with men and women alike, not with their bodies, but with their minds. Every conversation with Dimitri was a journey, an education, a revelation, and above all an amusement. I recall many an occasion where I would go to Dimitri's desk to ask about a detail and come back an hour later with tears of laughter on my face. Dimitri loved to recount the past, but he lived fiercely in the present and always brought me and others there—to the immediate moment—to contemplate the challenge of architecture. These qualities, combined with his deep knowledge of design and building technology, made him an incredible teacher. He engaged you, he wiped away your petty concerns with a joke, a pantomime, or an anecdote, and then brought you into the moment of deep analysis required to solve the thorniest problem. For Duff, myself, and many others, he was the spiritual and technical centre of the office. Asking not for rank or title, he simply commanded respect (and gave it sparingly). If he respected you, you were blessed, because this meant he would share the riches of his experience.

Born in Thessaloniki in 1927, Dimitri moved to Munich as a young man to begin his architectural studies. The untimely death of his father brought him back to Greece to settle his family's affairs, but he soon developed a new strategy to pursue his one true vocation. Moving to Melbourne, Australia, in his early 20s, Dimitri juggled full-time work in the architectural division of the municipal government, night courses in architecture at the University of Melbourne, and the raising of a young family. A *Reader's Digest* edition with articles on rising architectural star Arthur Erickson and Prime Minister Pierre Trudeau convinced Dimitri that Canada was an enlightened society where architecture was supported at the highest level. In the early '60s, Dimitri and his young family moved to Toronto, where he soon found work at the ascending firm Webb Zerafa Menkes Housden. Over 27 years he contributed to some of Toronto's most notable office towers, including the iconic Royal Bank Plaza and Atrium on Bay, Canada's first mixed-use atrium complex. The recession of the early '90s found many firms facing mass layoffs, among them this recent graduate and

An early model for the library and civic square

Dimitri, who was then 65 and considering retirement. Family-friend and fellow Greek émigré Terry Fitsialos had recently become a partner at Shore Tilbe Irwin and brought Dimitri on board to solve some thorny technical challenges.

Dimitri brought an incredible legacy to STIP and reveled in sharing the experiences behind some of Toronto's most notable structures of the 1970s. Whether it was explaining the complex details behind the gold-mirrored façade of Royal Bank Plaza, or recalling his former boss Boris Zerafa playing a soaring violin solo at the office Christmas party, one got a glimpse into another time with courageous people living courageous lives and making courageous architecture. Dimitri was a designer at heart, but red tape had blocked the translation of his Greek professional qualifications to licensure in Ontario and he was relegated to a technical support role. If he resented this, it wasn't apparent, for he simply lived to engage in an architectural challenge, and the difference between a grand master plan and a technical detail was simply a question of scale: They all matter, they all need to be beautiful, and they all need to endure. For Dimitri, beauty that didn't last wasn't real beauty.

I love to draw, I live to draw, and I thought I was pretty clever back in 2002 as we began to develop the design for Whitby Library, but I soon realized that there were some gaps in both my conception and perception of architecture. Dimitri taught me how to conceive of architecture as a built assembly in three-dimensional space. This requires a combination of a simultaneity of vision with a sort of X-ray vision. Today we easily understand compositions through parametric models that we can rotate on our screens, cut into, turn layers of on and off, and hence see all the constituent elements of in any sequence and from any angle we desire. Dimitri taught me to do that in my head, and then test and communicate it with a pen and paper. I learned to create a feedback loop between the mental construct of architecture and an exploratory drawing, where one built and informed the other, so that the drawing would gain layers of understanding and meaning with each cycle. The process of architecture is just this, iteration, distillation, refinement, and reiteration until the builder is standing at the door awaiting instructions for the site. Hopefully you have it together by then.

Whitby Library was my first major commission, my first opportunity to lead a small team toward a complete conception of architecture that integrated landscape, public realm, built form, and interiors. The building stands as a major milestone in my career not only because of its success and recognition, but because of everything that I learned doing it. I visited the building last year to mark the retirement of Ian Ross, the head librarian who so tirelessly supported our vision for the design throughout. I found Ian to be well and the building to be looking almost brand-new after 15 years of hard use and hard Canadian winters. For the longevity of the interior, we must thank the meticulous maintenance staff at the town of Whitby. For the preservation of the exterior, we must thank Dimitri.

As I walked the perimeter of the building, I marveled at the studied execution of the building exterior. The building form is articulated as a set of clear abstract volumes rendered in Indiana limestone and copper. The simple planar expression is uninterrupted by extraneous flashings and trims, which are so often deployed to mitigate the impact of water, snow, and ice. At Whitby, sheer plains of limestone turn the corner to articulate a true mass or meet the sky with a fiendishly clever and, it turns out, very durable limestone coping detail.

I recall sitting with Dimitri day after day as we worked our way around the building envelope, probing, sketching, and then detailing, with a series of exacting hand sketches, every possible built condition. There were no stock details, but rather architectural concepts at 1:10, 1:5, and 1:1 scale. I sorely regret that I cannot show you the drawings that Dimitri generated, but only the sketches that I did to communicate the intent to him. From this you will see only half of a conversation and have to imagine the rest. Dimitri drew with a set square or free hand on 8½-by-11 graph-paper sheets. He crawled around the building, slicing in plan and section, generating hundreds and hundreds of exploratory ideas to inform the design, engineering coordination, and final contract documents. He did this all day, every day for hundreds of projects that came out of STIP and then Perkins&Will Toronto, building a culture of architectural understanding that has served two generations.

Dimitri eventually retired in 2010, at the age of 84. I hadn't talked to him in several years until I phoned him in February of 2021 to ask if he had any of those marvelous drawings about. Sadly Dimitri informed me that in a tragic mishandling of both individual property and firm legacy, his drawings had been left at the Dupont Street studio and then, he imagined, discarded. He had been told by a rather overbearing office manager that all drawings belonged to the firm and could not leave the premises. He had left without his treasured archive. I recalled the successive and rather violent office purges from which I barely managed to rescue my own drawings. Dimitri's tidy piles of 8½ x 11 graph paper were unlikely to have survived. Although I am still looking, the personal archives of Duff and other colleagues who worked with Dimitri have not born fruit either, and at the time of this writing, all I have are my recollections and these words to bring the drawings and the spirit behind them to life.

When I spoke to Dimitri that day, I was transported back to our time working together. I had meant to squeeze my conversation in between two meetings and thought that half an hour would do. Dimitri soon disabused me of that, bringing me out of my harried and distracted state of mind and into the moment—a moment with Dimitri. For nearly two hours we spoke about his time working in architecture, the relationship between building and drawing, the meaning of true love. Dimitri's wife of over 50 years had recently passed from cancer, and he described the battle he had fought to bring dignity and comfort to her last days, as they navigated the callous mechanism of our overburdened public healthcare system. He was now in the final stage of his life, a time of reflection, and I was honoured to join him in his reverie. The themes of endurance and imagination wove their way through our conversation. He spoke to me of the consolation of nature and of his friends, the squirrels, who every day outside his window would share the intricacies of their busy lives. He described the storage space the squirrels had created in the hollow knot of a branch, complete with a removable hatch fashioned from a walnut shell.

"Did you know that all animals are architects? They have perfected their designs and repeat them. We foolish humans are still trying to arrive at the right design, and we keep changing and making more mistakes."

While Dimitri may have something there, I think that we have made some rather fine mistakes together.

Client	Town of Whitby and Whitby Public Library
Location	Whitby, Ontario
Size	6,300 gross square metres
Date	2002–2005

Terraced pools on the west end of the civic square

WHITBY PUBLIC LIBRARY

The library's south entrance and drop-off plaza

A bay window overlooking the building entrance

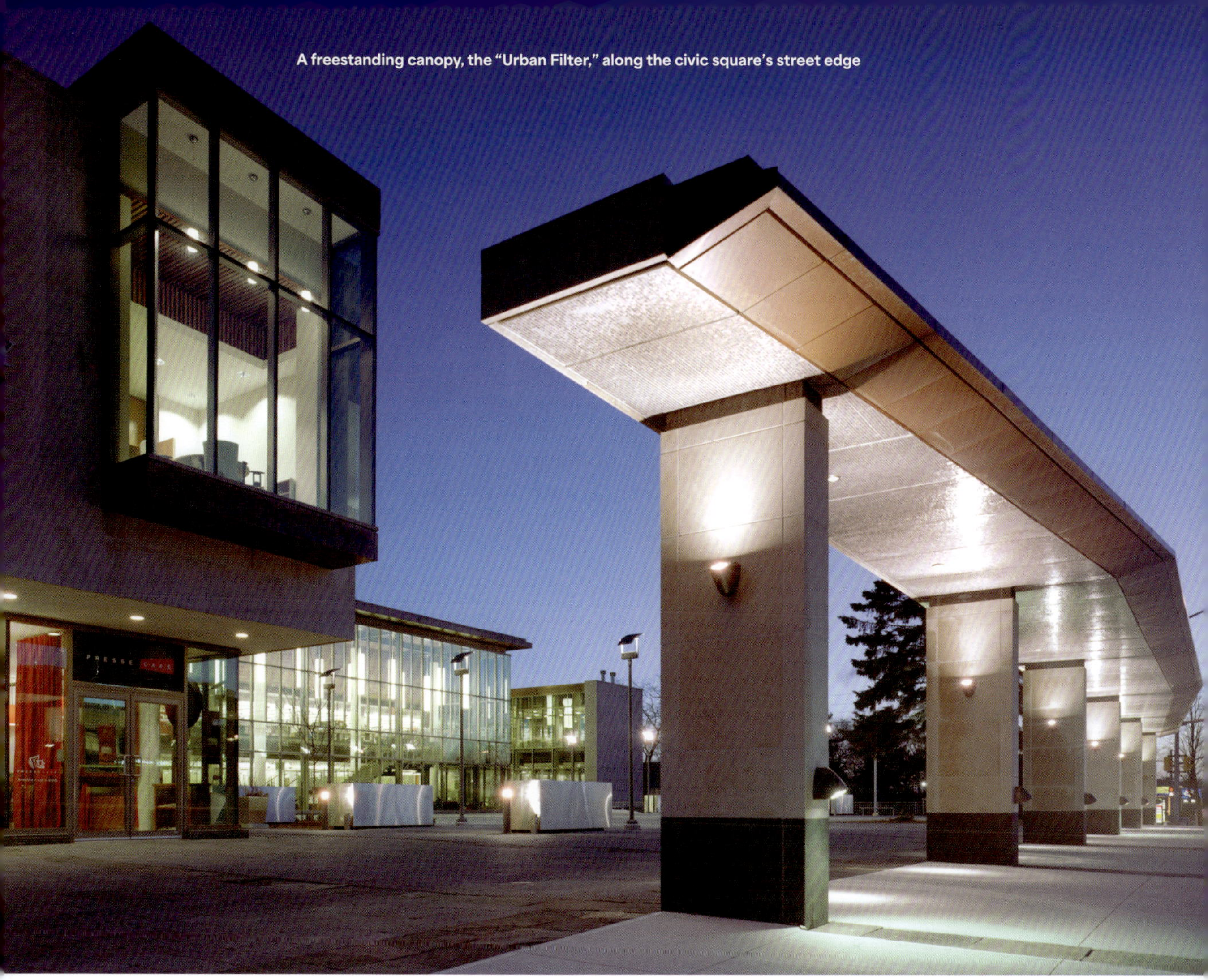

A freestanding canopy, the "Urban Filter," along the civic square's street edge

The civic square and the reading room beyond

North Elevation

South Elevation

East Elevation

West Elevation

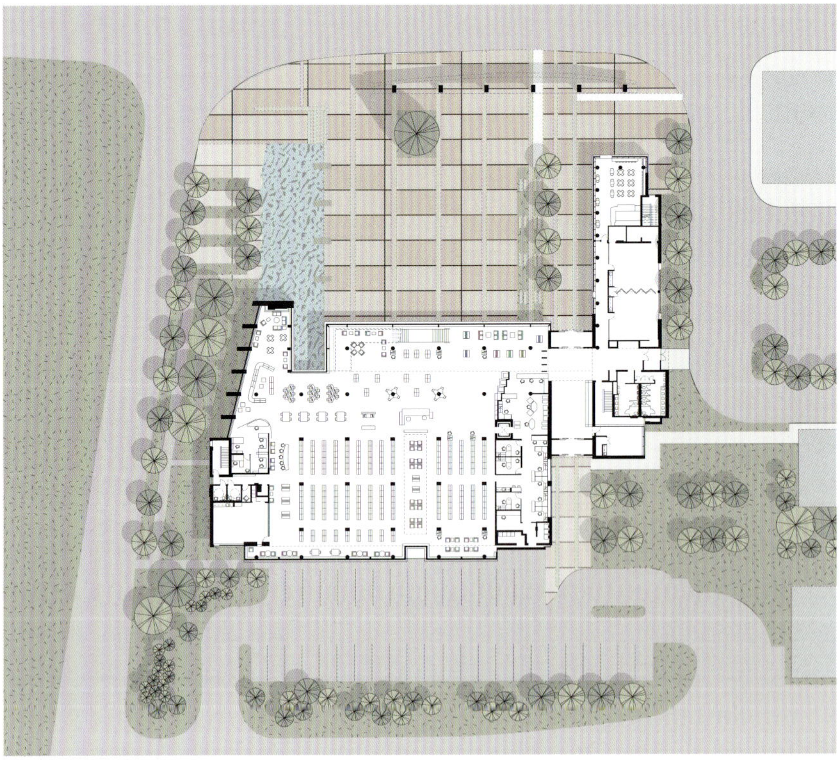

Site Plan

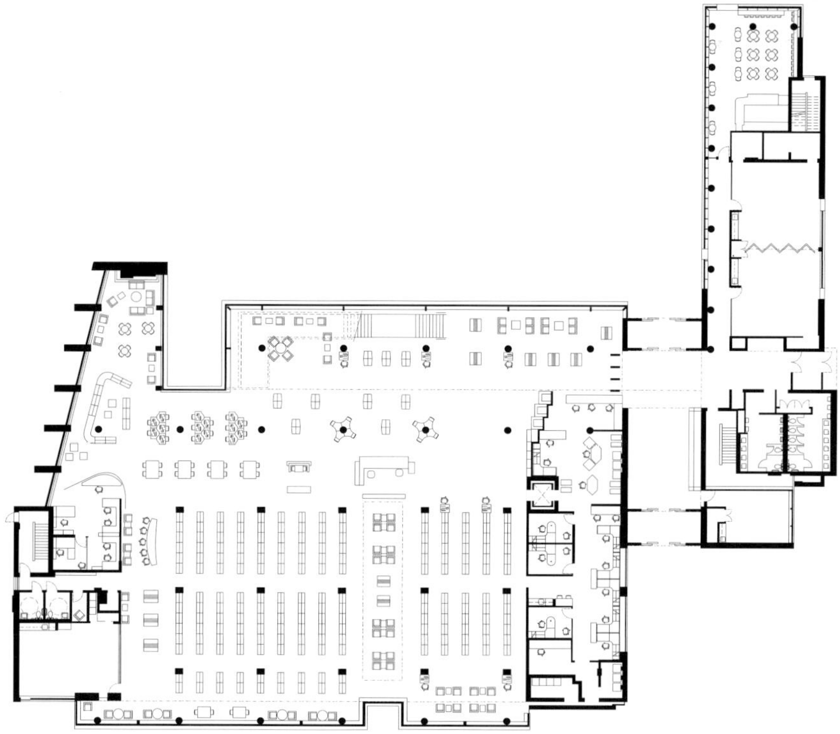

Level 01 Plan

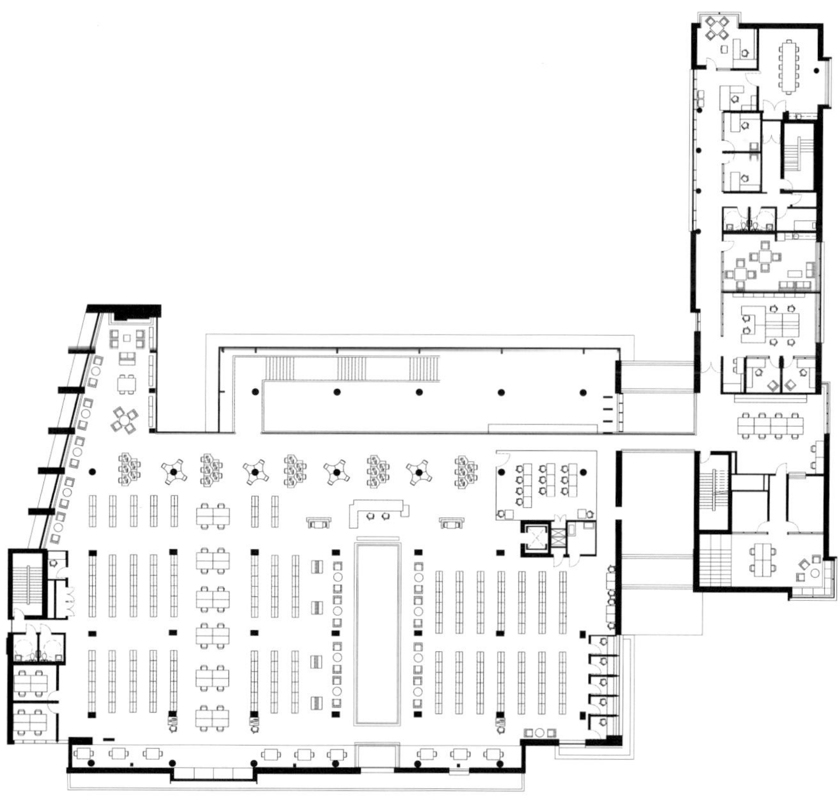

Level 02 Plan

Dimitri

The reading room looking onto the civic square outside

The south-facing reading bay window

The adult reading lounge and fireplace

A multistorey light well bisecting the stacks

Clerestory windows capping the light well

The Puzzle Box

Hazel McCallion Academic Learning Centre
University of Toronto Mississauga

Mississauga, Ontario 2003-2007

"At the outset your library is an intricately crafted box of weathered stone which conceals a second box—a finely crafted cabinet of wood and softly radiating coloured glass. This inner cabinet contains a great treasure—knowledge. Within the radiating cabinet, deep in the heart of the library, thousands of books move in tall metal cases, gliding silently on steel tracks. The box lies in a meadow at the northern edge of the campus, the purity of its rectilinear form disturbed only by deep joints in its cladding. Imagine that we begin to play with this puzzle. If we lift it, it rises above the ground, hovering above an inner sleeve of glass. At the same time a great slab of stone remains behind and a huge monitor window hints at the glowing treasure within. In lifting the box lid we have left a piece of the roof behind and now the sun streams into a southern terrace. These are but hints and only fuel our desire to get inside. Pull on the right-hand side and a large piece of the box slides over. This parting of the box opens a long vista, which carries our eye to the centre of the campus. A gate has opened. Within the gateway the pulling open has taken some floor plates with it and left others behind. The result is a zigzag chasm which draws our eye up to the left. There, suspended in space, touched only by the slender bridges which penetrate its lustrous shell is the inner cabinet—the repository of knowledge, symbolic heart of your experience, beginning and end of your journey."

The room was silent. I looked up from the typed page and the rickety wooden model I had been feverishly manipulating to meet the fixed gaze of the chief librarian. The various university functionaries (campus architects, facilities planners, and project managers) drifted out of focus as I waited for her to respond.

"I can sell that!"

She exclaimed, her stern mask breaking into a cautious smile. And with that, the journey was launched and a new covenant of trust established between client and architect. This was perhaps my first and most poignant experience with the sort of unwritten contract that informs architecture to a great degree. It goes into effect when the owner of the project vision on the client side sees that vision interpreted, amplified, and reflected back to them by the architect. Mary Ann Mavrinac, chief librarian at the University of Toronto Mississauga, was not technically the client, and I was not the lead architect, but at that moment, after she had received my little piece of prose and somewhat spastic manipulations of the maquette, we both assumed our respective roles. From that point on, we led the vision for the University of Toronto's first digital library together.

A week earlier, I had presented essentially the same architectural proposition to the same people. I had spent the last month running rogue and ignoring the advice of my firm's senior partner, Steven Irwin, whose architectural predilections were, in my opinion, out of sync with both the client and the times. This was the moment to show the firm and the university that I was the "new visionary."

But it didn't go that way. After presenting a complete set of plans and lovingly crafted perspectives for the better part of an hour, I looked up to see a veritable Mount Rushmore of inscrutable faces. To the few perfunctory questions asked, I made halfhearted responses. I knew something was way off but hadn't the strength or insight to figure out what. The meeting adjourned with a series of noncommittal remarks, and we went our separate ways. Two weeks earlier, I had seen these same people visibly moved as I presented my vision for an architecture that wove the natural fabric of the campus into its composition while defining opportunities for new public space. This approach had won us the commission and in the subsequent weeks, I followed the same line of inquiry to develop what I thought was a layered and ingenious accommodation of the new library program. How had I failed to make contact this time around?

"She felt an emptiness inside. She went home after your presentation, and she talked to her husband about it, and she just couldn't get over it. She couldn't sleep. She felt nothing."

Irwin looked up with a demonic twinkle in his eye. He had called me into his office first thing in the morning and sat me down in one of his greasy Le Corbusier loungers to relay the news. He, as the lead architect, had received a call from the chief librarian the night before and was now exacting the perfect revenge for my insubordination, with a barely concealed glee. Well, there was no backing out now.

"Nothing? She felt nothing? Give me two days and I'll give her something!"

I blurted out, storming from the office.

I had two days, so there was no point in redesigning what I thought was an elegant scheme. It was going to have to be a repositioning. In a way, Irwin, with his tendency to embellish every communication with a slightly misanthropic narrative flair, had set me off on the right course, for I had just enough time to write a story.

There was already a kinetic quality to the design, inspired by the university's mandate to put all the bound collections in mobile compact storage units. We had organized the units centrally on each of the building's four storeys into a block we had dubbed the "cabinet." The perimeter of the floor plan had been liberated for people to work collaboratively and engage with the campus's natural beauty. A series of public-space voids organized light, views, and movement. The creation of these voids had been accomplished by shifting programmatic elements outward, away from the central cabinet, giving the exterior volume of the library a dynamic quality.

Coming out of Irwin's office, I grabbed my partner in crime at the time, Marc Downing, and we retreated to the nearby Rex Hotel to strategize.

AF *When in doubt, build a model, but make it small because we don't have much time.*

MD *Let's make it move. Like a puzzle!*

AF *My uncle (he's an architect) spends all his free time making these insane wooden puzzles out of exotic woods. You move this piece and that and hours later it might open.*

MD *What's inside?*

AF *In his, nothing, but we better have something. Knowledge! It's a library after all.*

The conversation probably continued in this vein for a while but was eventually interrupted by the demands of the looming deadline. Fortunately, there was a precedent for our imagined puzzle in the centuries-old

Japanese puzzle boxes that served as precedents and inspiration

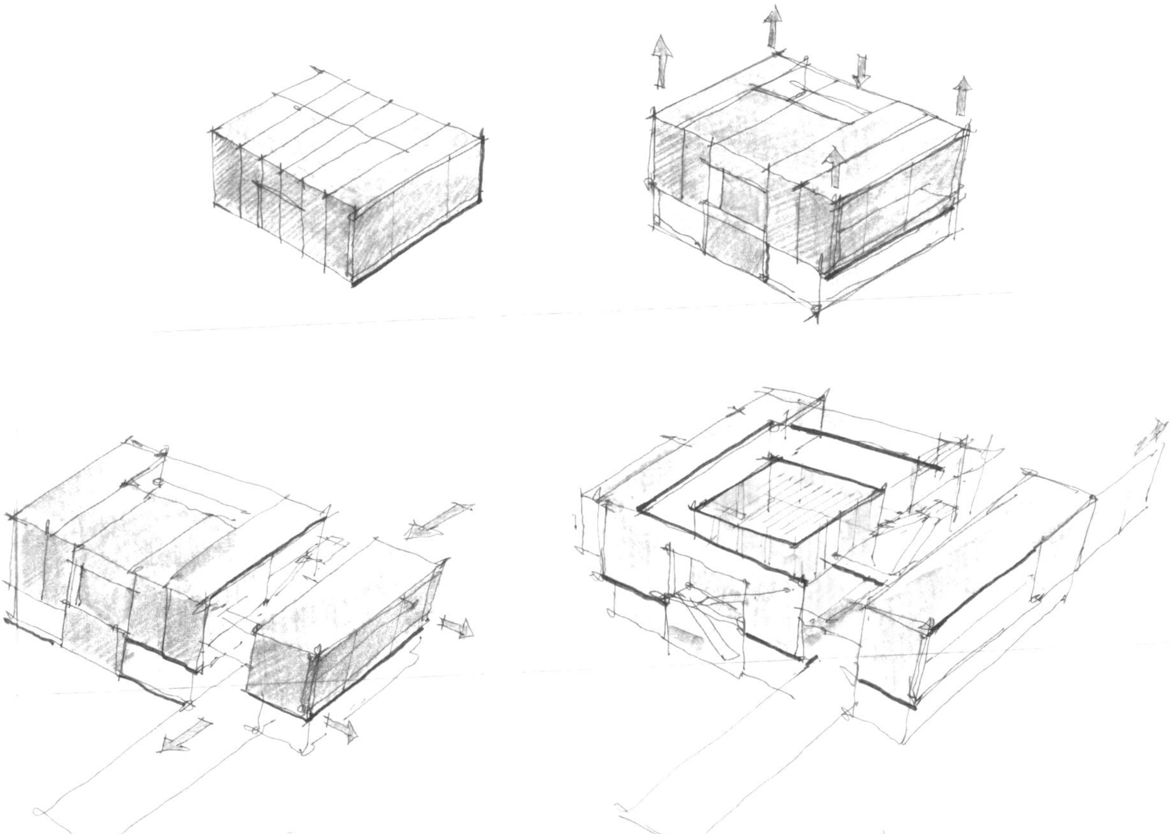

Sketch instructions for the puzzle-box maquette

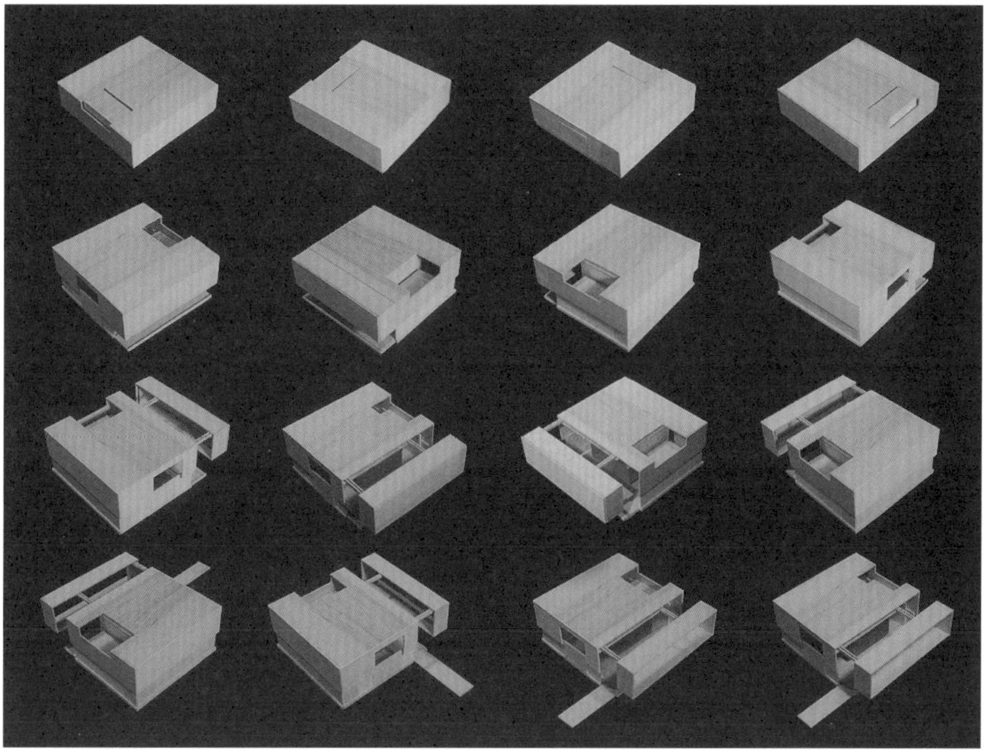

A series of operations: the puzzle-box maquette in its first iteration

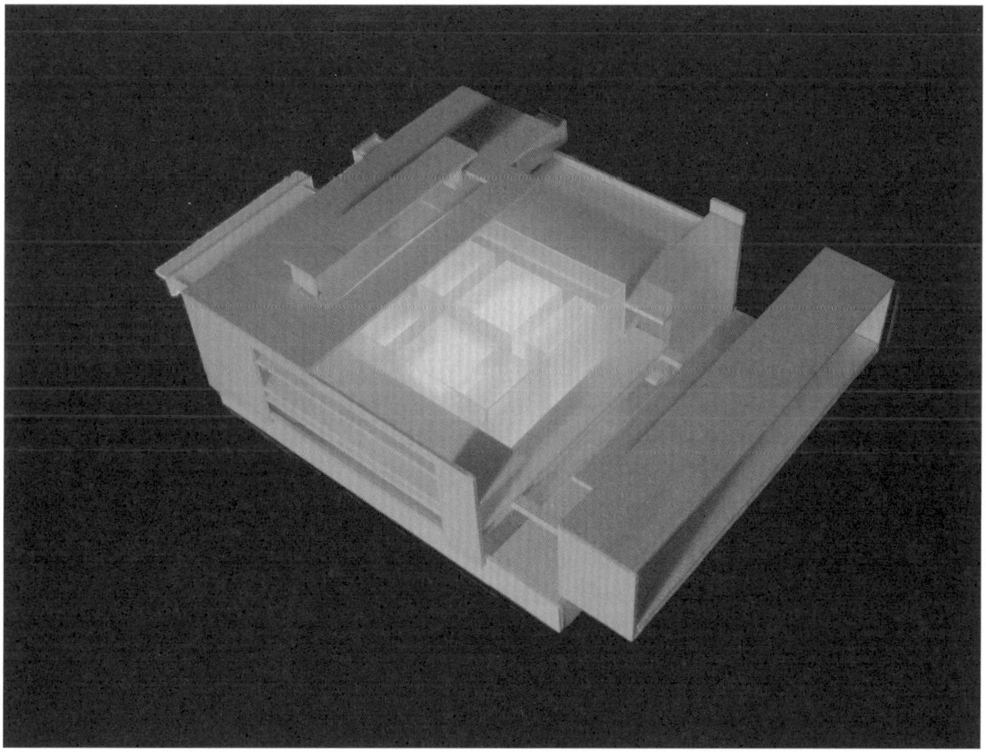

The second-generation maquette, shared with university leadership and potential donors

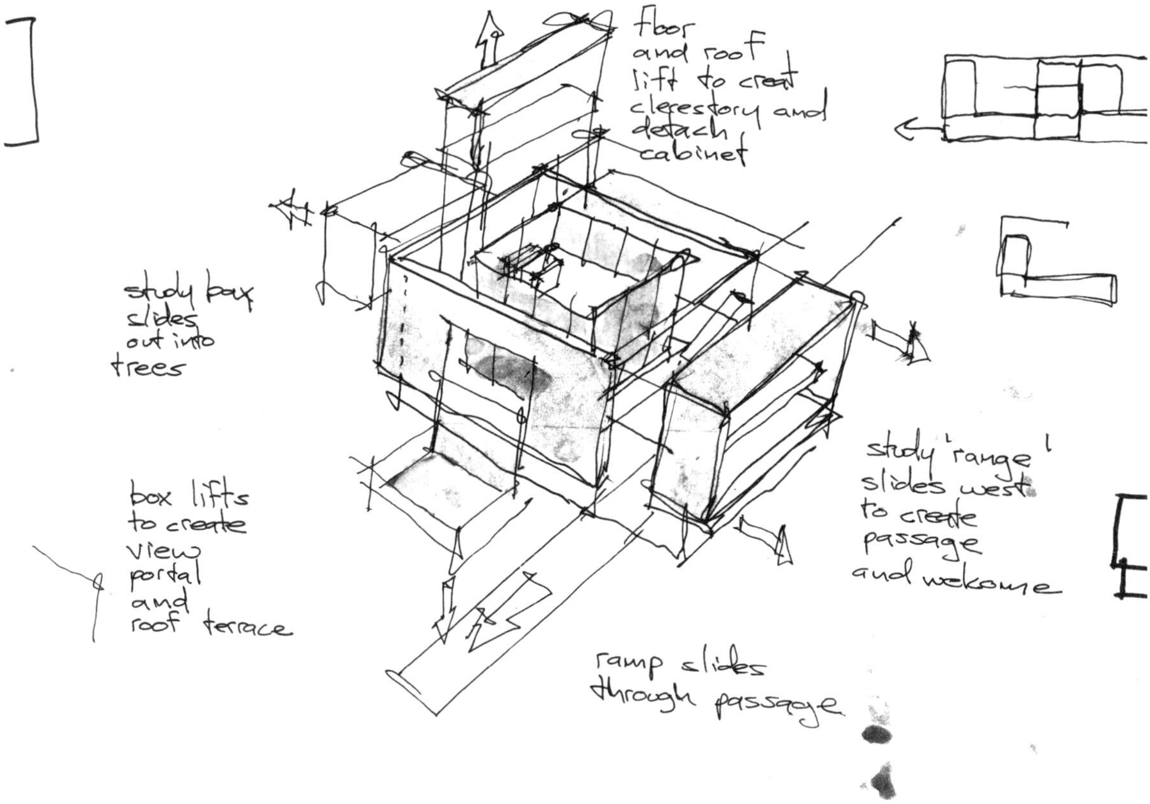

The library imagined as both a journey and a set of formal operations

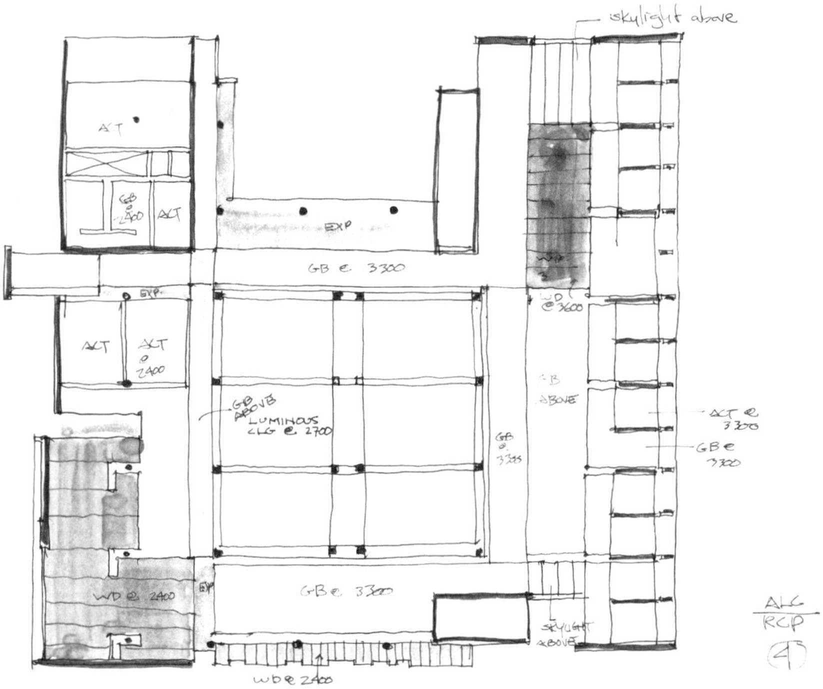

Sketch study for the Level 03 ceiling plan

A perspective study for the structural hanger system required to suspend the Level 04 reading room

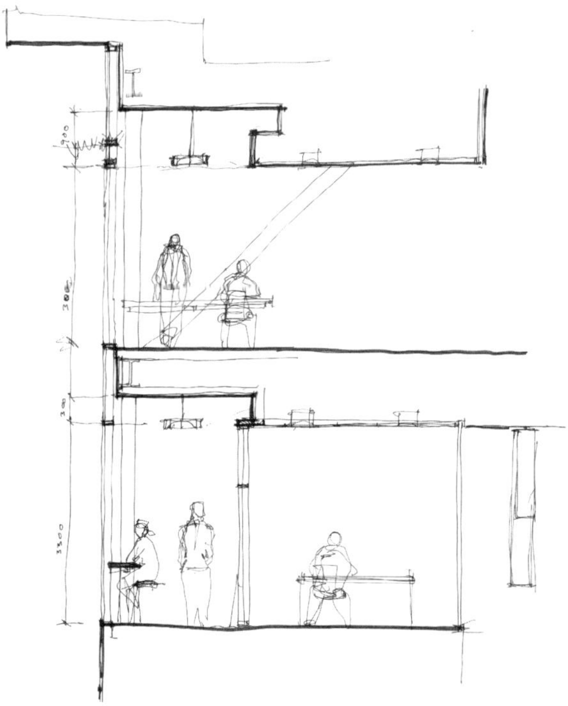

A section study for the structural hanger system

Japanese tradition of intricately crafted wooden puzzle boxes. This gave us the basic metaphor that we hoped would elucidate the merits of the existing design, or something very close to it. Over the next 48 hours our task consisted of reverse-engineering the building plans into a 6-by-6-by-3-inch wooden box that could, through a series of manual manipulations, be opened up to resemble the building's architecture. The physical prop was to be accompanied by a one-page text that was at once a poetic invocation and a sort of instruction manual.

The trick worked and provided a valuable lesson. People struggle to understand the abstract language of architecture. Having worked with many librarians, I can tell you that a little storytelling goes a long way. Stories may help clients to access our propositions, but we need them as well in order to guide our work. Over the months following the presentation, we developed several iterations of the model. These informed the building's form and materiality with increasing clarity and intent. The rather baroque materiality described in the original text gave way to a much more explicit and reduced palette: wood, black stone, and glass. Each took on a role, describing respectively the outer casing of the puzzle box, the anchoring elements, and the voids left by displaced volumes.

The puzzle-box metaphor extended to the most intimate details, with the planes of the exterior façade overlapping and parting to communicate the implied sliding action. Interior finishes followed in sync, with cherrywood substituting for the phenolic wood-veneer panels of the exterior.

After the building opened, my colleague Duff Balmer, an excellent designer, mentioned that the building looked like a '70s teak console with operable sections concealing a stereo, a television, a liquor cabinet. While he may have meant this as a critique of the rather relentless use of the phenolic cladding, I was pleased with the comment. If the building communicated craft, operability, and hidden delights, then it had achieved its intent.

In our era we have become increasingly used to buildings that have had "things done to them" to arrive at a form. I would argue that the measure of these buildings has to be not what has been done to them, but what they do. What is the benefit derived from a formal manipulation? At the same time, we have all become quite used to buildings that claim a metaphorical intent. Actions speak louder than words, so I would again ask what is a building doing with all of its story telling?

While the puzzle box may have grown out of a desperate need for a hook at the time, circumstances and a committed client allowed us to deepen the metaphor, extend its influence, and leverage it to create a unique set of spaces for people. As the box opened, it created light-filled lower levels looking onto sunken gardens, sectionally complex light wells and atria that connected communities of learners, and new public-space routes through the campus. The metaphor also provided an accessible piece of campus mythology—a story behind UTM's most visited building that conveys the sense of discovery that accompanied the advent of digital learning.

Project	Hazel McCallion Academic Learning Centre
Location	Mississauga, Ontario
Size	9,100 gross square metres
Date	2003–2007

The learning centre's north façade

The south façade with the landscape terraced down to the bottom floor

Approaching the library from the northwest

Detail of the west façade

The library's cantilevered northwest corner

Aerial view of the campus

The learning centre from the east

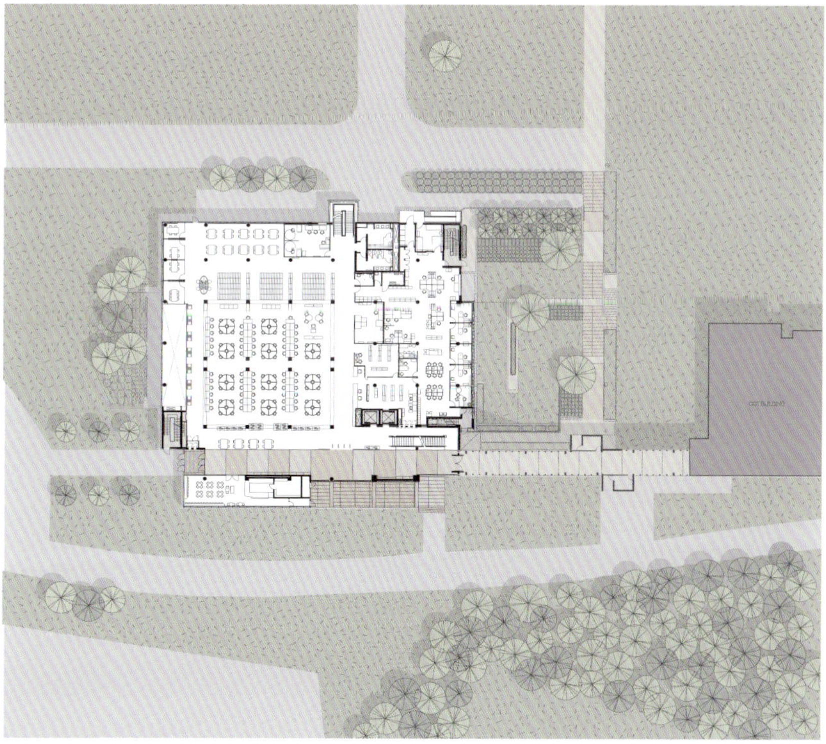

Site Plan

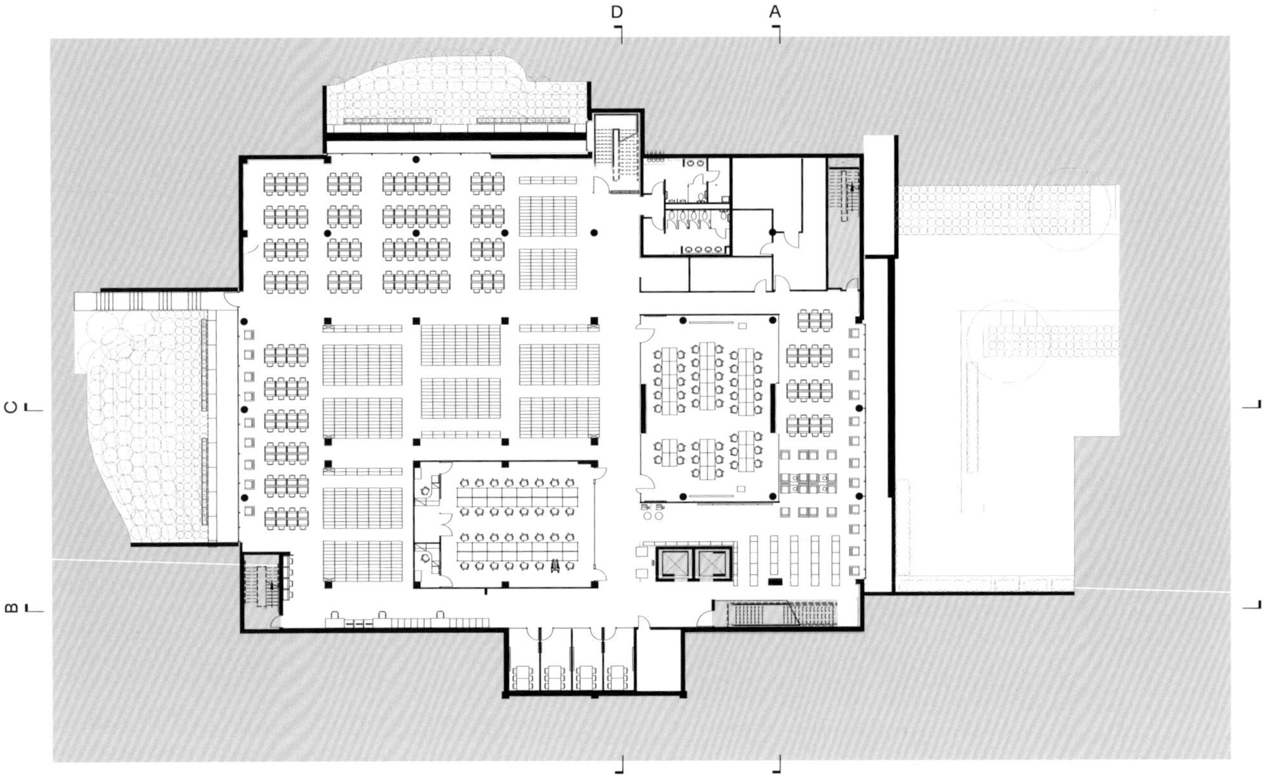

Level 01 Plan

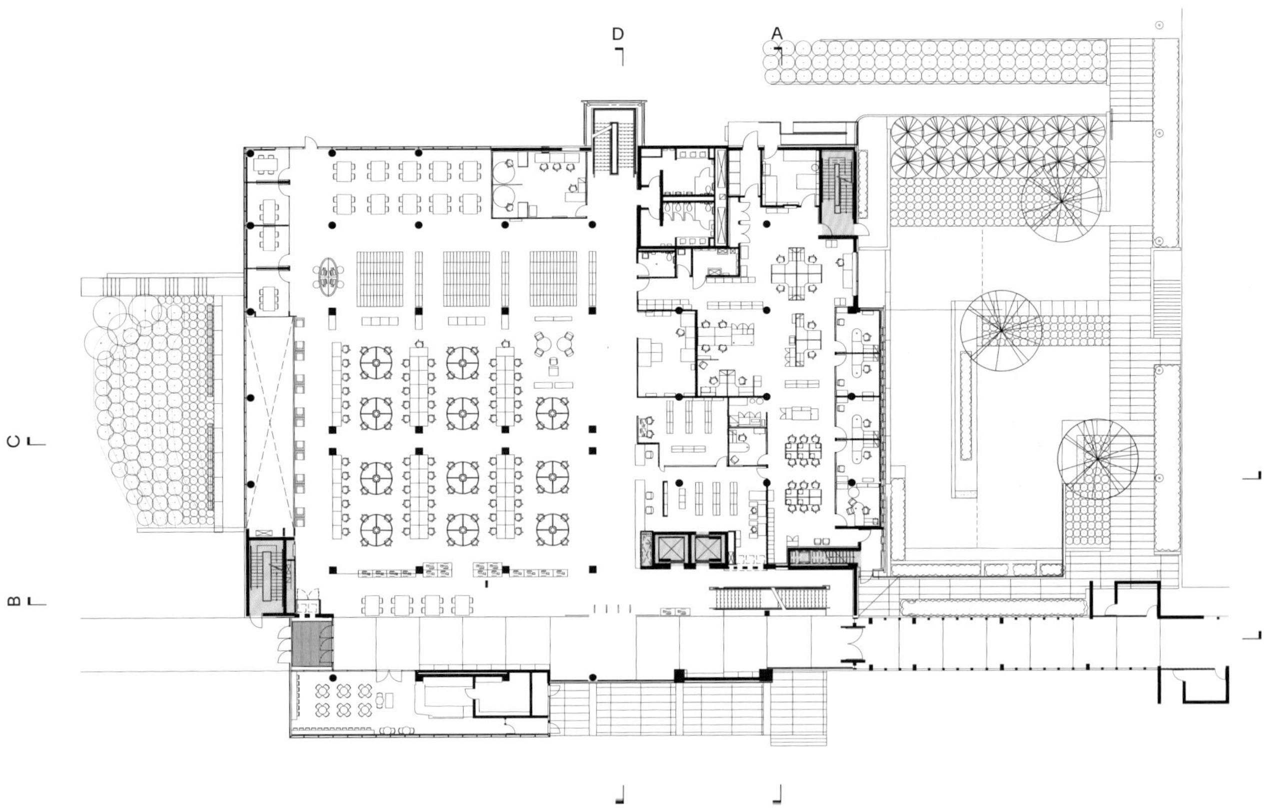

Level 02 Plan

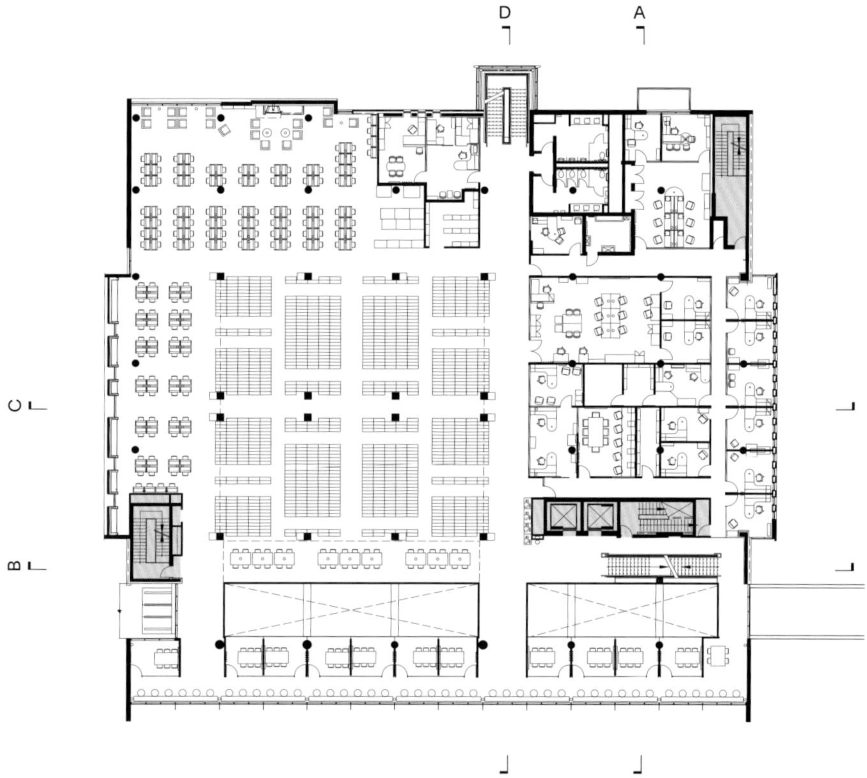

Level 03 Plan

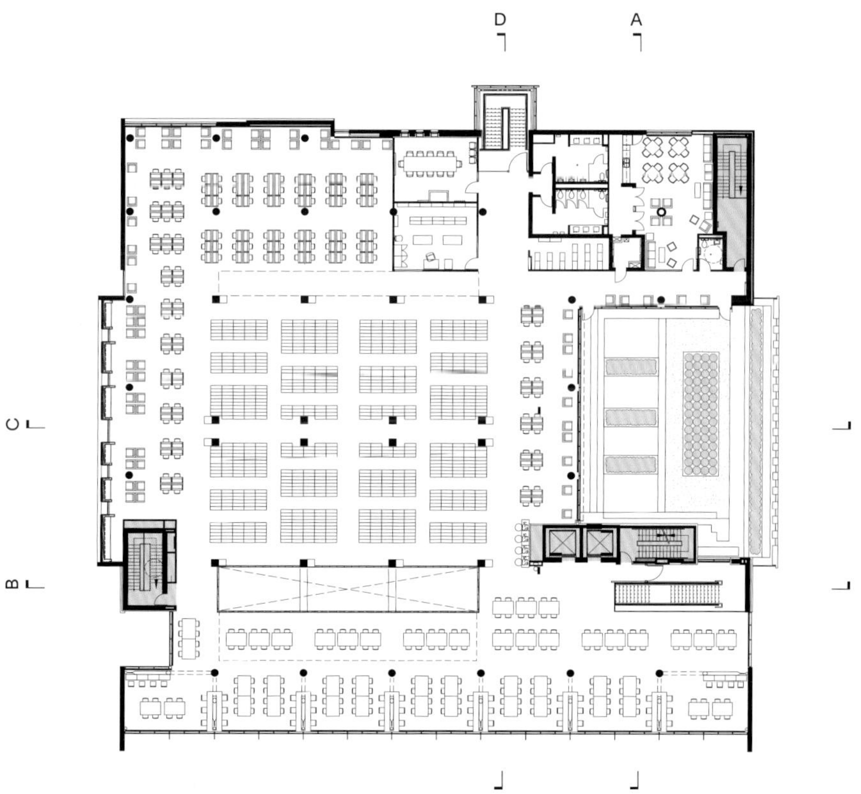

Level 04 Plan

Approach from the south through the campus link

The Level 04 reading and quiet-study area

Staggered voids connecting reading areas on three levels

The Level 03 reading area overlooking the campus link

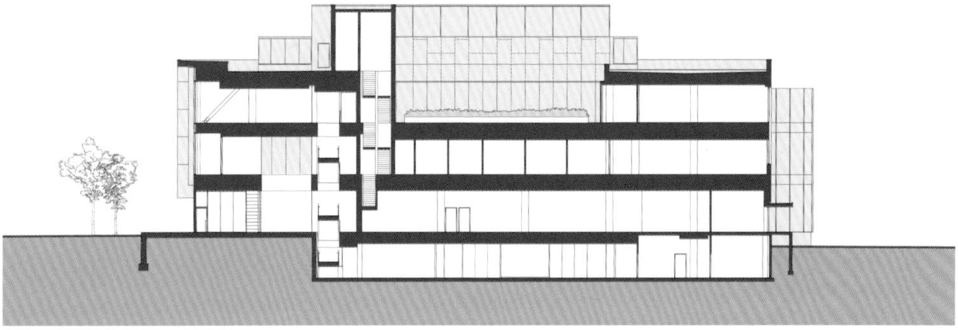

East-West Section A

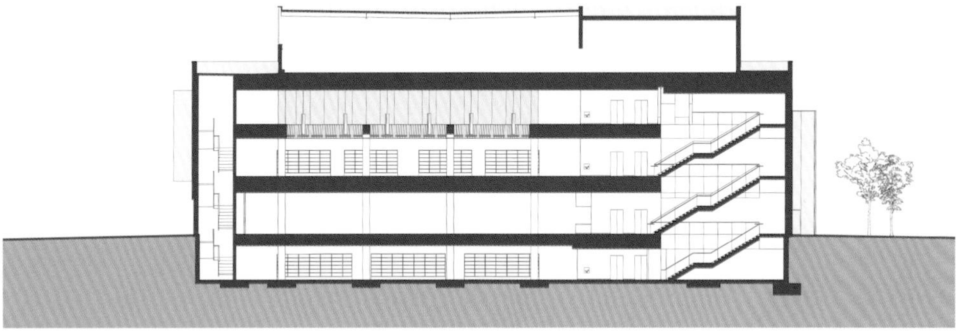

North-South Section B

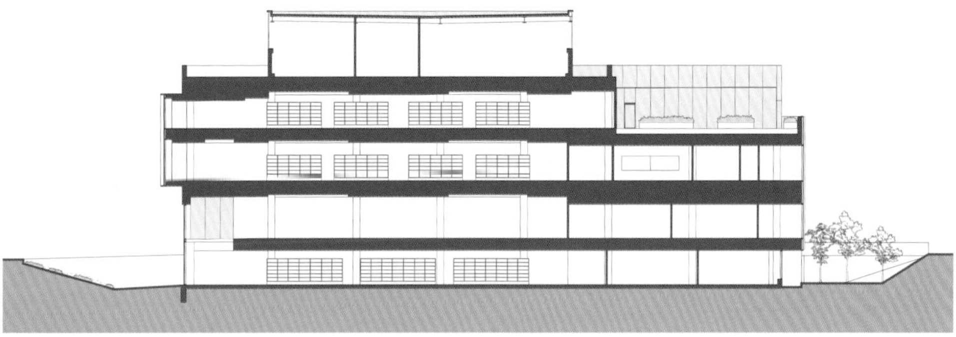

North-South Section C

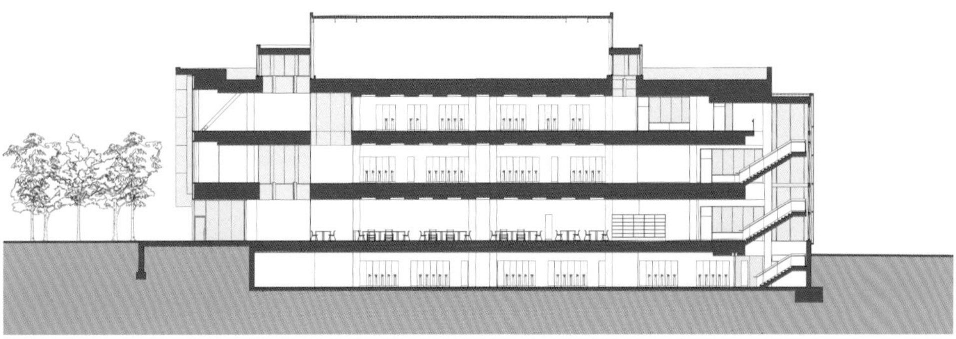

East-West Section D

Area for quiet study on Level 04 looking down to Level 03

The Builder's Hand

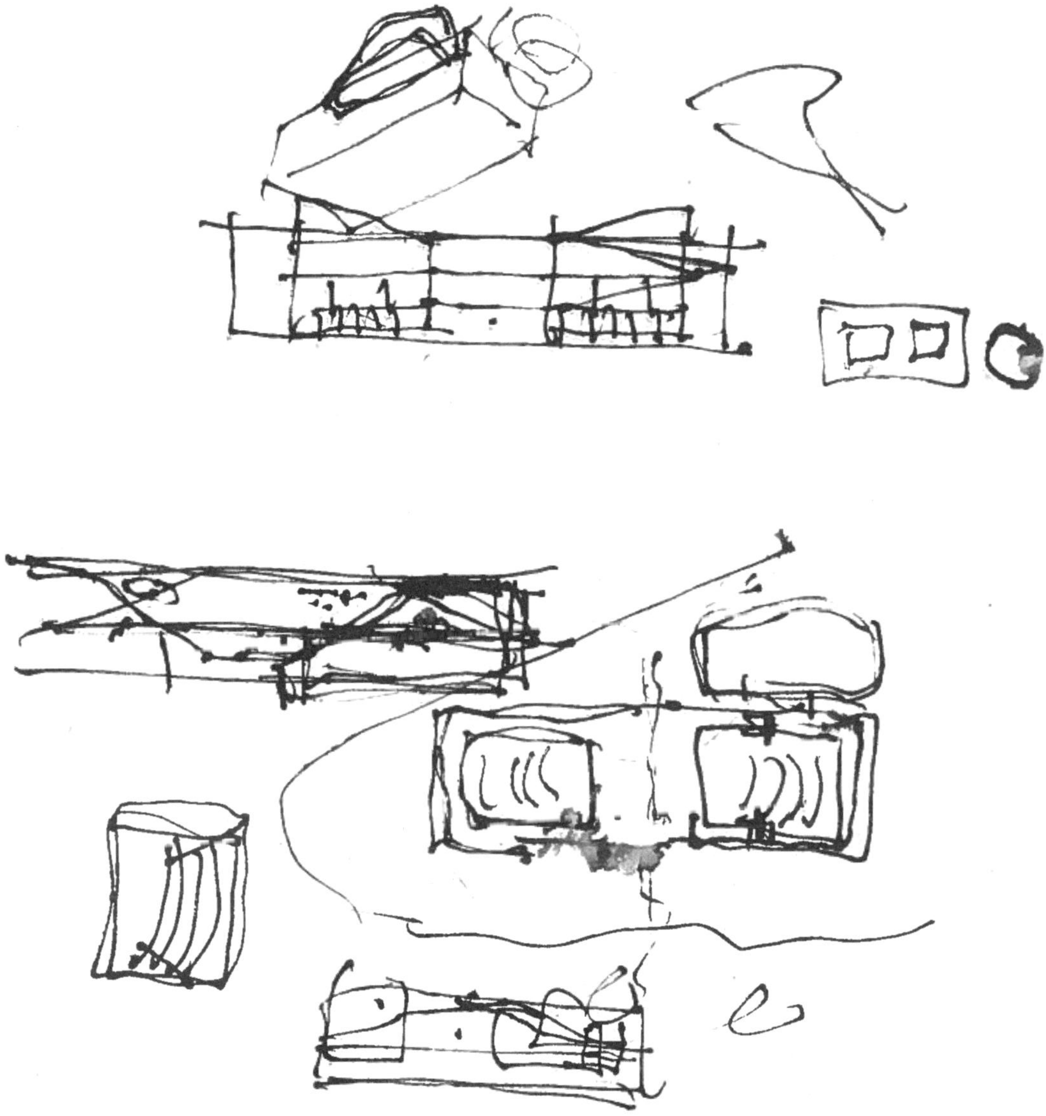

Instructional Centre
University of Toronto Mississauga

Mississauga, Ontario 2009–2011

Zahner in Kansas City, Missouri, has one of the most sophisticated computer-assisted design and fabrication facilities in the United States. The company specializes in custom materials and assemblies for architectural façade systems. In the summer of 2010, I toured their shop with Eric Zvaniga of Eastern Construction, who was leading the construction process for our latest design commission, a new classroom building at The University of Toronto's campus in Mississauga, Ontario. The building was being delivered through a design-build methodology with an accelerated schedule. Technically Eric was my client, but unlike many design–builders, he was also highly collaborative and recognized the value of a quality design. We had traveled down to Kansas together to finalize the details around one of the building's most important design features—its skin. Zahner is a family-run business that dates back to the late 19th century, when Andrew Zahner discovered the potential of zinc mined in the region to be used for specialty items such as cornices and decorative roofing profiles. That day in Kansas City, it was one of his great-grandsons, Bill Zahner, who received us and toured us around the facility. Bill showed us a series of complex prototypes for the façade of Frank Gehry's 8 Spruce, then under construction in Lower Manhattan. As we marveled at the sophistication of the facility and the architectural innovation that they were supporting, we could not help but feel humbled. The challenge that we had brought to Zahner, while very particular, would not even scratch the surface of their technical capability. We were in fact asking them to do something so basic, so ancient, that it had all but fallen out of use in design and construction.

Leaving behind the hum of computers and robotic arms in the cool space of the high-bay factory, we stepped out into the blinding sunlight, heat, and humidity of Zahner's back lot. Bill led us across the shimmering gravel surface to a large white tent along the property's back fence. Gathered in the shade was a group of six men, who looked at us expectantly as Bill addressed them in Spanish. Along the line of the tent, three 6-foot folding tables had been arranged end to end and covered with a long canvas drop sheet. A paint roller and a gallon pail marked "patina solution" sat alongside several 6-foot lengths of the copper siding extrusion we had chosen for the building.

Bill turned back to Eric and me and said:

"Well, if you want to take a shot at a mock-up, the guys will follow what you're after."

Luckily, I had done lots of mural painting in my younger years and knew my way around a brush, roller, and palette. I had been studying the building elevations in a series of Photoshop collages, imagining a range of textures and scales for the patination. My point of reference was Arthur Erickson's Bank of Canada Building in Ottawa, where the patina looks like it was sprayed on with a fire hose, leaving long, heavy streaks with extreme contrast between turquoise highlights and black shadows. The fine stipple roller Zahner had provided was not going to achieve this kind of intensity, so I asked if a course brush was available. In the end, we settled on a combination of modified broom, large paintbrush, and coarse roller. After experimenting for about 40 minutes with a range of stipples, splatters, and streaks, we arrived at a suitable aesthetic—one that provided colour and texture that would communicate at a variety of scales. Our goal was to create a copper skin that would evoke the forest surrounding the building site as well as the notion of catalytic transformation—the building skin as a living thing. It was to be seen at a distance but also intimately, as it came into the building interior. When we had developed a series of four panels that worked to create sufficient variety when repeated, we broke the process down for the work crew. Each of the four panels would receive a different sequence of application using the available tools. Four panels, each with three steps—roll, splatter, stipple—in different orientations and scales of gesture. Defining the application sequence and teaching it to the crew took the rest of the morning, and by one o'clock we were drenched in sweat and hungry. Ultimately, six men in a tent in Kansas City would use a couple hundred gallons of patina solution to hand-patinate 1,200 square metres of copper cladding. There were dual ironies at play in this scenario. The first stemmed from the fact that we were standing outside one of the most sophisticated digital fabrication suites in North America. The other came from the fact that we were in a mad rush.

With our control samples established, and the crew busily executing a batch of each panel type, we went to experiment with the application of a different substance—Kansas City barbecue sauce. After sloshing ammonia around for three hours, I was not as receptive as I might have been to this unique culinary experience. Mopping the sticky red sauce from Styrofoam containers with slices of Wonder Bread, Eric and I mused over the tactile quality that the new building was promising to project. How would we counter the richness of the patinated copper skin? Although we were in Kansas City securing a long-lead item, for a building whose foundations were already poured, many elements of the building's finish remained undetermined. Eric held up a floppy slice of fresh bread.

"It can't all be meat and sauce, you need some bread. Bread is cheap, quick, and I can buy it anywhere."

This sort of handy metaphor was already becoming familiar to me after six months of working with Eric. He wanted me and my team to design something great, but within tight parameters of time and money.

Our journey together had begun the previous autumn when our practice had partnered with Eastern Construction to respond to a hastily assembled call for design–build teams issued by the University of Toronto, which had just received a government infrastructure grant to build new teaching facilities at its Mississauga campus. The University of Toronto is one of the largest and most exacting sponsors of architectural projects in Canada, and their built legacy is a point of pride. The design–build methodology is traditionally chosen by risk-averse clients looking for cost-effective and expeditious solutions, and for whom design excellence is a secondary concern. Going design–build was not only an unusual choice for U of T but went against the very grain of their well-established campus design standards and design excellence framework. Having completed an academic library on the same campus two years earlier, I was familiar with the expectations of the university's dean of architecture and the design-review panel that he chaired. But this time, the university had no choice but to put speed of delivery above all other considerations, as the $54 million Knowledge Infrastructure Program grant came with strings attached: The building needed to be both "shovel-ready" before funds could be released, and substantially complete within two years of the grant award.

There was no time for the university to host a design competition, so the team would be selected based on their vision, reputation, and presentation of a credible schedule of overlapping design and construction activities. With our previous experience on the adjacent library site and Eastern's track record of executing several high-quality buildings for U of T, our combined team was able to convince the selection committee that we were sensitive to the overall architectural makeup of the campus, well-versed in their design-review process, and ready to design and build something very beautiful, very quickly. By the time we were awarded the commission, there remained just 22 months to design and build 150,000 square feet of state-of-the-art teaching space with high bars set for design excellence, student experience, and sustainability. Given that the 100,000-square-foot library had taken 42 months to design and build following U of T's standard process, the proposed schedule was, to say the least, aggressive.

The win was galvanizing, as it offered the opportunity to build beside our own recently completed project, frame a campus gateway, and sow the seeds of a larger master plan vision for the north end of the UTM campus. The approach we expressed in our proposal and interview focused on defining a chain of public space around the existing campus green, on weaving built fabric into the existing forested perimeter of the campus, and on defining a set of unique and sympathetic material expressions in tune with nature and the dynamic seasonal shifts of our Canadian climate.

The selection committee was evenly divided along two lines—those in favour of an expedited design-build process and those who were, to say the least, skeptical. It turned out that we had a "friend in court" and vocal advocate in the campus's chief administrative officer, Paul Donoghue. Paul and I had worked together in 2003, during the design stages of the library, and I knew him to be an excellent administrator—the kind of person who is born to get things done, who is inclined to empower his team, and for whom bureaucratic inertia and ponderous discourse are anathema. Paul had recently been in Egypt, where he built an 800,000-square-foot desert campus for The American University in Cairo in mere months, as if conjuring a mirage. He had returned to U of T with his long-held convictions buttressed by the experience and with a desire to revolutionize the way projects at the university were delivered. U of T's focus on design excellence had produced some remarkable pieces of architecture in recent years, many by foreign architects of note, but cost overruns, delays, and technical deficiencies had begun to compromise the ability for people like Paul to deliver what mattered most in his mind—a great education and experience for students. Paul had seized upon the opportunity that the grant presented.

Not only did the funding allow the addition of much-needed student-gathering and teaching space to his growing campus, but it also provided him with a chance to prove his conviction that high-quality design could be delivered quickly and predictably with the right team and a supportive client process. As the administrator of a satellite campus, Paul was a David to the Goliath of the central St. George Campus, whose planners, architecture faculty, and design review panel were firmly opposed to being so unceremoniously rushed. The money and the conditions attached to our project were, however, pointing to a new way of doing things. The UTM group was given the license to organize and launch this first design–build endeavor. St. George still held the reigns, albeit with a looser grip than usual. As for me, I had been deemed a suitable lead designer for such a venture in that I could tolerably respond to the expectations of both sides of the selection committee. The library had proven to be an award-winner so the St. George crew could reluctantly allow themselves to accept a designer of my pedigree, and Paul Donoghue had found me to be a reasonable person to work with. As he later confessed, while we toured the completed project:

"This is the best design I can get without hiring an asshole."

The design process and culture that evolved to make this project happen are unique in my professional experience. All of the inertia, bureaucracy, indecision, and competing agendas that usually plague publicly funded projects fell off the back of this fast-moving vehicle. Paul Donoghue and his project team had pre-consulted the users and defined the functional program down to the last plug. The program was bound together with the university's various technical design standards, its public realm and landscape guidelines, and the campus master plan and sustainability objectives, and passed over to the design–build team. Paul was characteristically direct with his instructions:

"That's all you will need and all you will get from us. There won't be any changes, so you can get moving."

Such a degree of certainty from a client organization is extremely rare. The objective had been captured in detail and fixed. The expectation was that the schedule and cost of the project would maintain a corresponding fixity. For this to happen, a very simple decision-making body was assembled that we eventually nicknamed "the triumvirate." The allusion to Shakespeare's Julius Caesar was not far off the mark, with an old way of doing things deposed and a three-headed leadership group of architect, builder, and client taking charge of all decisions moving forward. We convened to discuss the needs of the university, the design vision, and the demands of the construction schedule and process on a biweekly basis, establishing and maintaining the priorities of the project. In hindsight, this process seems expeditious to a fault. In so many of my design experiences, the nuanced voice of a complex and diverse community has been critical to inspiring the design response. The voices left out, the perspectives not considered, seem conspicuous today as casualties of a schedule mandated by political interests.

The drive to build, stimulate the economy, and show demonstrable growth before the next election cycle would override the purported benefits of creating a new "knowledge economy."

Whatever this fast-tracked approach may have left behind, it did benefit us as architects and the built outcome. If there was meagre fodder in terms of client culture to inspire the design, this was compensated for by a necessary focus on the essentials of architecture—material, form, light, and tectonics. Collectively the design and construction team were obliged to work as a highly integrated collaborative, with three simple objectives: create something beautiful, accommodate the program, and, above all, meet the schedule.

Eric and his team at Eastern established a "pull-planning" schedule that mapped in great detail every conceivable activity the large team of architects, engineers, and contractors would need to carry out in order to reach the finish line 22 months hence. Paul Donoghue had leveraged the university's considerable influence with the City for Mississauga to negotiate a phased approach to both planning approval and building permits. Instead of a standard design process, where a concept is developed and the entire architectural proposal moves iteratively towards a complete set of technical documents, the fast-track process saw our team creating complete technical packages of an incomplete design to be released for either municipal approval or construction on a constant basis, as the schedule demanded. Alan Mortsch, a very thorough and gifted technical architect, kept our talented but green team focused and motivated through a blur of tender deadlines, client presentations, and visits to the building site and fabricators shops. We were literally designing the building while it was being built, which proved to be an incredible learning experience for us all. The process influenced our understanding of technical assemblies and the constructability of our designs as well as the way we approached the overall concept. The concept needed to be dead-simple and open to multiple interpretations. It also needed to be fundamentally aligned with the logic of construction. If we were to be successful, two questions—"What is it?" and "How will we build it?"—needed to have the same answer. This is how the three "teaching towers" came to be.

A mere two weeks before machinery went on-site, we developed a simple wooden model to communicate the architectural concept, the arrangement of the program on the site, and the way that a single crane could work without interruption to service the entire construction process. For any construction project, cranes cost money and idle cranes are a sign that things aren't happening as fast as they could be. Removing redundancy and downtime became key drivers in the way that the built elements were arranged. We were fortunate in that the simplicity of UTM's program ultimately supported an expeditious construction sequence but also allowed us to establish some strong public-realm concepts that would form the DNA of a new master plan for the north end of campus. The program consisted of three basic ingredients: classrooms of varying sizes, crush space, and student study and lounge space. At a master-plan level, our team was interested in breaking up the mass of the building and creating public-space connections between the campus's verdant inner heart and its outer ring road, where the new building was to have its main address and transit drop-off. This impulse aligned with a need to manage the crowds inherent in such a large aggregation of teaching spaces. At class turnovers, the public spaces would be under enormous pressure to accommodate the comings and goings of thousands of students. How our design would support their navigation around the building and the campus as a whole became a critical question. It was Eric who hit on the confluence of agendas:

"Where the kids want to go, that's where we'll put the crane."

These combined drivers led us to the arrangement of the three teaching towers, each with large auditoria on the ground floor and smaller classrooms and seminar rooms above. A main atrium and a secondary passage created the public-space voids between the towers and facilitated the movement of students between classes, both vertically and horizontally. The public-space passages between the towers linked to a linear, south-facing gallery with entrances at each end. The crane tower would find a home in the main atrium and facilitate the erection of formwork and pouring of concrete for the columns and long-span post-tensioned beams of the large auditoria. During the curing period for the beams, when no further vertical progress could be made on the teaching towers, the crane turned south to build the three-storey gallery structure. When the gallery was complete, the crane returned to serve the second and third levels above the long-span beams, which by this point had cured and been tensioned to receive the new loads. In this instance, and in many analogous situations, the flow of construction activity was maintained thanks to an architectural arrangement founded on construction logistics. I came to realize that building fast isn't about sprinting up and down a ladder, but rather about avoiding a wait at the bottom.

Within three months of starting the project, construction hoarding was up, the site was being stripped and leveled, and we were called to present our first design ideas to the university's design review panel. The review was structured much like an end-of-term critique in architecture school: A chair makes opening remarks, the designers present, the panelists ask clarifying (and often leading) questions, and then a round of comments and open discussion ensue. At the end of an hour and a half, the chair verbally summarizes the panels' combined recommendations, which are later issued as a written directive. A team can proceed based on the comments or be requested to return at a later date. This is exactly what Paul Donoghue wanted to avoid at all costs. Larry Richards, the panel chair and then dean of the architecture school, set the stage by expressing how disappointed the panel was at the speed of the design and construction process, as it would likely preclude the possibility for a second visit to the panel. To compensate, the panelists would have to be doubly exacting and precise in their critique to ensure that the highest level of architectural quality could be achieved

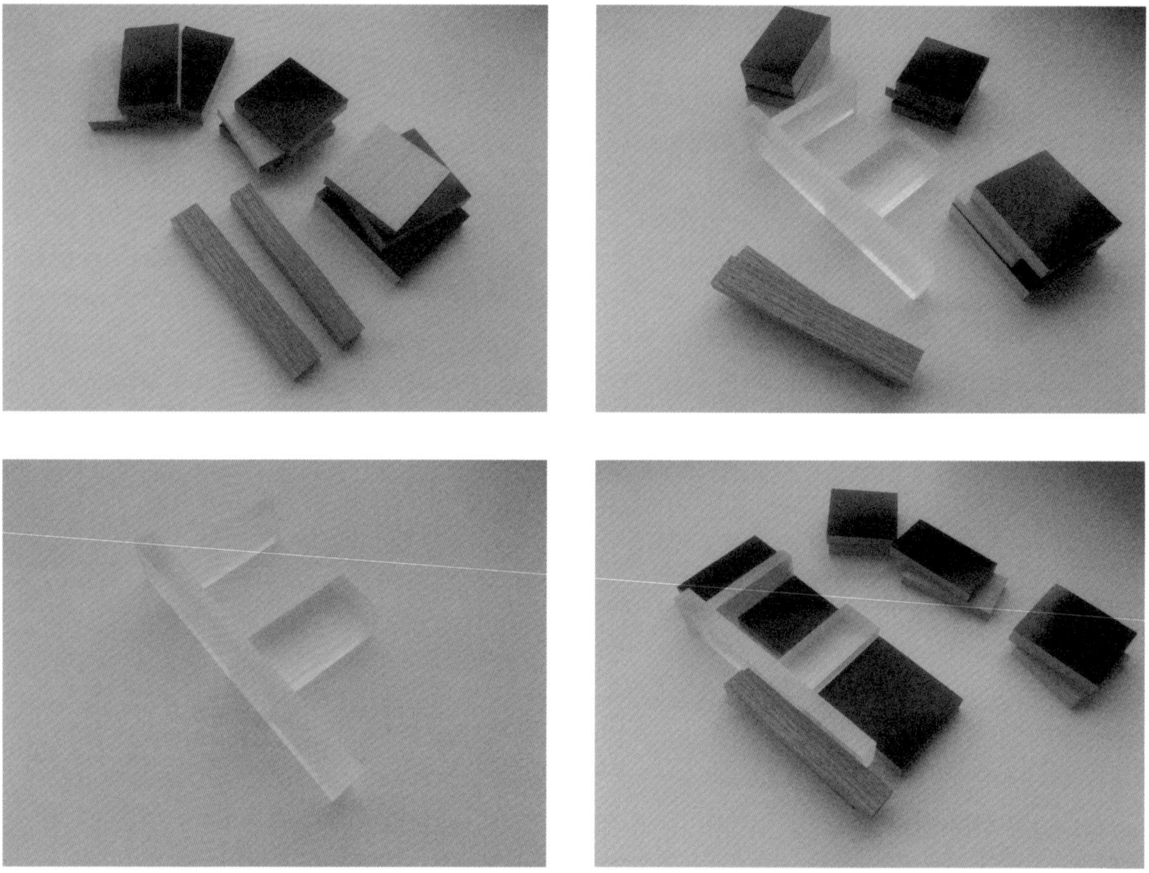

A conceptual maquette used to describe program-stacking, public space, and construction logistics

The maquette assembled

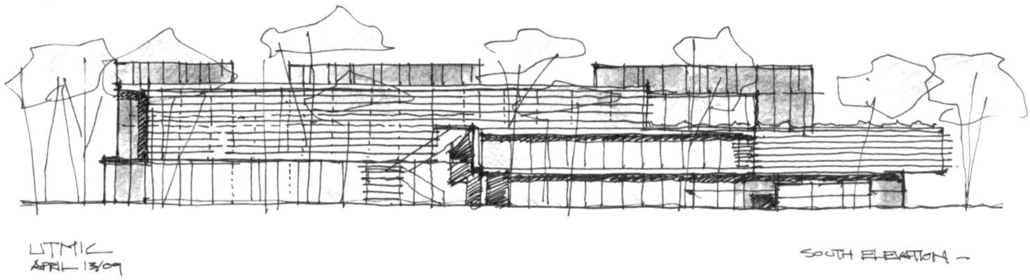

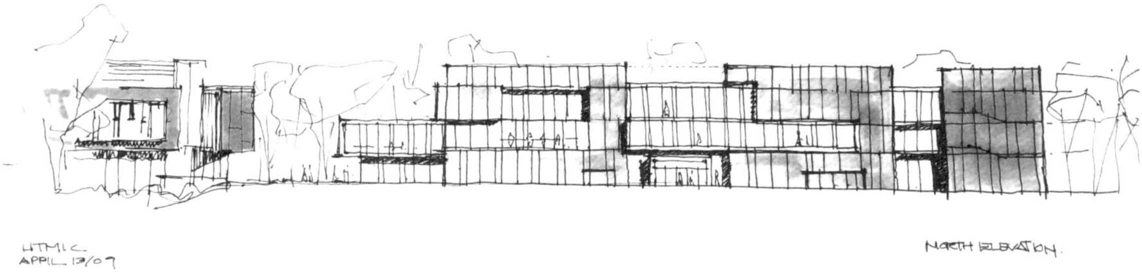

Early sketches studying context and composition

given the limited forum for discourse. Personally, I felt the need to compensate for the design–build process and went into the review hoping to convince everyone that the design would stand on its own merits and not be compromised by the frantic pace at which it was being executed. I probably came across as rather manic, having been amped up by a series of rolling deadlines in the weeks leading up to the presentation. As I paced back and forth in the glare of the projector bulb, I could see Paul and Eric out of the corner of my eye. Paul, in particular, was looking rather uncomfortable as I waded deeper and deeper into what, for him, was surely a quagmire of impenetrable architectural discourse.

Some architects design well but are not inclined to communicate critically. For academics, critical discourse may be their stock and trade, but they are often at a loss to practically apply their knowledge to a built proposition. The architect who is at once a thinker, a communicator, and a builder is a surprisingly rare bird in my experience. Panelist Brigitte Shim of Shim-Sutcliffe is one of those special individuals. You admire her work enormously, so you want to listen to what she has to say. You can actually understand what she is saying because she builds beautifully herself, and you can see the ready application of her ideas. If the review panel had one opportunity to make an impression on the clay that was setting so rapidly, Brigitte took full advantage by meeting the design process and construction sequence on their terms. She accepted the building's organization of program and form on the site as a fait accompli that, in her opinion, worked. It was, after all, disarmingly simple and tied to both functionality and sound public-realm principles. For her, the design would live or die by its material and tectonic manifestation. Would the three masses of the teaching towers be legible? Would the space of the campus readily flow between them to support both conceptual and master-plan objectives? For these things to happen, the proposed patinated-copper skin would need to come inside the building, defining the teaching towers and characterizing the spaces in between them. Such had been my desire from the outset, but I had not been able to convince Eastern that the expenditure was either necessary or viable. I had in a way invited this bit of critique and publicly embraced the recommendation, using the design-review panel to soften the resistance of my client. While the maneuver was risky, I hoped that Eric and Paul would see the change as a reasonable tithe to pay for getting through the design review panel otherwise unscathed.

As we left the chamber, I turned to Paul and Eric to gauge their reactions. Paul didn't like these meetings, finding the rhetoric to be insufferable, and he was frantically unwrapping a cigarette package in an attempt to regulate his blood pressure. Eric seemed to have enjoyed the whole thing, as if he'd been on holiday in a strange land. I expected him to be irate about the copper interior and my public commitment to seeing it through. But he was unbothered:

"It's fine with me, we just keep the trades on site and get them inside. It will be faster, and now the decision is made. It will cost, but we are buying in bulk. Now, the rest

of the building will have to be dead simple. Whatever we make it out of, that's what it is. I'm willing to pay the masons to make block walls, because when they're done the finish is done. The longer I can keep the drywallers out of the building the better. They make a mess and get in the way of everyone else. Let's avoid finish trades wherever possible. So yes, you overreached, but in the end it simplifies things."

For a design-build contractor, unresolved design decisions and uncertainty in general are deadly. "Slaying the dragons" was a term that Eric used to describe a prioritized approach to getting the big, expensive, and risky elements of the building underway and paid for as quickly as possible. The concrete structure, the heating and cooling infrastructure, and the building envelope were the key targets up front and, by following the design-review panel's suggestions, we had just added the signature elements of the interior to the pile of dead dragons. From that point on, our team was given very strict instructions regarding the remainder of the interiors:

"Pick one surface, the rest is background."

Fortunately, the conceptual organization of the building supported a strict delineation of interior language. Outside the teaching towers, the finishes were rich, as part of the exterior public realm. Inside the towers, they would be dead simple: linoleum floors, acoustic ceilings, three neutral walls, and one signature surface. To this end, we developed a strategy of wood acoustic walls that would face students as they entered any of the building's 24 teaching spaces—the singular focal point drawing people into the space of learning from the space of movement and social interaction.

What proved to be most instructive to our team as designers was the degree to which the logistics of the fast build focused our efforts on what really mattered and what could realistically be achieved. In many cases, this clarity of intent, at first seemingly focused on the build, in the end also benefited the design outcome. There is a rugged simplicity and power of voice to the expeditiously named "Instructional Centre" that I doubt we could have achieved if we had taken all the time in the world.

Lessons of the Fast Build

- Design it in the order they build it.
- Detail it the way they build it.
- Don't draw what you don't need to.
- Simplicity saves you time and money and leads to beauty.

Project	Instructional Centre
Location	University of Toronto Mississauga
Size	11,000 gross square metres
Date	2009-2011

Detail of the patinated-copper façade

The three teaching blocks along the campus ring road

Framing a campus gateway with the Hazel McCallion library

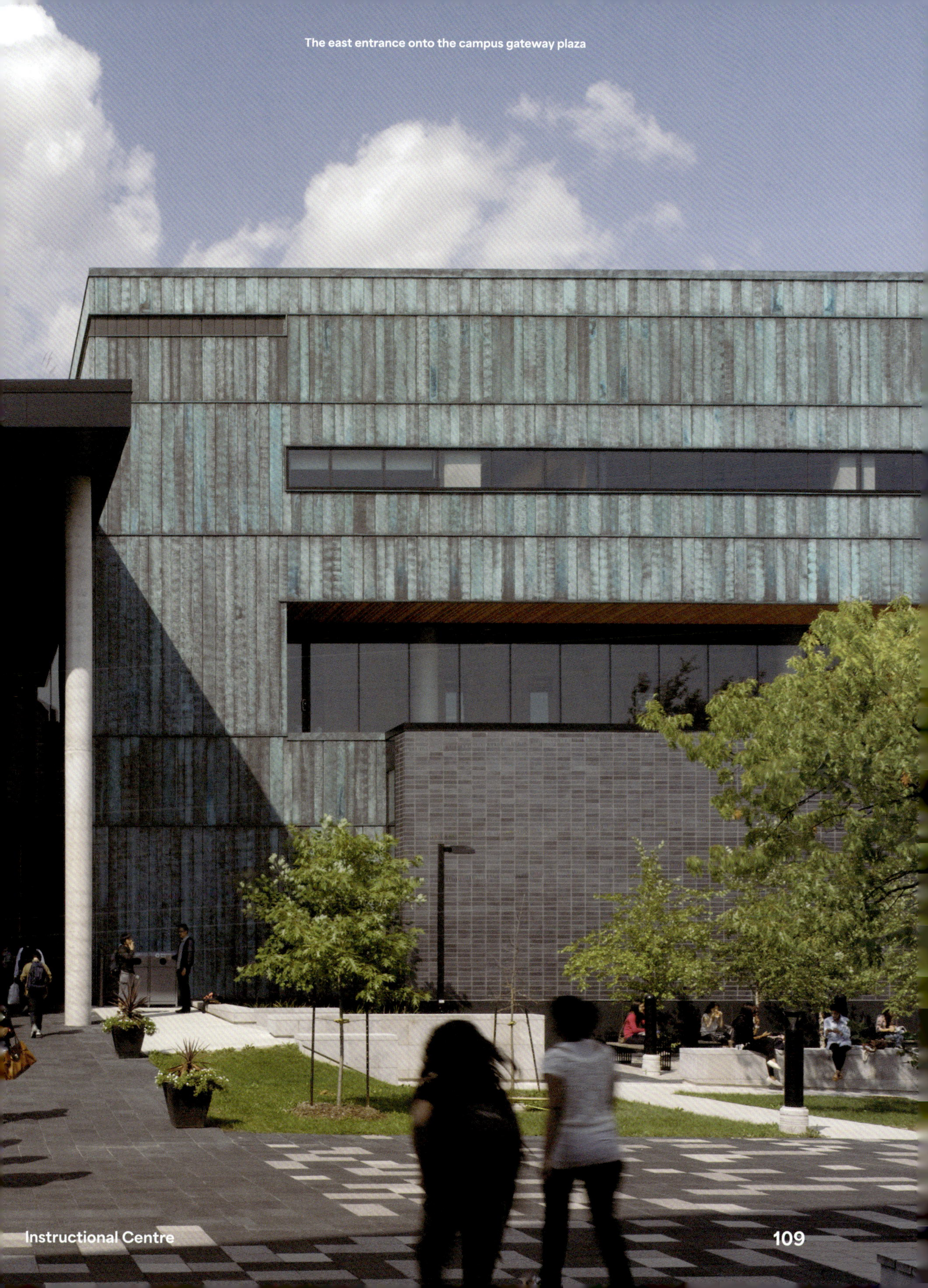

The east entrance onto the campus gateway plaza

Café and study spaces facing south onto the campus green

BOUNDLESS ENTERPRISE

Patinated copper volumes framing the north entrance onto the ring road

The south-facing gallery

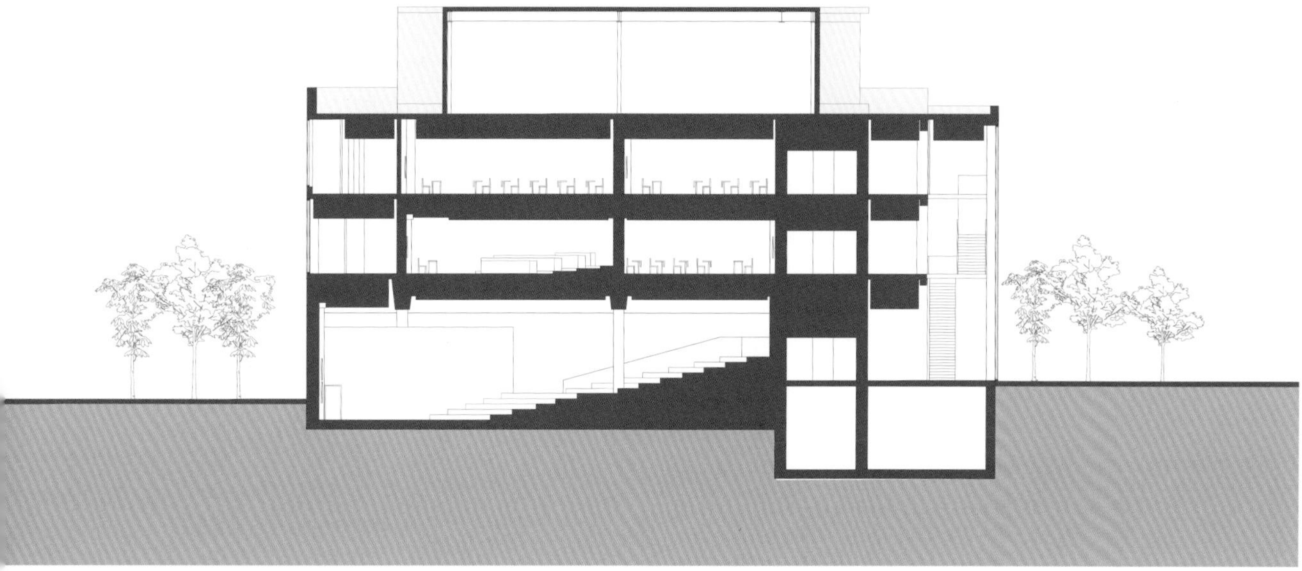

North-South Section A

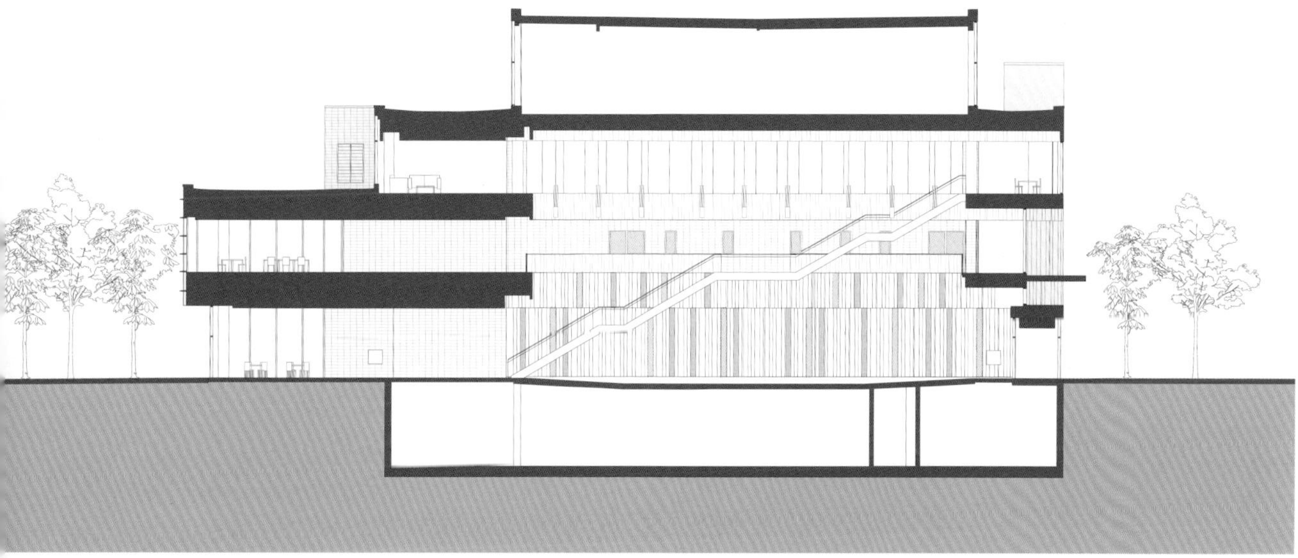

North-South Section B

Aerial view of the campus

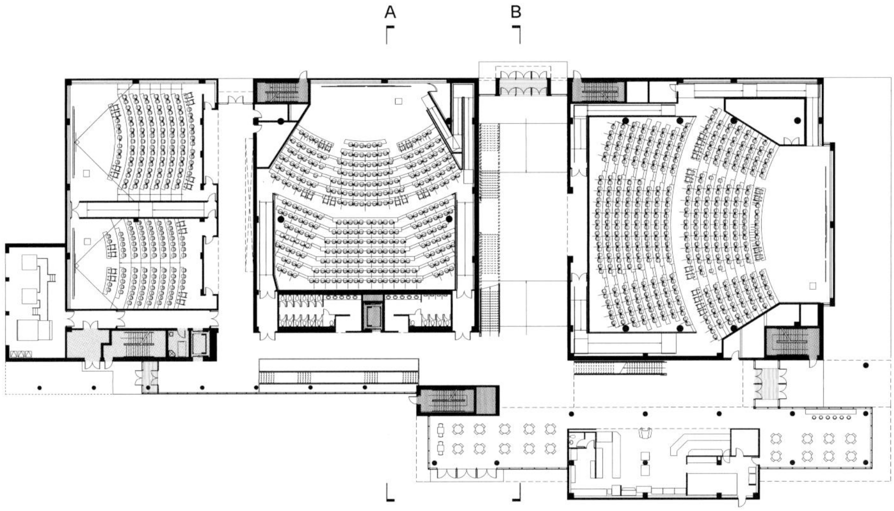

Level 01 Plan

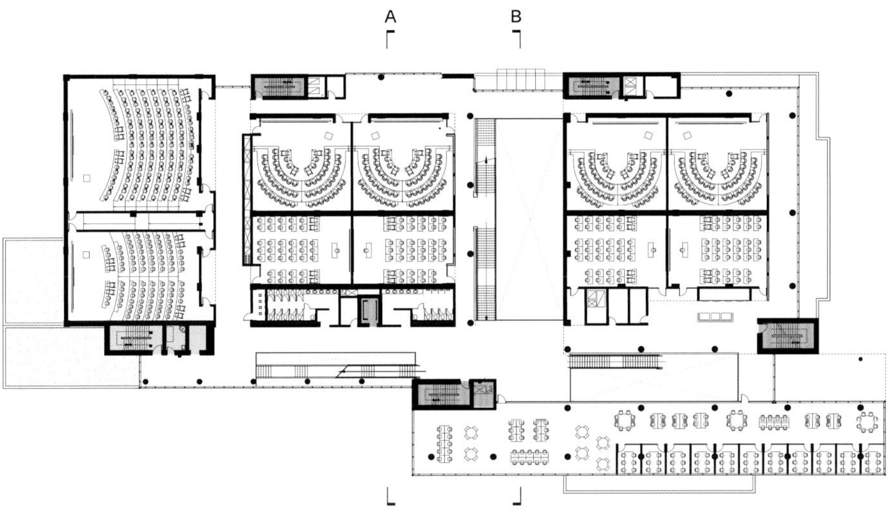

Level 02 Plan

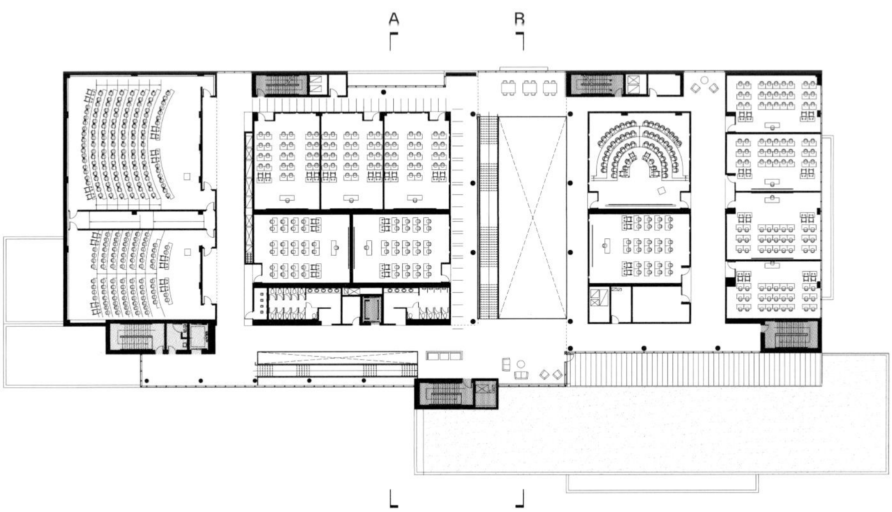

Level 03 Plan

The central atrium

Staircase on the building's south face

A passageway on the building's north side

Looking north in the central atrium

A 500-seat auditorium

Study spaces on Level 02

The east entrance at dusk

Fail Forward

Engineering 5 and 7
University of Waterloo

Waterloo, Ontario 2007–2018

It was a strange sort of homecoming, driving the winding regional highway towards the twin cities of Kitchener-Waterloo and my alma mater, the University of Waterloo. I felt an odd sense of apprehension, déjà vu, and excitement. I had stayed in touch with the School of Architecture through sporadic teaching and visiting-critic roles, but the school had moved off-campus to the nearby hamlet of Cambridge, and I hadn't been near the main campus in years. The University of Waterloo campus is not a pretty place, and it held no sentimental attraction to me. As architecture students, our time there had been focused on the studio, and we had all viewed the rambling, late-modern campus with its ring road, windowless bunkers, and generic landscaping with indifference. A place to be endured until the next co-op term transported us to intern employment in some big city with real architecture, real culture, and real adventures.

Waterloo had been founded in the late '50s by a local industrialist and engineer, Douglas Wright, who had seen the pressing need for a new generation of engineers to solve the challenges of a growing postwar society. Training young engineers to enter the workforce as quickly as possible with the highest level of skill and knowledge was to be the new university's primary objective. Starting in the fall of 1958, Waterloo began to offer its first semesters of co-op education in engineering, math, and the seminal field of computing. To accelerate the pace at which students could contribute to the labour shortage, and to forge ties with regional industry, they would alternate between four-month semesters on campus and four-month work placements in their field.

Today, Waterloo's co-op education program is world-famous, having born multiple generations of tech-savvy entrepreneurs whose global network is ever-expanding and self-perpetuating. Waterloo's connection to industry is solidified by the incredible success stories of its alumni, who continue to nourish and collaborate with the university.

I attended Waterloo between 1984 and 1991, and during that time I subscribed to the quasi-nomadic existence that accompanied the co-op education model. I eventually whittled down my personal belongings to a pair of large duffel bags and a guitar case, as I alternated academic terms on campus with work placements in Toronto, Kingston, Montreal, and Rome. I recall that we were vaguely aware of the massive engineering faculty, and that we often scoured their sprawling assemblage of brutish buildings for underutilized nooks and crannies that would afford a scholarly refuge from the chaotic camaraderie of the architecture school. I had little sense of the people who inhabited these buildings or what they were doing. I would say that this lack of identity and sense of place pervaded the entire campus. The campus was an instrument of the co-op program. It was used, but not lived in. I'm sure that there were identities and cultures corresponding to a variety of groups, but one would have to dig deep and, as architecture students, we didn't have time for that.

In 2007, I was returning to the campus, driving west on University Avenue with my colleagues John Potter and Werner Sommer. We were all Waterloo grads, sharing a combined sense of excitement and dread as the white cubic silhouette of the campus library came into view. Two weeks earlier, Dave Mitchell, one of the senior partners in the legacy firm of Shore Tilbe Irwin & Partners, had taken a call from Waterloo's campus architect Daniel Parent. Dave was then administering the tail end of several smaller projects on campus that the firm had done over the years. For Daniel, STIP was a reliable source for executing projects. The fact that the firm hadn't delivered any visionary design solutions for Waterloo was just fine with him. Daniel liked things simple, predictable, on time, and on budget, but this time was obliged to offer and ask for something more. Waterloo had just received a notable donation and was under intense pressure to deliver 150,000 square feet of engineering offices, research labs, classrooms, and space for student teams and classrooms as quickly as possible. With no time to go to market, Daniel was proposing to extend our existing on-campus contract, effectively sole-sourcing a prestigious, $50 million commission. There was one condition, stipulated by the director of the School of Architecture and head of the president's advisory committee on design, Eric Haldenby. The condition was that I lead the design with a team of as many Waterloo architecture grads as we could muster. This singular event clearly outlined the strength of the Waterloo network. Rick had been, at various times, my professor, my mentor, and, while I served as a teaching assistant to his Waterloo Rome Studio, my employer. He was now asserting what influence he could over the level of design on campus.

So there I was, approaching the campus with two very proud and very different Waterloo Architecture grads. John Potter was my long-time friend, my former college roommate, and a relatively recent addition to our team. John was going to be my design assist. He processed concepts at an incredible rate, bringing a torrent of creativity and knowledge from the widest range of sources to every conversation. Creative, restless, childlike, and irreverent, we nicknamed him "the pollinator." Werner, the assigned project architect, was, on the other hand, taciturn, stoic, methodical, technical, and professional. He lived by a series of simple maxims: "black lines on white paper," for instance, and "bring something new to every meeting." In the crucible of this fast-tracked project, their differences would create a distinct and occasionally volatile chemistry. It would become my job to mediate and channel these frictions towards the design solution that we eventually derived.

The first day on campus, we met the client team led by Sue Gooding, assistant to the visionary engineering dean Adel Sedra; Daniel Parent, the campus architect; and Ron Venter, the former provost and dean of mechanical engineering at the rival University of Toronto. Ron had been brought on to lead the academic planning and programming of the large new facility. This group would be augmented by the voices of departmental chairs, researchers, and students along the way, but the aggressive schedule required an efficient and decisive project culture. Ron Venter would be our greatest resource in translating the dean's vision and the needs of the various users into a highly detailed functional program. Ron introduced the vision. The new building, rather expediently christened E5, was to create much-needed expansion space for the growing departments of mechanical and mechatronic, electrical, and systems engineering. Ron described the new building as the first of two phases that would act as "decanters," allowing uses to move out of the faculty's earliest structures, freeing them up for renewal and expansion. Ron was skilled at the management of a complex space and equipment inventory. He also had very specific attitudes to architecture and how it affected the student experience. Adel Sedra's vision for the new building was that it provide a showcase for student talent, a magnet for recruitment and advancement, and a bold identity for his top-ranked faculty. Ron decried the "corridor syndrome" which dominated the existing building complexes, keeping research and creativity in the dark, stifling culture and collaboration.

That afternoon, we toured the rambling mega-complex of the four interconnected "E" engineering buildings. What we saw was surprising on a number of fronts. The first set of revelations came with a tour of the various star research initiatives. I had naively put engineers together into a homogeneous lump, not realizing how broad and inspiring their enterprise actually is. We saw windows into biomechanical engineering, robotics, structural and material investigations, and complex fluid analysis, to name but a few. I came to realize that engineers are, fundamentally, problem solvers, applying and inventing techniques to shape the world and its processes. Like many architects, I am prone to hubris, and I was humbled that day by the depth and diversity of the engineer. I found myself wishing that I had studied engineering as I marveled again and again at the ingenuity, creativity, and passion buried within the labyrinth of the existing complex. It was obvious that many of the spaces were dark, tired, and undersized for the activities being carried out. Creating ordered, well-serviced, and daylit environments to support the faculty's research activities would be paramount. But it was clear that the fix would need to go far beyond the technical requirements. In all of the four existing buildings, there was just one space that could be described as cultural space, the tall brick atrium of Carl Pollock Hall (E4). Within this dim, cavernous volume, a student-run coffee shop, a collection of battered lounge furniture, and a large cork pinup board told the story of the student experience. The cork sheet was completely covered in handwritten Post-its—testimonials to the harsh rigors of a demanding academic program, nomadic lifestyle, and pervading sense of isolation that were at times heartbreaking. Werner, John, and I were given pause to reflect on our own experience at Waterloo and what cold comfort the built environment had provided. In my mind, E5 would need to go beyond its role as a program container and showcase. It would need to provide the framework for a supportive culture for students and faculty alike. It would need to be a home.

Parameters and Principles

Apart from these initial observations on the existing program, space, and culture, several key project parameters would guide our thinking:

- The proposed site was a large surface parking lot located across a regional rail line from the campus boundary. While this would provide the opportunity to define the face of a new engineering precinct, it would create challenges with regards to connecting to the main campus and the rest of the engineering spaces.

- The program featured some very specifically defined, highly technical spaces such as high-bay labs for undergraduate team projects and hydrogen vehicle research, fabrications shops, and an anechoic isolation chamber. The remainder of the proposed 150,000 square feet was to be assigned to office, research, and teaching space for the various departments. Consultation with the departmental chairs was ongoing and the specifics were still to be ironed out when we put pencil to paper. We were encouraged by Ron and Sue to think of part of the building as being highly adaptable and in a constant state of flux.

- E5 was to be the first of two interconnected phases and the cornerstone of a master-planned engineering precinct. Whatever we designed would need to anticipate a major addition within a decade.

- The design schedule was to be highly compressed, with only seven months available to complete programming, master planning, detailed design, and construction documents. We would need to design fast and in an open-ended way that would accommodate program changes and serve speed of construction.

In the early days of our engagement, we immediately dove into the technical and logistical challenges presented by the high-bay vehicle labs at the base of the building. We came to understand the need to separate people from cars, and academic uses from the "industrial occupancy" classification required for the use and testing of hydrogen fuel cells. This complex program would potentially drive the design towards two buildings: an academic building stacked on top of an industrial building. With the client's stated desire to showcase all the building activities, we would need to explore ways to integrate the two worlds both visually and spatially.

While Werner was diving into the particulars, I was getting used to my new creative collaboration with John, which tended towards an open-ended conversation. Sensing Werner's mounting impatience, I decided to pin down some of the main themes. Acting as a kind of verbal editor and graphic stenographer, I generated quick doodles to crystallize our design conversations and the project's guiding principles. I always meant to go back and create a more polished diagram, but never did. The following seemed to capture the energy and intensity of the project and served us for both phases over the better part of a decade.

The Daylight Factory

Inspired by the rich industrial tradition of the Kitchener-Waterloo area, the architecture of the E5 building would be characterized by a modular structural bay, articulated service cores, and abundant perimeter glazing. Raw, lofty, and highly adaptable, the new building would be at once the support and display system for all manner of research and exploration.

The Universal Container

The E5 building would be configured as a universal container with a modular bay and a regular form, articulated only by the major spaces of movement and public interaction. The façade would feature abundant transparency for showcasing high-bay labs and serve as a unifying conceptual mask behind which a multitude of ongoing adaptations could occur.

Two Buildings, One Experience

The building would offer two distinct types of spaces: the factory and the academy. These spaces would be visually and sectionally interconnected by a public realm that offered a simultaneity of experience while connecting E5 to the campus at large.

Engineers in Motion

The design of E5 would celebrate the need for engineering students and faculty to navigate between E5 and the main campus. The public-space system would be designed as a promenade that put the people and research of Waterloo Engineering on display. The movement of projects, equipment, and vehicles would be woven around the threads of pedestrian movement, using the section to physically separate but visually connect incompatible uses.

In the first four months of the design, these principles allowed us to communicate the design intent to ourselves, our clients, and their stakeholders. They also helped us to adapt in an aligned way to a variety of project disruptions. When at the end of schematic design, the project was tracking over area and over budget, our team was able to course correct by removing an entire six-floor bay from the south end of the building. The conceptual drivers of universal container and daylight factory allowed the building to maintain its aesthetic and planning intent despite this sizable reduction, precisely because it had been conceived as an expandable or contractable modular system.

Past Futurism

As we defined these guiding principles, we were also mindful of the aesthetic language that they would imply in combination. For several weeks, we toyed with inspiration to be found in the region's industrial vernacular or the modernist tenets of the Bauhaus, but we ultimately found them to be backward-looking and not reflective of the University of Waterloo's intense spirit of innovation. Architecture is in many ways the laggard of cultural expressions, as its reliance on labour in the field renders it fundamentally low-tech in its final realization. The fact that every building is a unique prototype means that economies of scale may be realized for individual components but never for the building as whole. Imagine fabricating all the parts of an automobile in a hi-tech factory and then dragging them outside to be welded together in the rain and mud, and you will have a sense of why buildings are fundamentally expensive and crude compared to Teslas, iPads, and high-speed trains.

In the end, it was the convenient moniker of E5 that began to suggest an aesthetic language based on a cinematic vision of the near future. John Potter and I have shared two passions over our long friendship: country music (not relevant here) and science fiction. Imagining a supergraphic "E5" stenciled on the side of a lunar shuttle, we began to revisit Stanley Kubrik's *2001: A Space Odyssey* as a template for the image of innovation. Kubrick's reductive approach to the interiors of the future were a touchstone, but we were more interested in the mystery presented by the film's silent protagonist, the black monolith.

The idea of an enigmatic, sculptural object that communicated the spirit of the future became a focus of the building's central public space. Working with Ion Luh, our lighting designer from Crossey Engineering, and Mike Moffatt, our structural engineer from RJC, we conceived of a communication stair that would not only serve to encourage social interaction between floors but function as an integrated design solution, providing movement, lighting, and acoustic control in one gesture.

The stair was planned as a set of stacked straight-runs that obliged its users to double back through each floor. We dubbed the atrium and its stair "the academic mixer"—an instrument for promoting interdisciplinary interaction. To achieve the desired configuration, Mike Moffatt designed the stair as a cranked truss that could bridge the 18-metre length of the atrium without interim support. John Potter developed the details of the stair cladding—perforated black aluminum acoustic panels with integrated LED-lighting reveals that transformed each cranked tube into a high-contrast graphic composition. At the apex of the atrium, a mirrored ceiling inset with a constellation of blue LED pin lights created a visual backdrop for the stair, allowing it to float in seemingly infinite space.

The atrium was set in the middle of the rectilinear plan with bays of adaptable modular space on either side. Within this framework, we were careful to avoid the pitfalls of "corridor syndrome" that plagued Waterloo's earlier buildings. A graduated hierarchy of breakout spaces and lounges were distributed on each floor, providing a complement to gathering spaces around the main atrium. Corridors were planned to terminate in natural light and views to the outside world. All perimeter spaces feature glazed fronts to bring borrowed light into the plan and express a community of layered space.

The accelerated schedule and the vision of the universal container drove the team to focus design effort on the central public space. The atrium was to be a magnet for interaction and exchange, which we viewed as a permanent fixture of the architecture. The bays on either side were detailed as cleanly and simply as possible with an eye to resilience and flexibility. This dual expression, differentiating what was fixed and what would inevitably change, also translated into the building exterior.

In an effort to expedite both the design and construction process, we had specified a unitized curtain-wall system for the entire building. Modular and prefabricated components would reduce

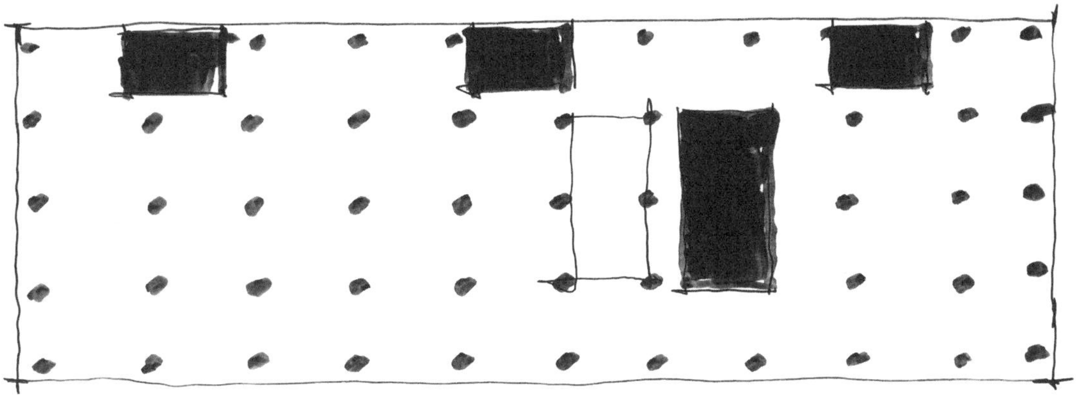

Sketch of the building as a universal container for research and learning

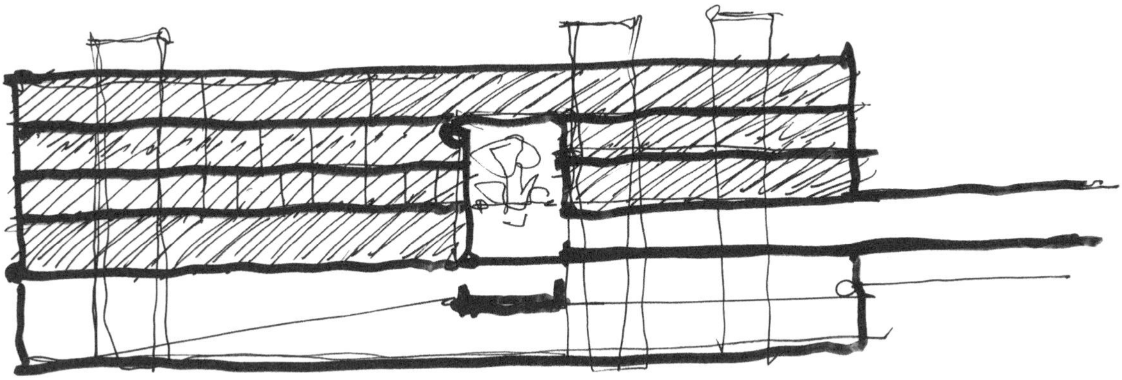

Sketch of two buildings in one shell: a factory and a laboratory

Concept sketch of the public realm expressed and a masked space for adaptive research

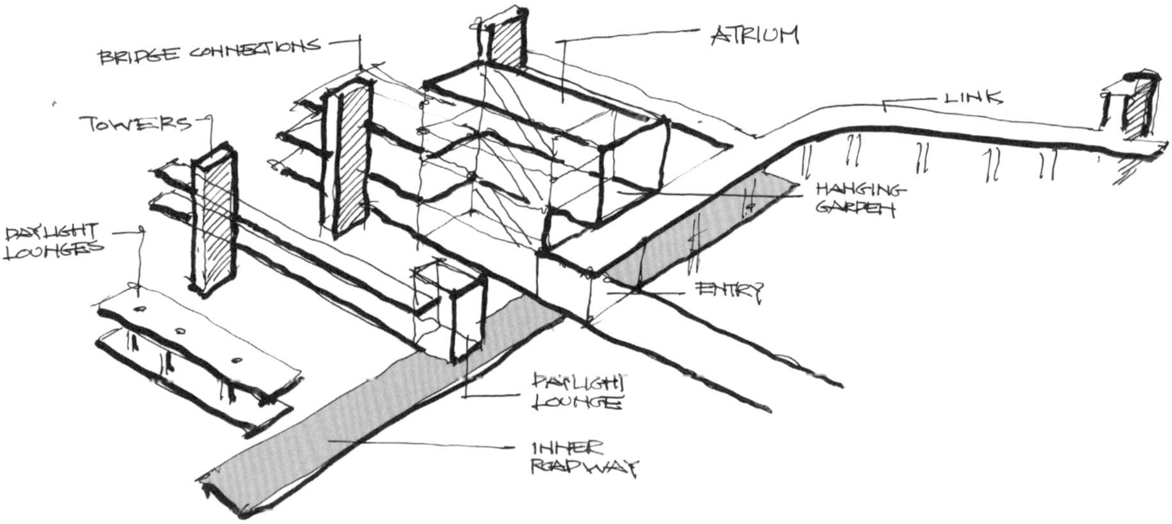

Concept sketch of occupant connectivity

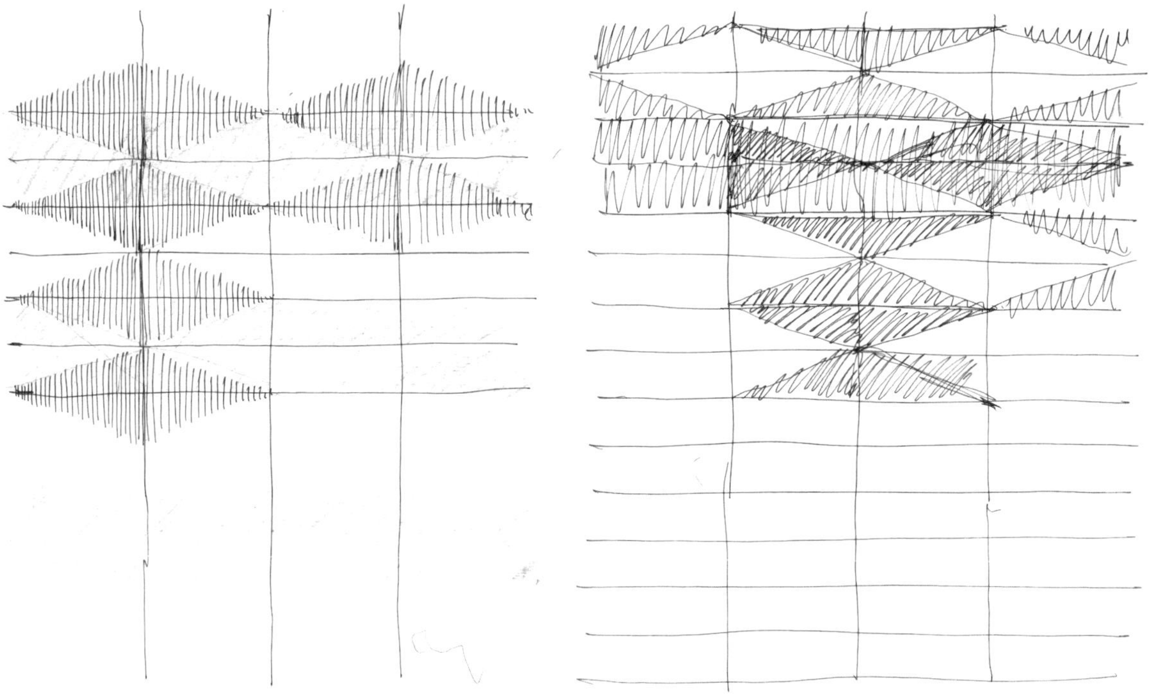

Sketch study of the trompe l'oeil façade

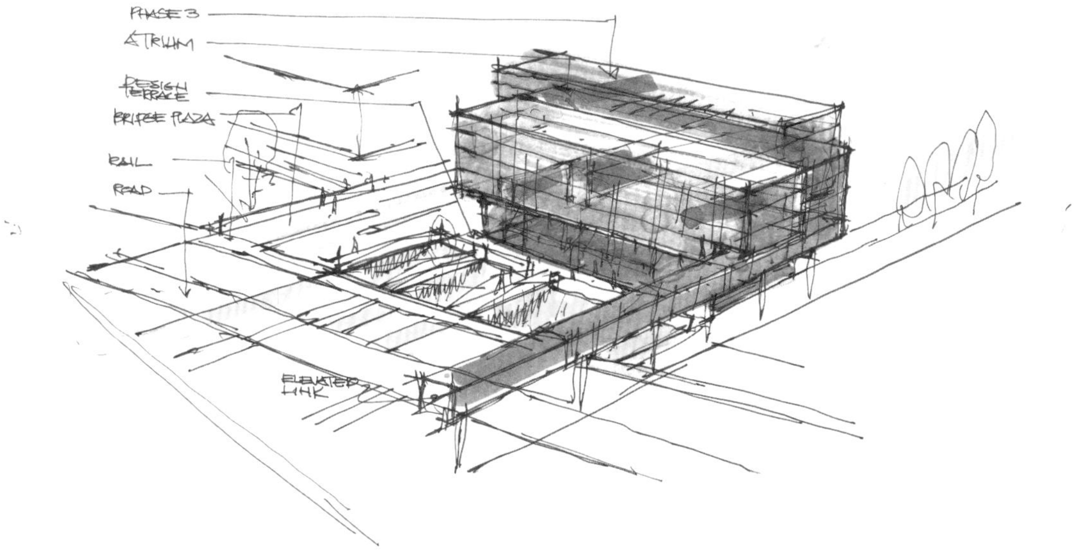

Early study for the two-phase build-out, forecourt, and bridge link

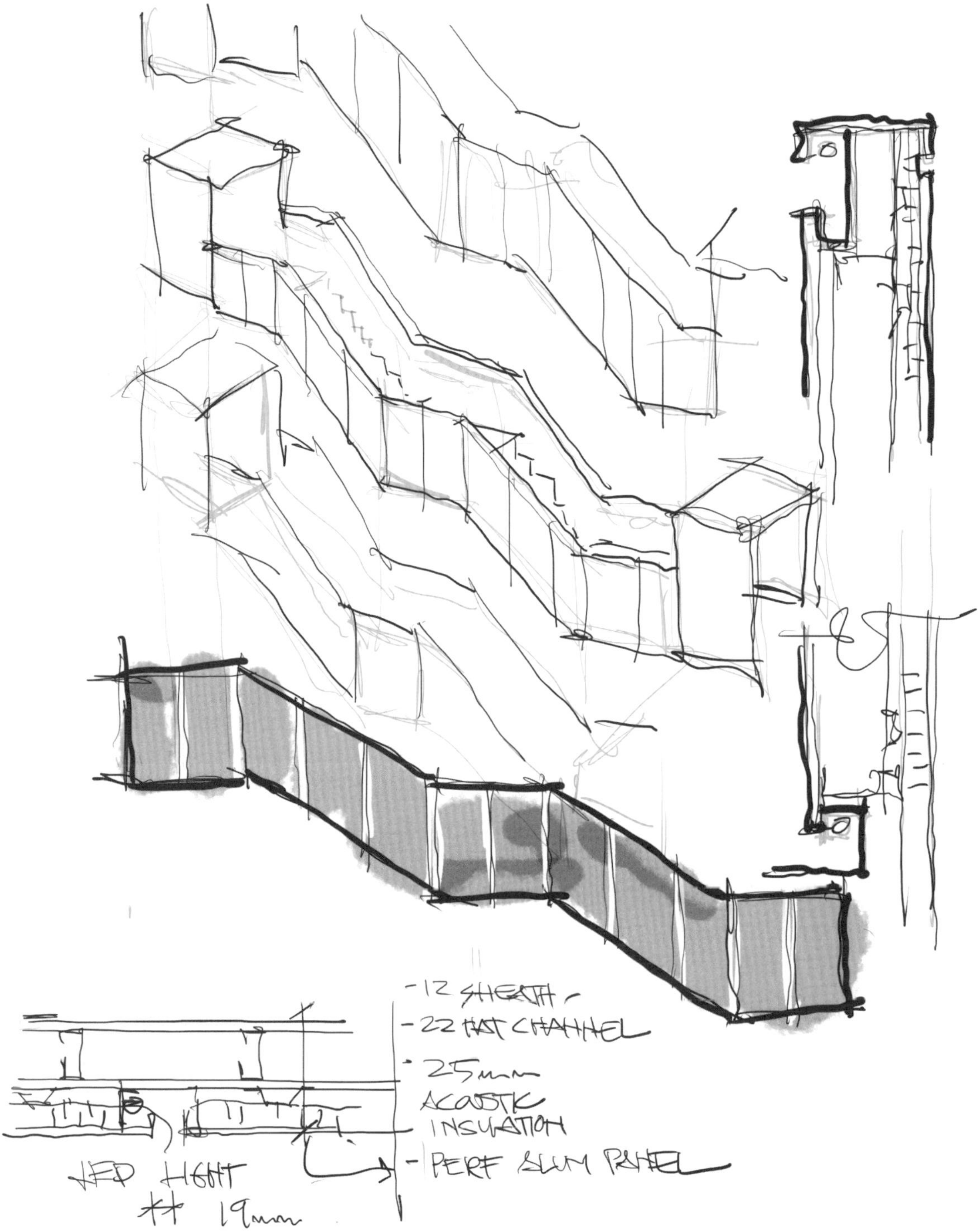

Studies of the E5 feature stair, integrating structure, acoustics, and lighting in one system time and cost while maximizing the quality of workmanship and precision of the installation. The resulting efficiency and simplicity of building form presented our team with a unique challenge. How would the building act as a flagship for Waterloo Engineering? How would its architecture communicate the spirit of innovation and the enormous variety of the enterprise within? We had to ask ourselves, "What is the expressive potential of flatness?"

Working with a series of cardboard sketch models, we developed the notion of a simple volume where different uses were communicated through the presence or absence of an architectural veil. We wanted to highlight the building's fixed spaces—the atrium, the bridge connection to the main campus, and a student design centre—through a high level of transparency. In contrast, the constantly changing and more cellular spaces of the research floors would feature a higher percentage of insulated wall and yet be unified and abstracted behind a continuous geometric veil.

While Werner coordinated the planning and servicing of our universal container, John and I continued to search for a suitable façade language. We knew what the design language needed to communicate but not what it looked like. While certain aspects of the project were deep into detailed design, others were lagging, most notably Ron's functional program, which seemed to have an ever-expanding membership. One particular late addition proved inspirational: the anechoic chamber. These specialized research spaces feature an adaptable interior shell formed by multiple carbon-coated foam-rubber pyramids that effectively isolate the space from the noise vibration and electromagnetic interference of the outside world. On a tour of such a chamber, I was immediately struck by the expressive potential of these pyramids in aggregate, as well as their metaphorical potential. Could the architectural veil of E5 take the expression of a reversed anechoic shell? Instead of isolating, its pyramids would create an increased surface area for engaging with the world. Instead of black, they would be light. Rather than volumetric projections they would be trompe l'oeil illusions.

Using the unitized curtain wall system as our canvas, the team explored multiple scenarios where varying densities of white ceramic ink would create a play of light and shadow suggestive of a three-dimensional pyramid. In 2007, ceramic frit was a relatively new process and, while architects were deploying it for solar shading, generating the aesthetic for an entire building based on the geometric arrangement of white dots on clear glass was unheard of. The end result is a building skin that is utterly dynamic. From certain angles and in certain light conditions, E5 can appear aggressively volumetric—a sculptural assemblage of metal pyramids. Before your eyes, it can flatten into a taut glass box and then a moment later it can dematerialize, as its mirrored coatings reflect a cloud-scattered sky.

Tethered to the brick bunkers across the tracks by a curving glass umbilicus, the universal container of E5, with its ever-changing shell, would form a singular and enigmatic presence at the edge of the campus for the better part of a decade. We had always planned E5 as the first of two research containers, parallel to and slightly offset from one another. In 2015, Dan Parent invited us back to complete the commission, this time with 180,000 square feet of research and teaching on seven floors, with an atrium between the two phases. Daniel, Sue, and Ron were back in their roles as client representatives, and Werner and I paired up again to handle the design and management of the project. Despite John Potter having moved on to a client-side role, it initially seemed that we would be embarking on a sort of reunion tour. At our start-up meeting, I dusted off the scrappy sketches that had served the initial guiding principles and the massing model that described the relationship of the two phases. Everyone present was in agreement that this framing of the project still seemed correct and would serve us well. But when we took our initial thoughts to the new dean, Pearl Sullivan, I realized that things had changed. E5 had been designed in response to a deficit of space for culture and interdisciplinary collaboration. Over six years, Waterloo's culture had flourished and transformed within its new home. It was now more diverse, more integrated, and more entrepreneurial. It had outgrown our assumptions and methodologies. We would now have to engage with it on its own terms.

I had met Pearl during the E5 project in her capacity as chair of electrical engineering, and I had been impressed by her insight and energy. Meeting her in her new role as dean, I soon realized that she had been holding power in reserve. Pearl was a force of nature with a bold new take on her predecessor's vision. Pearl was tireless in her promotion of women in engineering and would not rest until the field was demographically and culturally transformed. For her, bringing diversity of thought, viewpoint, and capability was the only way to solve the world's most complex problems. She challenged her peers and students to fail publicly. Not just to experiment, but to take big risks and share the embarrassments and lessons learned. Pearl was not afraid of corny slogans, as long as they were impactful, and "Fail Forward" became the motto of her tenure.

Pearl saw the new atrium between the phases as a huge theatre from which the open and unabashed risk-taking would always be on display. It would be a cultural space, supporting, commemorating, and broadcasting Waterloo's new vision.

I was excited by Pearl's vision and was careful to impress upon our clients that it could not be achieved with the rather expeditious and closely controlled process that had been used on E5. To create a cultural space on the scale that Pearl imagined, we would need the input of lots of people thinking freely and speaking openly. It would get messy before it came into focus. In the end, we reached a compromise that suited the university's need to tightly control budget and schedule while still allowing the potential for new programmatic, spatial, and behavioral paradigms. The concept of the universal container continued to serve us. Werner led a dedicated technical team in the planning and servicing of the seven-story research wing for E7. The "hard spaces," with their fixed program requirements, could proceed at pace while I led an exploration into the more open-ended cultural realm of the atrium.

Cultural spaces tell stories and I felt we needed to add a storyteller to our team. I invited Keith Curtis, the leader of Perkins&Will's branded environments

Sketch study of the view into the student work bays from the E5 lobby group, to run a series of visioning and design workshops focused on the culture, history, and future vision of engineering at Waterloo. I had watched Keith lead a similar visioning session for our client at the Bank of Canada two years previously and had been thoroughly impressed. Keith combines charisma and an almost intimidating physical presence with a disarming empathy that draws people in and the stories out. Over four sessions, a diverse group combining leadership, faculty, students, and alumni shared their perspectives on life at Waterloo across six decades. What shone through most consistently was an enormous collective pride, combined with the sense that all of the amazing accomplishments of the school were still hiding under a bushel. While E5 was recognized as a great showcase of undergraduate teamwork, there was still no one place on campus where a visitor, a new student, or a prospective recruit could feel a sense of awe.

Following the visioning session, we began to develop the atrium as a manifold cultural container combining elements of an event theatre, museum, gallery, social hub, and super lab. We worked with Keith and his team to develop a series of design elements to tell the Waterloo story both in physical space and in the space of social media. The illuminated red stair, the mirrored monumental sign, and E5 and E7's distinct graphic skin work in concert with signature program spaces such as the two-storey robotics hub, the entrepreneurs pitch zone, and the ideas clinic to create a powerful story about the past, present, and future of Waterloo Engineering.

In the fall of 2018, I joined my colleagues and over 1,000 invited guests to watch Dean Sullivan preside over the grand opening of E7. Pearl was then in the final stages of her battle with cancer, but she managed nonetheless to bring the house down with her impassioned account of progress at Waterloo and the brilliant future it could anticipate in its new home. I have attended a hundred grand openings, and this was by far the most joyous. The ecstatic crowd was a testimony to the changing face of engineering. They were young, diverse, and dare I say beautiful in the passion and pride on their faces. I thought back over the long arc of my relationship with the University of Waterloo, and particularly those despairing and anonymous testimonials that engineering students had once pinned up in Carl Pollock Hall. I too felt proud, for my colleagues and I had been part of a bold transformation. We had been given two great opportunities: the first to create a space for culture to grow, and then to shape another space for that culture to express itself. If we failed along the way, it served us well in the long journey from no place to pride of place.

Client	Engineering 5 and 7
Location	Waterloo, Ontario
Size	39,500 gross square metres
Date	2007–2018

Detail of the trompe l'oeil façade frit

The E5 west

The ring road and rapid-transit line separating E5 from the rest of campus

The south entrance to E5 and E7

Façade detail of E5 before the second phase

The north entrance and plaza

The south entrance and engineering work yard

The atrium between E5 and E7

The student-run food and beverage service

Crush space outside main lecture halls

The structural frame expressed in the skylit atrium

Detail of the E7 feature stair

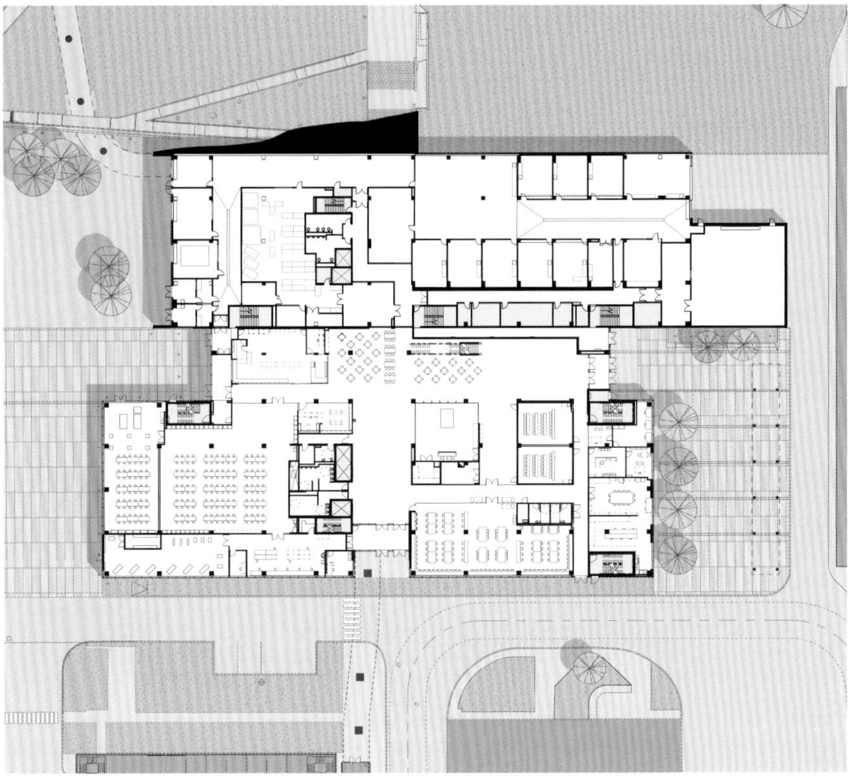

Level 01 Plan

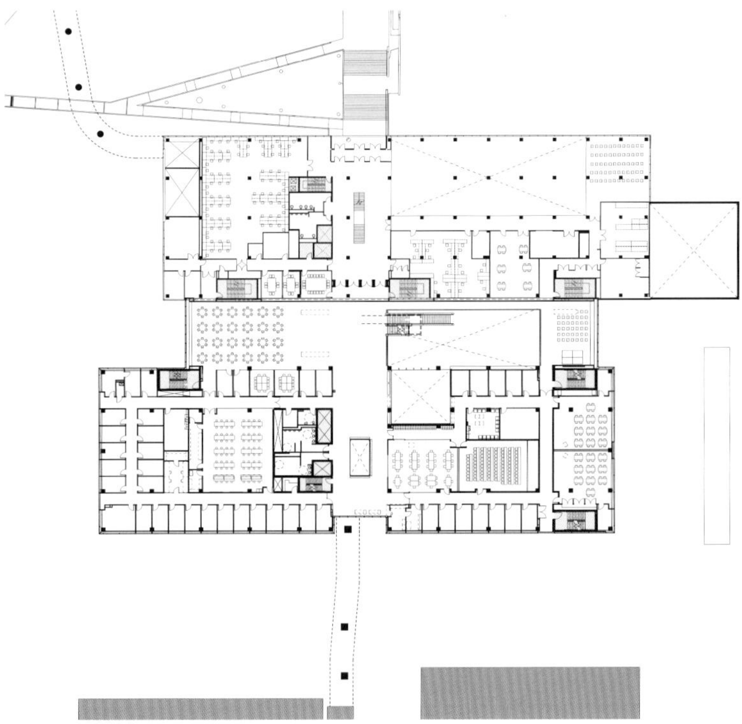

Level 02 Plan

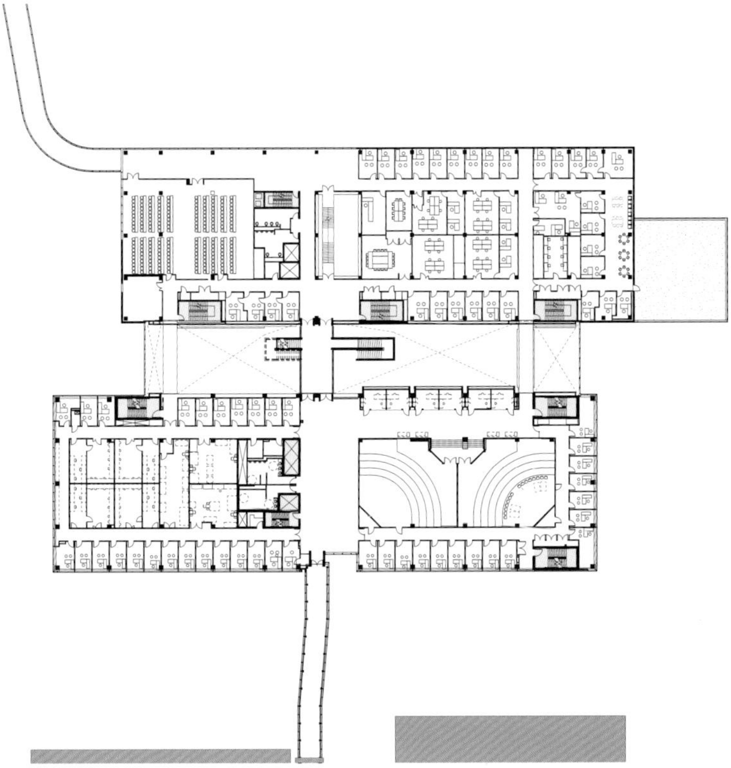

Level 03 Plan

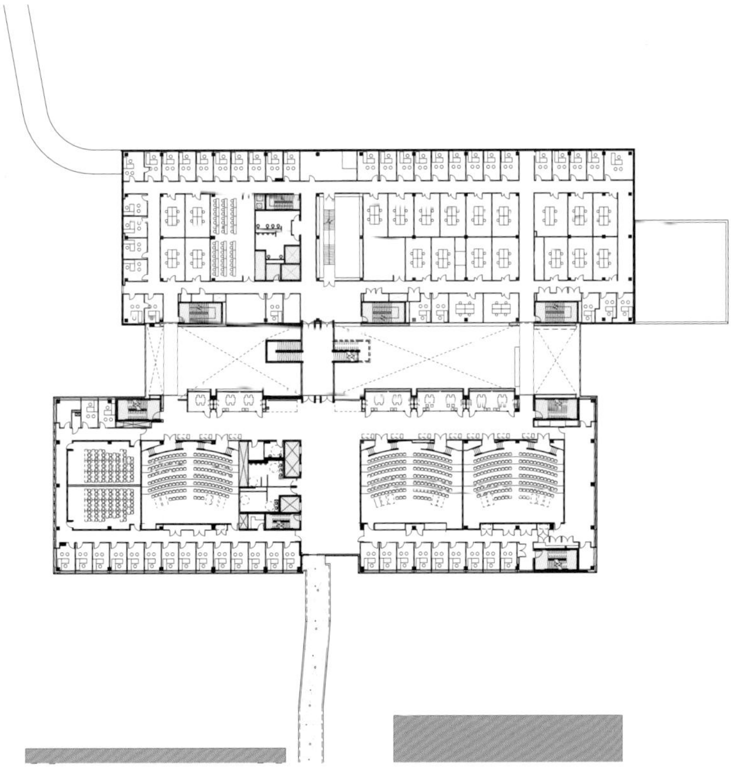

Level 04

E5 lobby and feature stair

E5 atrium and feature stair

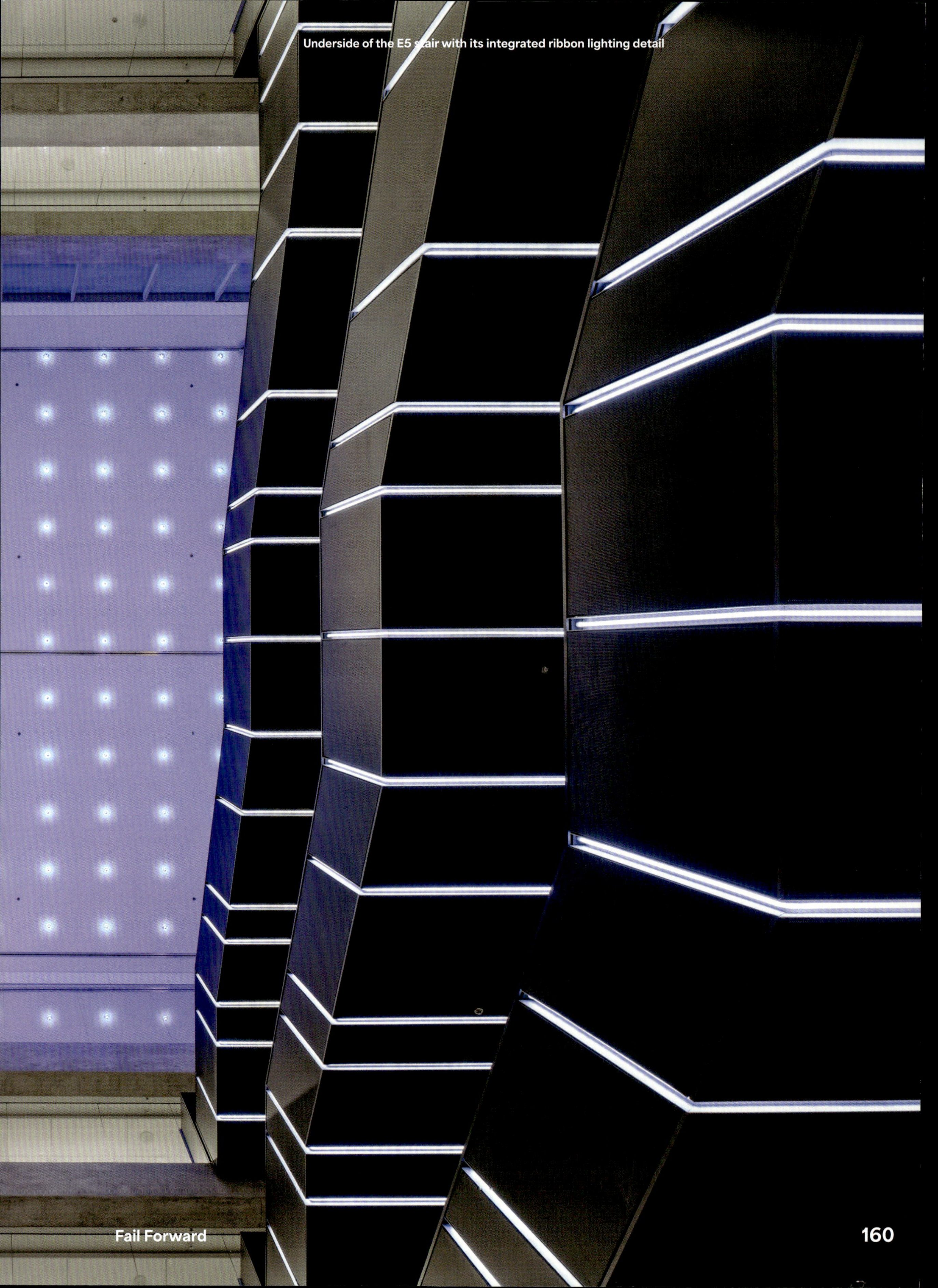

Underside of the E5 stair with its integrated ribbon lighting detail

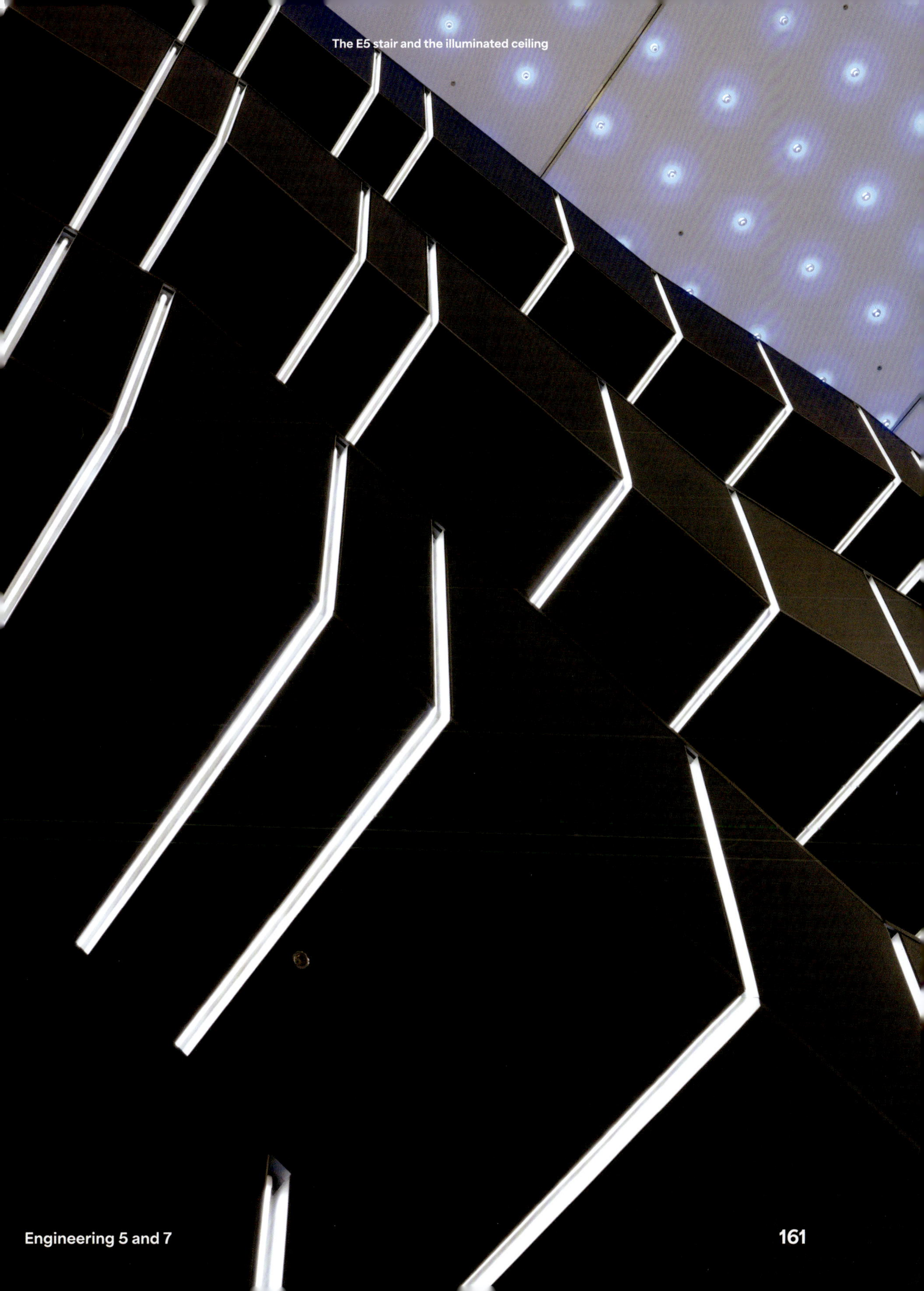

The E5 stair and the illuminated ceiling

The E7 robotics hub seen from the atrium

Looking from the robotics hub into the atrium

410
411
409
408
418
416
415

The Ideas Clinic, an undergraduate space for team-based ideation

The Charrette

Bank of Canada Head Office Renewal

Ottawa, Ontario 2012–2017

"I think you are a good commercial architect and maybe not even that."

Those are tough words to hear. Softened by the fact that I didn't hear them directly, but that they were received by my colleague Fred Vermeulen, the managing principal on our project to modernize Arthur Erickson's iconic Bank of Canada headquarters in Ottawa. Sharpened, however, by the fact that they were delivered by none other than Phyllis Lambert, the grande dame of architectural sponsorship and our nation's principal curator of all that is modern and good. Phyllis had been drawn in by the Royal Architectural Institute of Canada to offer a rebuke to our practice and demand a corrective course from the client in the proposed transformation of their corporate home. Controversy around the proposed modification of the two mirrored-glass towers and 12-storey winter garden, designed by Arthur Erickson between 1972 and '77, had begun several weeks earlier. Erickson's winter garden had appeared in the North American Registry of Endangered Public Spaces, a now defunct online forum championing the public realm across North America. Prior to this article, our client had been steadfast in the resolution that their asset was under no heritage listing and that it was theirs to do with as they liked. All of this changed when Maria Cook, then architecture critic for the *Ottawa Citizen*, published a damning editorial that admonished not only the perceived secrecy surrounding the project, but also the early design proposals our team had offered for the plaza in front of the bank. For the article, Cook drew upon experts from Heritage Canada and Heritage Ottawa as well as Phyllis Lambert herself. Our client, no longer free to go about their business in peace, was obliged to meet with an assembled panel of critics to justify their position and propose an acceptable route forward. While the Bank was under no legal or contractual obligation, as an arm's-length agency of the federal government, they were not immune to public opinion. Fred's meeting with Phyllis was the first of several defensive forays, which eventually gave way to negotiations toward a mutually acceptable solution.

The bank wanted to preserve, modernize, and transform their headquarters. The critics wanted nothing on the building touched seemingly without the blessing of Erickson himself, which since his death in 2009 has been often sought but never received. In Canada, architecture of the modern era is only beginning to be recognized as having potential heritage value. An official framework for protecting architecture for its inherent qualities, regardless of its era, doesn't exist. The ambiguity surrounding an impulse to enshrine the bank's architecture was further complicated by the fact that, while it was designed by a great architect, the Bank of Canada building is not universally liked and holds at best a secondary status in the catalogue of Erickson's collected works. It came late in the architect's critically lauded period and in terms of architectural preoccupations veers away from the muscular, landscape-inspired modernity that characterizes his best work. Erickson himself excluded the project from his second self-published monograph, and the complex is conspicuously absent from Erickson's writings or lectures of the period. Peer reviews and publications of the project are scant and one of the only extant publications, a 1979 review of the partially completed complex appearing in *Canadian Architect,* compares it somewhat unfavourably to the new crop of mirrored-glass office buildings springing up across North America. From a conservancy perspective, Arthur Erickson's Bank of Canada sits in a grey zone where the architect who dares to take on a complex renovation must forge their own way, use their own insight, buttressed by extensive research into what has aesthetic, technical, and historic value, and be prepared to meet with criticism as part of a due process.

In the fall of 2012, six months before Fred's run-in with Phyllis, we had mounted a multi-office pursuit to win the prestigious commission to renovate the headquarters of our nation's central bank. The brief was complex, calling for a complete technical and programmatic overhaul of the 800,000-square-foot edifice. Energy efficiency, structural stabilization to meet contemporary seismic codes, and a complete overhaul of the security systems and protocols were at the core of the technical brief. Programmatically, the bank was looking for a reimagining of their workplace culture, with a movement away from a series of departmental silos towards a technologically enabled, highly integrated, and mobile workforce, collaborating in teams across disciplines. Heritage was a stated concern, ironically not for Erickson's atrium and glass towers but for the 1939 limestone bank building that Erickson had built his complex around. While neither exemplary nor innovative for its day, the Centre Block, as it was known, was old and therefore would be treated with the greatest deference. For the rest, it was open season within the confines of schedule and budget.

When the storm of public critique broke over our team, I recall Fred and I commiserating over the injustice of the attacks, for we had been the champions of Erickson's legacy at the bank from the outset. While not considered a seminal work, Erickson's bank, seen from the perspective of our time, is an incredibly innovative articulation of the corporate workplace. Joe Connell, creative collaborator, Perkins&Will's lead workplace strategist, and a scholar of modern corporate architecture, saw incredible potential for Erickson's architecture to support a collaborative and mobile workplace culture. The building's deft interactions of open-concept workplace floors and a series of dramatic interior landscapes anticipated our current preoccupations with open and collaborative work cultures as well as the need to embrace nature into every aspect of our lives. If Erickson had been able to take advantage of wireless networks, mobile computing, and smart building systems as an integral part of his design, its fate might have been very different. While in the end, the overlaying of contemporary technology has unleashed the potential of Erickson's architecture, the designers of the late '70s seemed blind to the information revolution that was less than a decade away. It is the advent of modern computing that in many ways compromised Erickson's architecture, as its owners struggled to integrate increased power requirements, data runs, and cooling loads. Changing technologies combined with a reluctance to accept the democratic ideal of the bank's open-concept floor plates had motivated a series of ad hoc interventions, which after four decades had obscured the beauty of Erickson's vision. These layered accumulations were alternately symptomatic and the cause of a deteriorating workplace culture, with hierarchical structures and departmental silos taking precedence over collective and individual wellbeing. An architecture of striking clarity, lightness, and openness had, over the decades, been rendered dark, stuffy, and labyrinthine.

As I have already mentioned, the Bank of Canada building was not particularly well-documented by Erickson's studio or the press of the day. Fortunately for our team, the institution had maintained a complete record of all the original construction documents as well as subsequent renovations. We had an excellent repository of technical information at our disposal. It was the cultural and creative legacy that proved more elusive. Jim Strasman, Erickson's lead designer and the bank's project architect, had taken exception to the bank's early investigations into a potential transformation and was resolute in refusing to have any involvement in the project. What we did have at our disposal was an incredible institutional memory in the form of Dale Fleck, our main client liaison and project coordinator with the bank. Dale had worked his entire career within Arthur Erickson's construct, having joined the bank in his late teens as a mailroom clerk and steadily worked his way up through the administrative ranks to finally oversee this wholesale transformation as his final assignment before retiring. There was nothing about the building's life or workings that he didn't know. Dale was tough, taciturn, decisive, and ultimately fair. He was at once an incredible resource and in many ways the author of the critical hot water we found ourselves in. Dale knew the bank, was of the bank, and felt a strong sense of ownership. While intensely respective of Erickson's legacy, he was suspicious of what he referred to as the architectural "elite" and was adamant that the design process be managed with the absolute minimum of outside stakeholder involvement.

During our early initiation into the challenge of transforming the bank, we were struck by the complexity of the task, but it was clear to us that a massive decluttering was at the core of the exercise. Embarking on an intensive research and investigation phase, we tasked ourselves with finding the essence of the architecture, removing all that obscured the original intent, and layering in the new technical and programmatic requirements as deftly as possible. If new interventions could not be invisible, then they would be precisely considered complements to Erickson's initial vision.

One of our key collaborators, architectural historian and preservation architect Julia Gershowitz, described Erickson's Bank of Canada as a Gesamtkunstwerk, or total work of art, with every piece contributing to a harmonious whole. I would generally agree with Julia's assessment when it comes to the broad architectural organizations and a series of beautifully considered details that articulate the main elements of the building skin, vertical circulation, and structure. The interior design finishes, led by Erickson's life-partner

Francisco Kripacz, had not survived in many instances, and where they had, they seemed incongruous with the architectural framework. Beige shag carpet, bronzed mirrors, and polished brass handrails clashed with the building's muscular base finishes of architectural concrete, split-face slate, and powerfully colourful and textured patinated-copper cladding. Similarly outside of any totalizing influence seemed to be the complex's interface with the city, as articulated in its landscape and public-realm elements. As the project's lead design architect, I saw these areas of weakness as spaces for a deferential but distinct set of contemporary interventions, which would be leveraged to achieve the required technical and programmatic upgrades while elevating the image and lived experience of the complex.

The most complex technical challenge of the project, and the core of the programmatic need, was the transformation of over 500,000 square feet of workplace, spread over the two 12-storey glass towers that framed the winter garden atrium. Each tower was based on an identical floor plate consisting of 15 structural modules wrapped around a centrally located elevator and vertical service core. Each module consisted of a 16-square concrete waffle slab with a central circular column. In Erickson's original conception, this was a total system design with rational planning, structural support, lighting, and ventilation all stemming from one repeated compositional element. This "structural tree" provided the architectural order and character, bay by bay, with a narrow gap between each tree creating a tartan grid of interstitial space for the routing of electrical and mechanical infrastructure. These pathways were narrow, shallow, and already packed full to bursting. Recognizing the architectural significance of Erickson's exposed structural system, our team was adamant in our stance that no new interventions should compromise the original intent. No dropped ceilings or new mechanical shafts would compromise the beauty of the open floor plan with its modular coffered ceiling.

Initially, Dale and his team were skeptical of our position, as the findings of a feasibility analysis and business case authored a year earlier by Ottawa architects Griffiths Rankin Cook had proposed a series of conspicuous interventions thought necessary to bring the building up to modern standards—dropped ceilings to conceal new duct work for heating and cooling, new vertical shafts to supply that ductwork, and a set of structural cross braces located at the building perimeter in order to strengthen the towers against a seismic event. To our minds, any one of these interventions would be a grave compromise, but in combination they would constitute a desecration. We set about a rigorous interrogation of the mechanical and structural briefs provided in the feasibility report and challenged our extended team of consultants to think differently, putting architectural legacy as a primary objective.

Fred brought in structural engineer Halsall, whose founding partners had worked on Erickson's team. They were given the mandate of creating a dynamic computational model of the original tree-column structure to be observed through a series of simulated seismic events. The results were surprising. While an earlier analysis had assumed little or no seismic strength to be gained from the

Existing conditions at the bank, including a typical office floor (top) and Banks Street Plaza (above)

Jason Sweers, Cornelia Oberlander, Andrew Frontini, Michael McClelland of ERA, John Hillier of DTAH, and Gregory Utas (left to right) working together at the charrette

John Hillier's sketch for the winter garden atrium

structural trees due to the lack of lateral elements and the relatively fragile structural linkages between each of them, the dynamic model revealed that this perceived weakness was actually a strength. In a simulated seismic event, the ability of the trees to move independently created a fluidity across the entire tower that dampened the forces of the earthquake. The system of lightly connected trees was shown to behave like structures in nature, accepting and dissipating hostile forces rather than trying to resist them through brute strength. Whether Erickson's team had intuited this hidden strength, or even seen the need for it, is not documented, however we know that Erickson began his career as a student of nature in British Columbia, surely affected by the forests and routine seismic events of this mountainous coastal region.

While the tree-columns had proven to be surprisingly resistant, the modelling revealed the need for a stiffening at the core of each tower. Imagine a strong trunk with swaying branches and you will have a picture of how we hoped the towers could perform in an earthquake. This approach would leave Erickson's open-concept plan and floor-to-ceiling glazing intact but would require the addition of structural sheer walls within the elevator cores. While our engineers had been conducting this analysis, our architectural teams had been testing the existing building cores for their ability to accommodate modern building code and accessibility requirements, only to find them wholly lacking. When the analysis revealed that 60 percent of the existing poured-concrete core would have to be surgically demolished and rebuilt, acting construction manager PCL stepped in and advised that even if this proved to be cost-effective, which they strongly doubted, there wasn't enough time in the schedule to complete even half of the floors in this manner. A detailed cost and schedule analysis revealed that the best possible approach would be to provide temporary shoring to stabilize each tower and then demolish the entire core, cutting a 16-storey hole from the roof to the sub-basement. We would then be free to plan the cores in the best possible way to achieve the manifold needs of structure, code compliance, and accessibility. This proved to be one of several radical surgeries that we would conduct on the body of the bank. Each time, we cut deep so that the patient would come back better than before and with little or no scar tissue.

We had challenged everyone's assumptions about how Erickson's architecture could be structurally updated, and we would do the same with regards to heating, cooling, and energy. When we first toured the office floors, Dale had described how typically uncomfortable the space was during the winter and summer months. Workers on the south side of the building would be sweating in their shirtsleeves while those on the north side would be donning sweaters and even winter coats. This spoke to us of a mechanical system that was at once overwhelmed and inefficient. Over the years, upgrades to the base building systems had attempted to address an increased need for cooling to mitigate the heat load created by thousands of computers, but getting the cooler air to the workplace in a comfortable and consistent way had proved impossible.

Ottawa has an extreme climate with arid winters that can drop to negative 40 degrees Celsius and humid summers that peak at plus 35 Celsius. The beautiful expanses of mirrored glass in which Erickson and his team had sheathed the bank provided scant protection against such extremes.

As we commiserated with the group of bank employees leading the tour, it struck us that the first step toward mitigating their suffering would be to somehow bring the extremes to which the cooling and heating systems were being asked to respond closer together. Although we, as a species, have done a pretty good job of modifying the climate globally, we couldn't modify Ottawa's climate overnight. Modifying the building envelope, at least from the exterior, was out of the question in terms of the building's legacy and the project's budget. Given these limitations, we began to explore the potential of what is commonly called a dynamic buffer zone—a building skin within the building that creates a sandwich of air where extremes of temperature can be brought closer together. We proposed a perimeter layer of frameless and highly transparent glass set 18 inches in from the existing curtain wall. The layer of air between the two walls of glass could be distributed around the building perimeter by return air vents and fans, evening out the differences of temperature between sunny faces and shady faces. This approach created more consistent temperatures throughout the whole floor plate, lessening the extremes to which the heating and cooling system needed to respond and consequently maximizing the overall capacity of the system. It's a bit like life—soften the edges, and everybody can take it a little easier.

With our peaks and valleys softened, we discovered that we could provide air solely for ventilation and deal with the narrower cooling and heating margins through radiant panels. The feasibility study had assumed the need for heating and cooling with air, all requiring large and invasive duct runs that Erickson's architectural framework could not have accommodated. Radiant technology uses warm and cool water, which takes up a lot less space. We challenged the engineering team to come up with a holistic approach to distribution that would update Erickson's original design intent—namely, that the coffered ceiling module be the singular organizing device for space and distribution of services. To this end, we devised a system of radiant panels that fit snuggly into the deep coffers of the structural tree. These same panels also concealed the electrical runs that served the lighting system and the piping for a new layer of fire-suppression sprinklers.

Through our research and challenging of stated assumptions, we managed to highlight the original vision of the workplace that Erickson had put forward, resuscitating it and rendering it relevant for the coming decades—a much greener, safer, more comfortable, and more adaptable version of its former self.

Given the ingenuity, deference, and sweat equity that we had deployed in our design of the transformed workplace, you can imagine how frankly hurt we were by the volley of criticism we faced. While technically demanding, the transformation of the towers was carried out with

Erickson's crystalline winter garden skylight with the Parliament buildings beyond

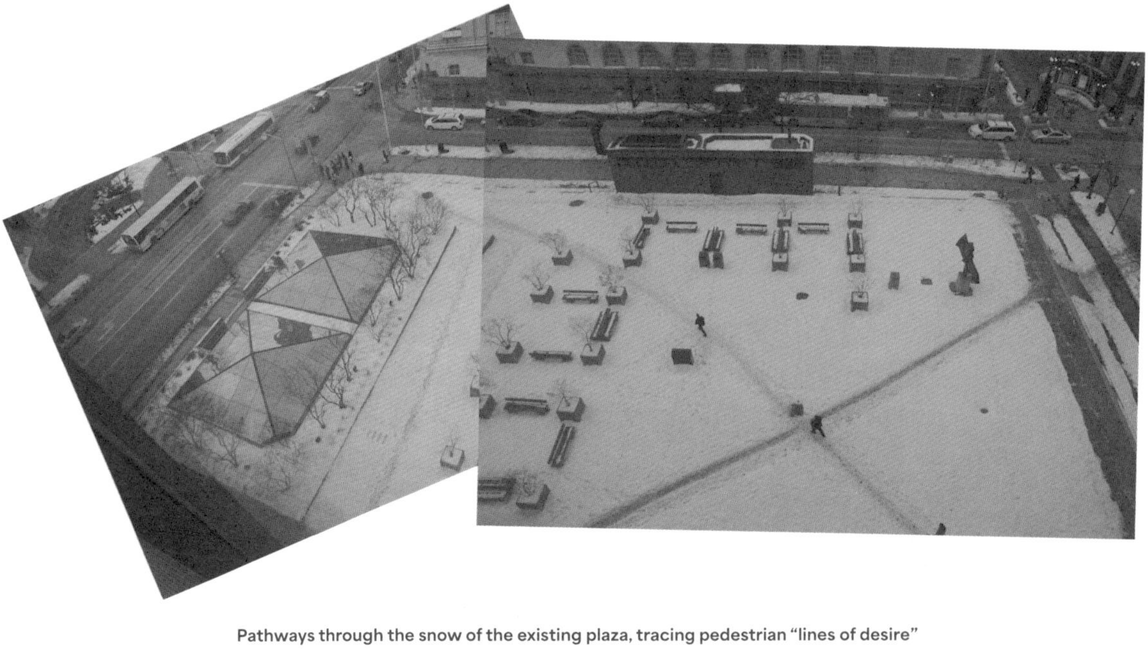

Pathways through the snow of the existing plaza, tracing pedestrian "lines of desire"

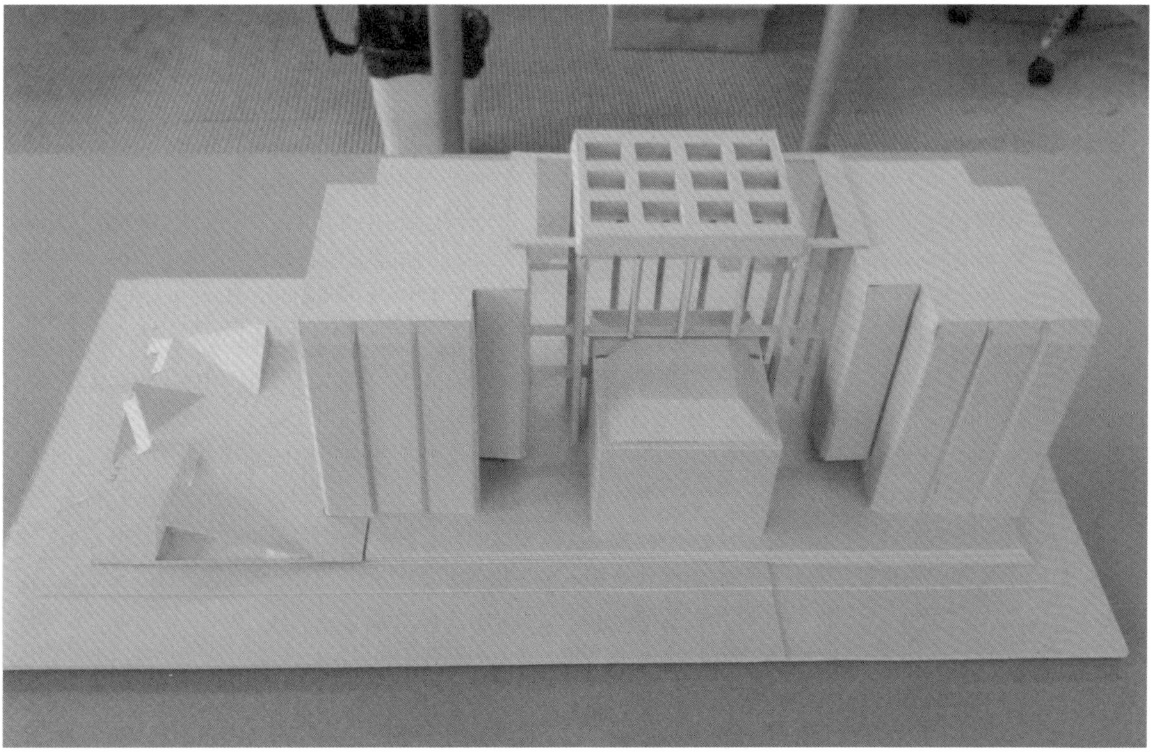

Early models studying the geometry and placement of new built elements in the plaza clear objectives relative to Erickson's legacy. When we met with our critics and explained our proposal, there was general concurrence that we were doing the right thing. It is precisely where Erickson's intent was incomplete or unclear—and where we had dared an act of interpretation—that we would continue to face vociferous opposition. Let me begin with an assessment of the bank's public realm proposition, what Erickson had originally intended, what was actually built, and what our initial proposals were.

Coloured renderings and plans generated by Erickson's office in 1970 indicate that Erickson had a vision for an interior landscape under glass at a scale that comparatively dwarfs the atrium that the bank eventually built. This vision included four towers framing a massive winter garden that covered Ottawa's Sparks Street for an entire city block. When we eventually met architect Keith Loffler, who had joined Erickson's team as a young job captain on the bank project, his recollections helped us contextualize these grand schemes. According to Keith and accounts provided in David Stouck's excellent biography *Arthur Erickson: An Architect's Life*, Erickson had pushed the idea of a grand indoor landscape far beyond the client's appetite or the project's budget. When the concept was finally rejected once and for all, the relationship between architect and client was strained, with Erickson's subsequent passion for and involvement in the project notably diminished. Seeking to appease the client, local executive architect Marani Rounthwaite & Dick stepped into a more present design role, further alienating Erickson from the ongoing design of the public-realm elements. The winter garden was eventually designed at a reduced scale, with the marvelous proportions and material treatments developed by Jim Strasman, but the exterior landscape seems to have drifted out of Erickson's control. A series of tentative landscape sketches from the period show a variety of incomplete propositions for an elevated plaza facing Bank Street at the east end of the complex. What was eventually built pales in comparison to even these tepid explorations.

When our team took on the commission, we were confronted with a raised podium clad in slippery and deteriorating green slate pavers, stepping inhospitably up from the surrounding streetscape. The barren plaza's sole articulations were a set of precast concrete strips delineating the structural grid of the building, a sunken lightwell since covered over with a sloped skylight, and two utilitarian bunkers housing mechanical equipment and an exit stair. The bank's maintenance department augmented this rather bleak composition with a series of large precast concrete planters when they were not busy replacing the English slate pavers that constantly heaved and cracked under the harsh conditions of the Ottawa winter. The plaza struck us as having enormous potential to forge a link between the continuous pedestrian route of Sparks Street and Canada's parliamentary precinct. We proposed that the bank could, at this location, give back to the city, offsetting the required closure of the winter garden atrium. Having established that the space was not part of Erickson's intended vision, we proposed that a contemporary intervention seamlessly integrating new required programs, security features, and public amenities could transform Ottawa's public realm. Our proposal would be bold, but it would be contained, a new landscape in front of, but discrete from, Erickson's mirrored glass towers.

A large part of our mandate involved bringing the Bank of Canada into alignment with contemporary security standards for an institution of its significance. I would offer that nowhere else in the world can one walk into a central bank with a backpack, unchecked, and meander through the ground floor of the nation's currency museum, while directly above you the bank's governor, deputy, and commissionaires are meeting to discuss national economic policy. But that is what hundreds of school children and members of the public did daily. While I remain deeply skeptical about the proliferation of security measures and restrictions in the post-9/11 era, even to me this seemed overly trusting.

Working with the bank and our landscape architect John Hillier of DTAH, we developed an integrated strategy towards landscape and architecture that addressed the core challenges of the bank's security profile. In our proposed scenario, the winter garden atrium would become a secure space, the museum would move out of the building proper and into an existing service space below the plaza, and separate public access to the museum would be integrated into the landscape. While this was a sound strategy, it created the necessity for an architectural element that would accommodate the museum entry on the plaza in front of the bank. At first, we struggled with an appropriate language for the tiny entry pavilion in front of Erickson's 12-storey glass tower. Eventually inspiration for an approach was to be found in Erickson's own oeuvre. During an early exploratory tour of the bank's endless supports spaces, my longtime colleague and friend, John Potter, took a photo over the roof of Erickson's winter garden, where the pyramidal plexiglass sky lights appear as a sea of icebergs or snowcapped mountains in the foreground of the Parliamentary clock tower. This image proved to be a touchstone that inspired us to think of the various programmatic events on the plaza as landscape elements rather than buildings. It also nudged us to look deeper into Erickson's own fascination with the Canadian landscape as a source of inspiration. Erickson's design for the Canadian pavilion at Expo '70 in Osaka, Japan, served as a precedent, with its sheer mirrored-glass forms alternating between a concrete evocation of icebergs or mountains and an atmospheric ephemerality, depending on the angle and nature of the light. But unlike the Osaka pavilion, our interventions would need to act as invitations to a subterranean museum. They would need to draw people and views down, while allowing some aspect of the museum to emerge.

John Potter and junior designer Martin Lariviere created a series of study models where the surface of the plaza was notionally cut and folded to create a set of tilted plains at once suggesting a topography, a sheltered landscape, and a connection between the city and the museum below. These early studies formed the basis of a design that would be presented to the design review panel of Canada's National Capital Commission. This panel is led by some of the most notable voices in

Canadian architecture, landscape, and urbanism, and is responsible for overseeing the character and quality of the built environment in and around the nation's seat of government. The panel was receptive to our public realm aspirations and the project's conceptual relationship to Erickson's design in general, but they sent us back to do more analysis around climate and program. How could the plaza be used and animated throughout the year?

We returned several months later with a detailed analysis of pedestrian movement, sun angles, and seasonal wind effects, which had influenced the design toward the creation of a set of seasonal microclimates supporting year-round programming. The final design proposal presented three tilted landforms enclosing respectively the museum entrance, a mechanical plant for the museum, and an exit stair. Together, these new landforms framed a sheltered and intimate urban space with an abundance of greenery and a strong sense of urban theatre. We anticipated ice carving, busking, and food festivals, and indeed all have come to animate this new public stage throughout the year. Our second submission was enthusiastically endorsed by the commission, and we felt confident that we were on the right track.

Our sense of accomplishment was to be short-lived, as Maria Cook's article for the *Citizen* broke the following week, and we now faced a new court of approval. Phyllis Lambert minced no words in her assessment of the NCC's critical praise for our design. "I don't give a damn what Donald Schmidt thinks!" (Schmidt is a leading Toronto architect and served at the time on the National Capital Commission's design review panel.) It was now going to be about what Phyllis felt that Arthur would have wanted. While our colleague and heritage consultant Julia Gershowitz assured me that scholarship trumps opinion, in this instance I was not convinced that would be the case.

The schedule of design activities at the bank was in large part being dictated by construction manager PCL. The base building elements, which included the museum and plaza as well as structural upgrades and mechanical infrastructure, were six months ahead of the interior fit up. This meant that while our design for the plaza had been developed in considerable detail, our thinking around the other major landscape element—the winter garden atrium—was in its early days. In fact, our team had been struggling with how to redefine the winter garden in the wake of its planned closure to the public. The bank was adamant that the winter garden become secure, a meeting place for employees only. The space was to be universally accessible and the odoriferous and leak-prone water features to be decommissioned. When we first toured the winter garden we were struck by how beautiful the architecture was, suffused with an incredible quality of light that played off the delicate structure and rich materiality of slate, mirrored glass, and patinated copper. The challenge lay in the ground plane, which with its decommissioned ponds, sickly tropical plantings, and multiplicity of level changes struck one as a space to be looked into from the towers above rather than occupied in any meaningful way. Our challenge was to create a cultural heart for 1,600 employees. I must confess that after six months and several false starts, we remained stumped by the problem. Under the circumstances, this turned out to be a blessing. What we hadn't designed couldn't be used against us.

It was December of 2012, and I was sitting in front of my computer in a daze. I had just gotten off a call with Dale Fleck and Fred Vermeulen. Our public relations problem was not going away, and although Dale wanted it gone, he was adamantly opposed to another meeting with Phyllis. It seemed that we were, for the time, at an impasse. Within an hour, the phone rang. It was Peter Busby. Now for those who may not know, Busby is the grandfather of sustainable architecture in Canada, a leading designer in Perkins&Will, and the person who convinced me that the firm Shore Tilbe Irwin & Partners, of which I was the youngest partner, should join Perkins&Will in the first place. He is well-connected and well-respected across generations of Canadian architects. He was speaking incredibly softly, as he always does when he has something very important to tell you.

PB: *"Andrew, I just got off the phone with Phyllis, and I have an idea how to get you out of this mess."*

AF: *"Peter, I'm all ears."*

PB: *"I know you are. Listen, you know I just finished a project with Cornelia Oberlander, and she's amazing. She's the greatest living landscape designer in the world, she worked with Erickson for years, and she loves me. Phyllis and she are friends—you know, the old, old guard. So you hold a design charrette, you invite Cornelia and some other notables, she comes up with some ideas for the winter garden, and she endorses the design to Phyllis. All of your problems go away.*

"She just lives up the road, I could walk up there and ask her if she'll do it. Like I said, the old bird loves me. Do you want me to do it?"

AF: *"Please!"*

Three weeks later we were gathered in a large conference room at Ottawa's venerable Chateau Laurier Hotel to begin a two-day design charrette on the future of the Bank of Canada's winter garden atrium. In short order, we had gathered an impressive cast of characters, thanks to the combined influence of Phyllis Lambert, Peter Busby, and of course Arthur Erickson. Fred and I presided over the assembly, which included heritage specialists Julia Gershowitz of FGMDA and Michael McClelland of ERA, landscape architect John Hillier, former Erickson collaborator Keith Loffler, and landscape architect Cornelia Hahn Oberlander.

The previous evening, I had been introduced to Cornelia and Keith over dinner. Keith was in his early 70s and had been running his own practice in Toronto since Erickson's Toronto studio had folded in 1984. Cornelia was 92 and still fully engaged in practice and teaching. They both impressed upon me the rich potential of later practice, where so much accumulated experience and wisdom can be brought to bear on any challenge. I could see in both that their practices were in fact sustaining and energizing them beyond the point where many people stop living in earnest. As we

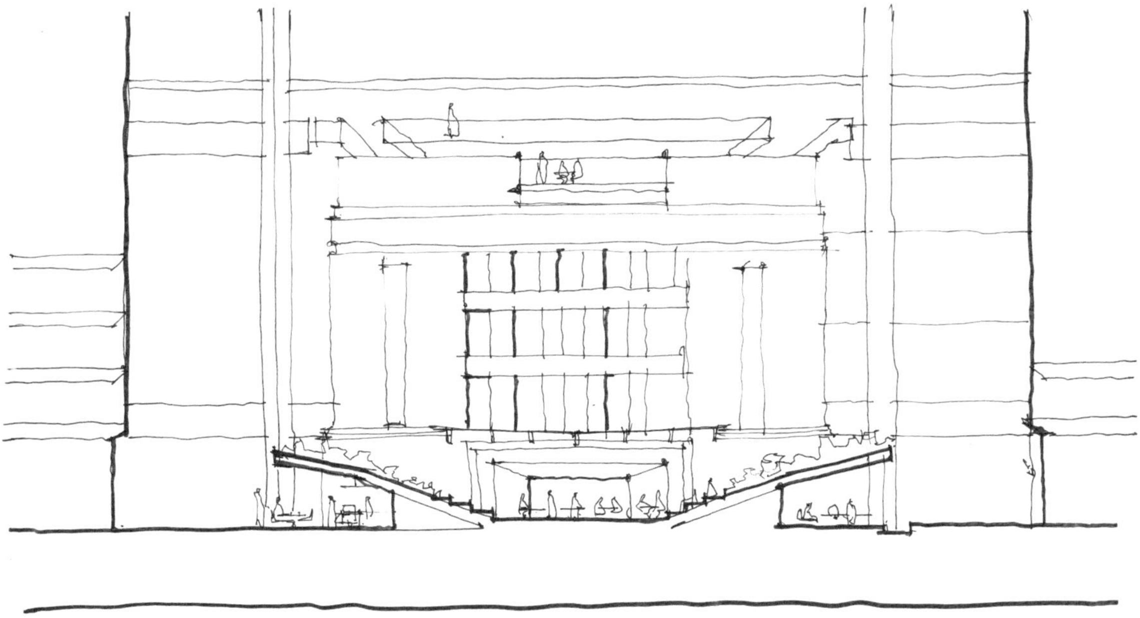

Sectional sketch showing one of many discarded concepts for the winter garden atrium

Sketch of a new digital library and media centre for the bank

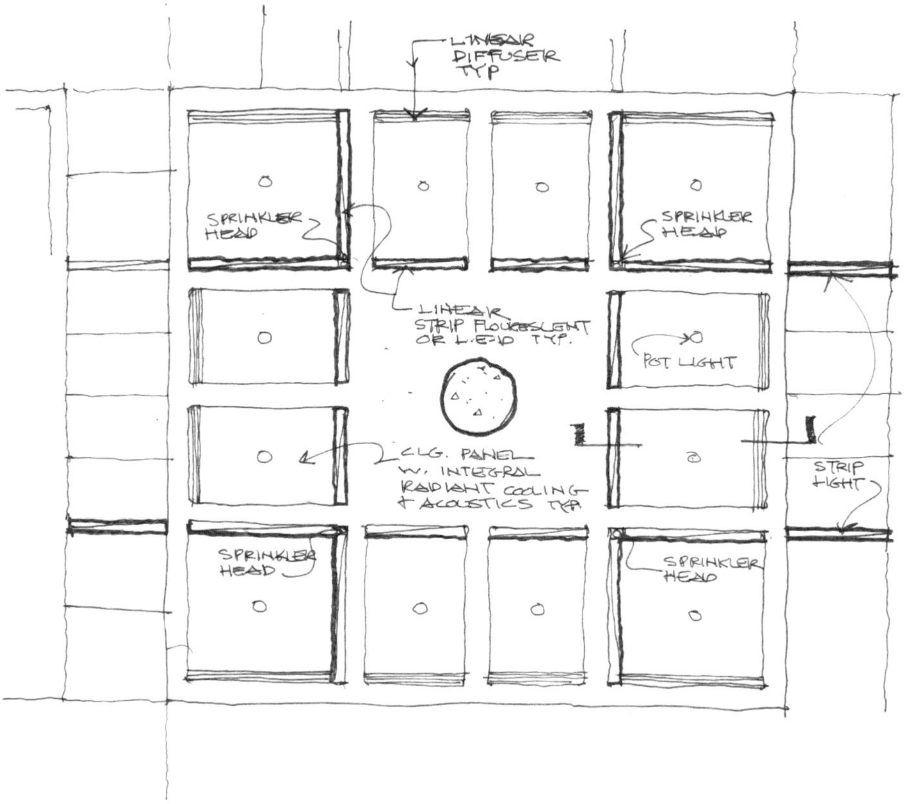

A reflected ceiling plan of Erickson's coffered structural trees, with new integrated systems

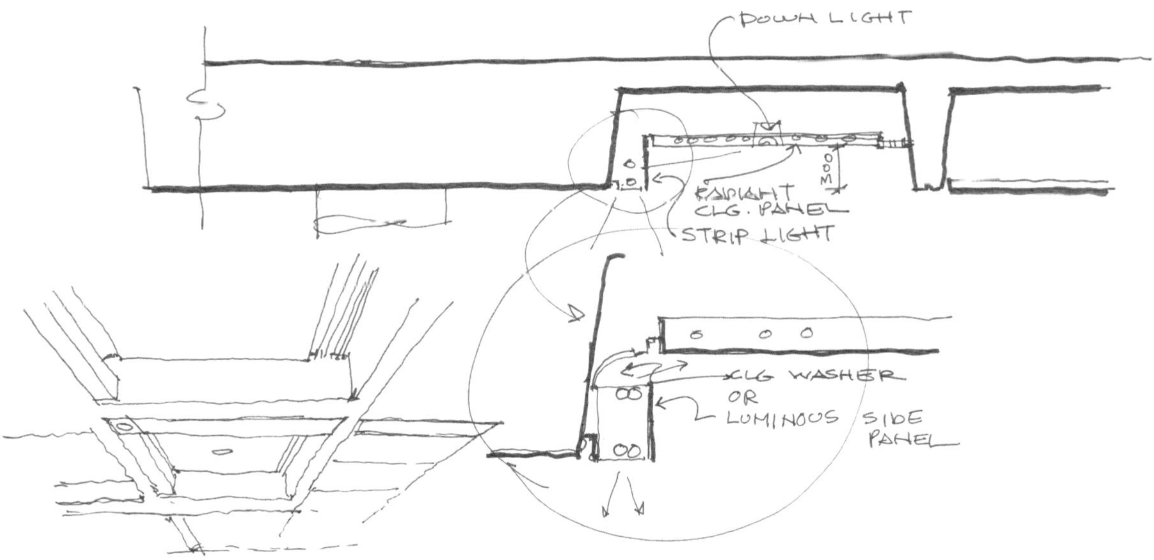

A detail section and perspective study of new systems in Erickson's coffered structural trees

walked back to the hotel from dinner, I suggested that we take the long route to avoid the set of stairs that connects the two-storey grade change between Sussex Drive and the ByWard Market District below. Cornelia would have none of it and literally bounded up the icy concrete steps at a pace that I struggled to maintain as a fit 48-year-old. That evening and in the months ahead, Cornelia would leave me feeling alternately very young and rather old. Young because her vast experience and keen insight were a constant reminder of how much I still had to learn, and old because in the tribulations of my daily practice I often lost sight of the pure joy that creation affords. This joy burnt like an inner fire in Cornelia's every glance and gesture.

The charrette began with my presentation of the research, technical investigation, and design exploration done to date, including the intended program and our tentative design options for the winter garden. While we acknowledged that our design for the museum and plaza had not won favour with Phyllis, we were resolute in our position. The design had passed through the NCC, submitted as part of the site plan approval process, and the contractor had already begun advance demolition work towards its execution. Today would be about the winter garden. After presenting for the better part of an hour, I opened the floor to questions and comments. The first person to speak was Keith Loffler, and his simple statement set the course for the next two days of the charrette—and the duration of the project. Pointing to a pinned-up copy of the only Erickson sketch that exists for the winter garden, Keith stated:

"I think we should just realize Arthur's vision for the garden. We couldn't do it at the time, but maybe we could now."

Loffler shared his memory of the course of events. Keith, then in his early 20s, had been thrust into the demanding role of job captain on the project and served as a critical liaison between Erickson, the local architect, and on-site activities. Erickson called him "the kid," and the nickname had stuck, being adopted by the client and contractor alike. Loffler recalls the last meeting that Erickson attended on the subject of the winter garden and the sketch he had brought to influence the course of events—which was increasingly out of his control. The sketch is a simple elevation showing two tree-covered mounds connected by a bridge-like element. Loffler explained that Erickson wanted to communicate the notion of a country united by its institutions—east and west linked by a timber bridge. Keith explained how the final execution had fallen far short of its author's intent. The soil couldn't be stabilized into a sufficiently steep grade and the idea of mountains was abandoned. Tropical plant species were deemed the only ones that would survive indoors, and Erickson's desire to evoke the coastal and boreal forests was also lost. At this point Cornelia piped in.

"But we know how to do all of this now! I have done it many times. I will show you."

Cornelia described the engineered soil cells she routinely used to create steep indoor topographies that are stable, lightweight, and promote the health, aeration, and irrigation of the soil. She also dove deep into the various plant species she used that, while in fact tropical, evoke deciduous trees through their structure, scale, and leaf form.

"*Ficus* 'Alii'! Not *Ficus benjamina*!"

She cried, referring to the variety of fig tree that she had successfully deployed in the atrium of Moshe Safdie's National Gallery next door. At our lunch break we walked over to the gallery to observe the trees, now flourishing in their fourth decade, and the variety of lush ground covers that Cornelia had chosen to weave this tiny indoor forest together.

She noted that the bank atrium would provide much higher natural light levels than the gallery and that we could expect our plantings to surpass even these. As we walked through the grove, Cornelia pointed out every species, the soil medium it was planted in, and the various nurseries in Georgia and the Florida Everglades where she had personally handpicked every tree more than 30 years ago.

Between them, Keith and Cornelia had set the conceptual and technical parameters of the design, and the rest of the day was spent working in small groups to sketch and physically model the way that the earth mounds, bridge element, and ground plane could combine to frame and support the various programmatic aspirations that the bank had for the space: a media lounge for catching the news in print or on video, a café, a series of small meeting spaces, and occasional town-hall gatherings.

By dinnertime, we had arrived at a well-fleshed-out scheme that was captured in a series of plan diagrams, a rough model, and some evocative pen-and-ink sketches by John Hillier. John and Cornelia would continue to collaborate on indoor topography and plantings for the project's duration. I know that John, who is in the late prime of his career and a leading designer of landscapes and public spaces in Canada, shares my gratitude for the learning opportunity that the charrette and its follow-through provided. You are never too seasoned to learn from the experience of others.

The second day of the charrette was dedicated to communicating our explorations to Dale Fleck. Dale was visibly moved as we explained how closely the vision would align with Erickson's original ambitions, far surpassing what had actually been built. He felt an enormous sense of relief, as he immediately saw that this approach would be completely defensible—as the Erickson that never was.

It was also clear to him that the proposed design would serve the bank's programmatic needs. At a deeper level, the design resonated emotionally. Dale spoke about the experience of looking down from the towers into the verdant landscape as a constant highlight of every day that he had worked at the bank throughout his adult life. The fact that this fundamental aspect of the architecture, so essential to its sense of place, would remain, convinced him that we had arrived at the right solution.

The design that we developed that day was the product of many hands and served us well both as a communication tool and a testimony to an inclusive process. Our critics could understand what we had proposed, its relationship to Erickson's vision, and the laudable pedigree of those who had contributed. I cannot pretend that I would have arrived at the final design proposal on my own, and even if I had, that it would have carried the authority that it needed to prevail. Cornelia stayed with us through the final execution and visited the construction site on several occasions to inspect and validate the progress. Towards the end of the project, I toured the site with Cornelia, John Hillier, and my colleague Matt Johnston, who has taken over Fred's role on his retirement. At this stage, the engineered mounds and *Ficus* 'Alii' trees were in place and the ground-cover species were just being introduced. Cornelia interrupted the on-site landscape crew, who were wondering what to do with a pair of geckos that had migrated with the trees from the Everglades, to inform them that they had supplied insufficient root coverage for the periwinkle ground cover.

We then proceeded outside to look over the nearly completed plaza. Standing in the centre of its informal amphitheatre, I admired the sloping green planes framing the West Block on Parliament Hill. To me this felt just right, a new theatre of urbanity brought to the doorstep of the nation's central bank.

"I am going to tell Phyllis that everything is just as it should be!"

Cornelia exclaimed. And she must have, because all of our problems went away. In the end, what had seemed to be an attack turned out to be a gift, bringing a pair of valuable lessons. The first lesson of the charrette is that collaboration is always a good idea. The second is that endurance is a critical ingredient of beauty, both in architecture and in the human spirit.

Client	Bank of Canada
Location	Ottawa, Ontario
Size	82,000 gross square metres
Date	2012–2017

View into a renovated open office

The new Bank of Canada Plaza viewed from above

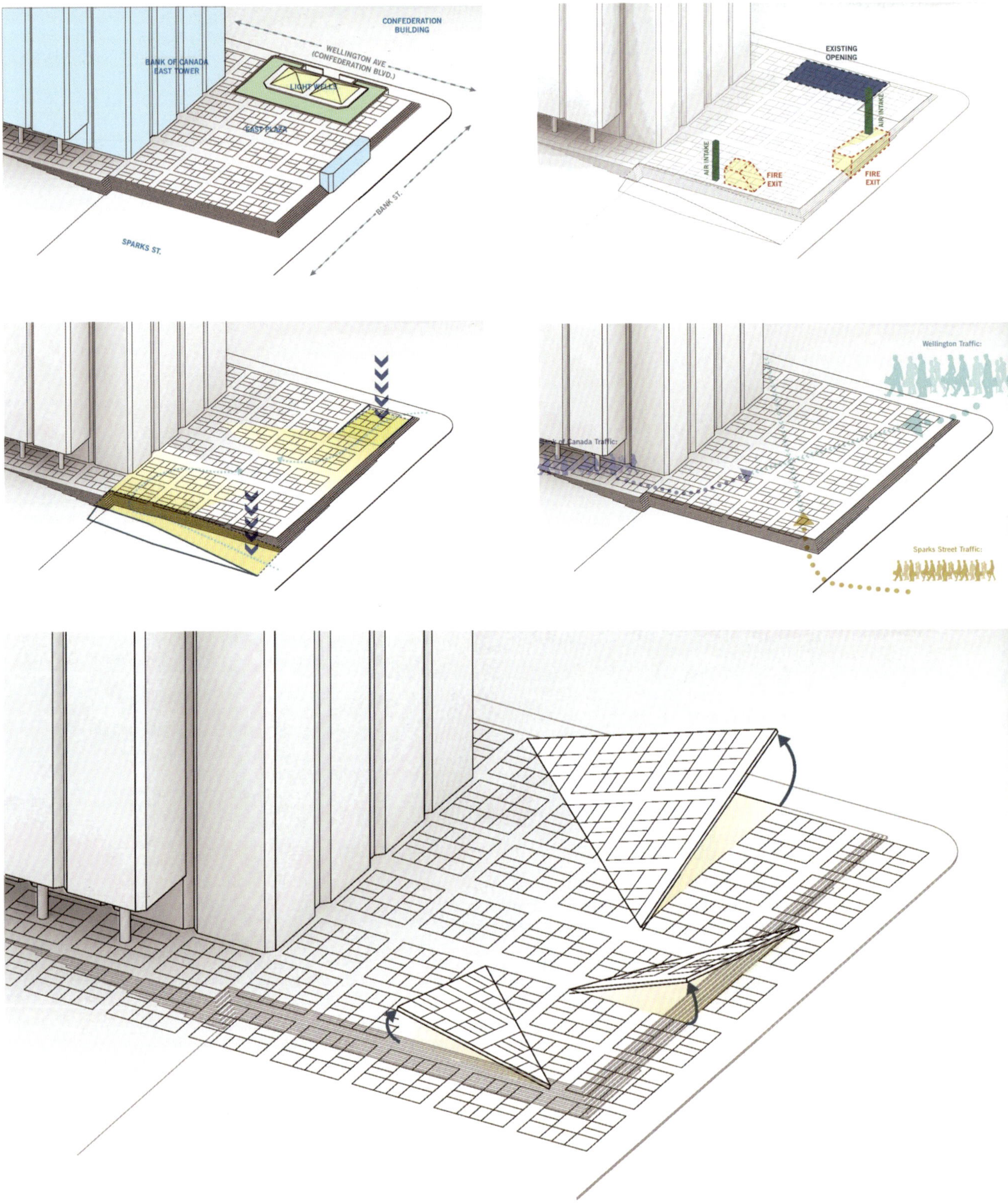

Analytical diagrams for the new plaza

Construction at the entrance to the new Bank of Canada Museum

ROLEX

Looking south across the new Bank of Canada Plaza

ROLEX
HOWARD FINE JEWELLERS & CUSTOM DESIGNERS

Landscape features in the new plaza

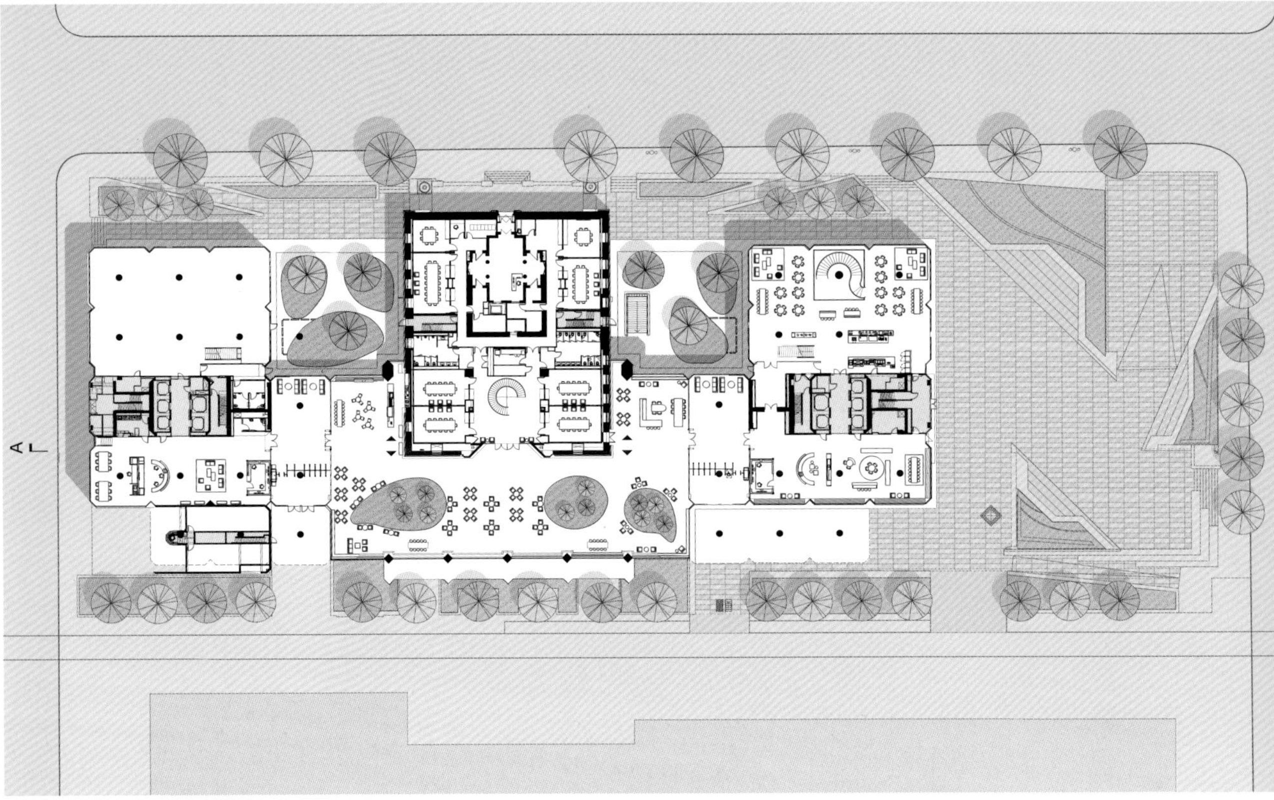

Level 01 Plan

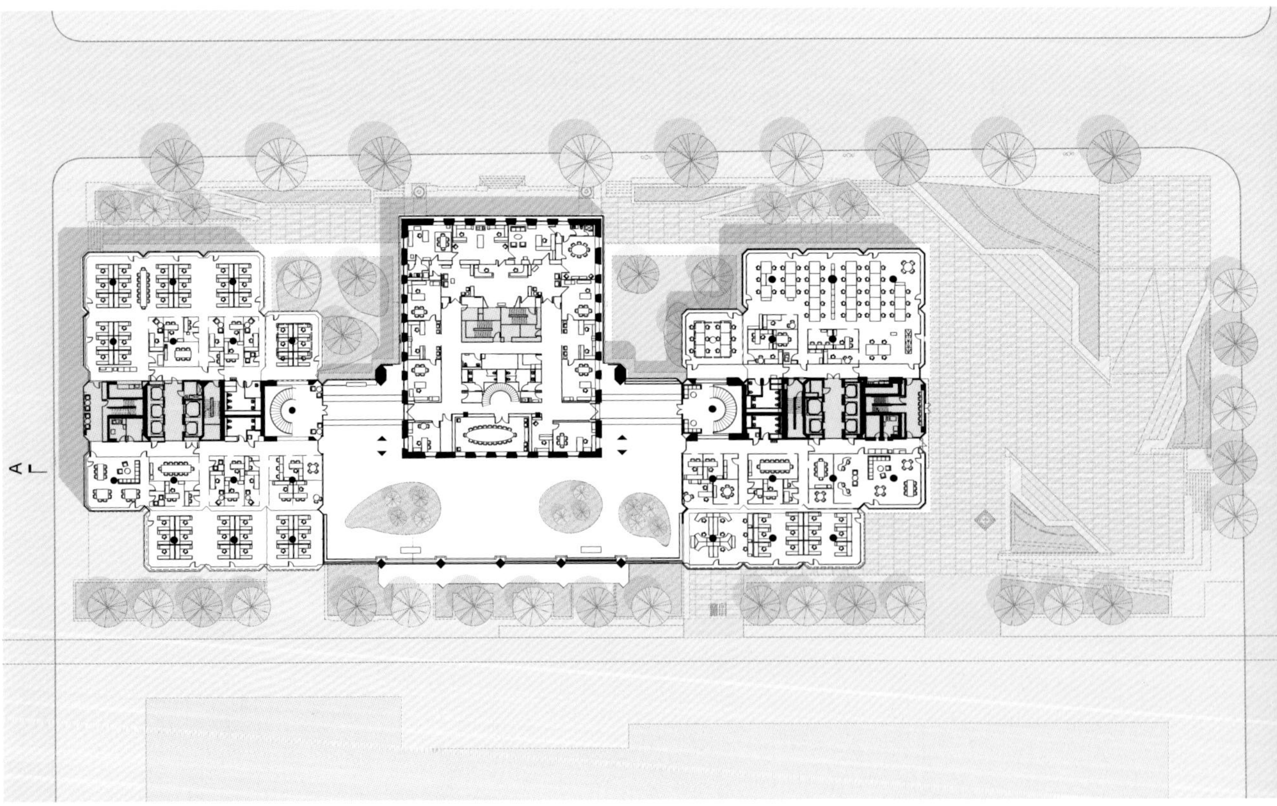

Level 03-05 Plan

Aerial view of the site and surrounding context

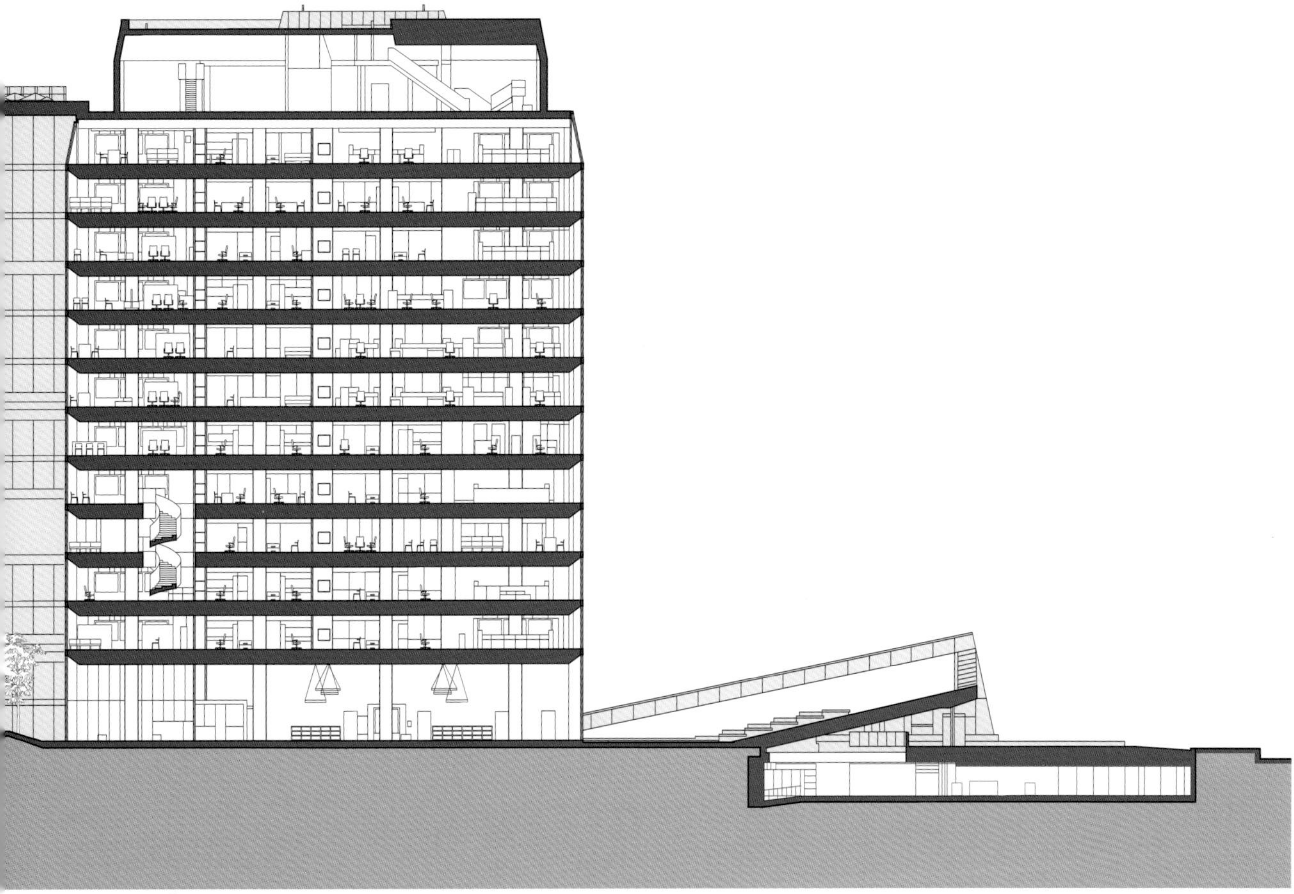

East-West Section A

The winter garden atrium under restoration

Looking east across the atrium from the seventh floor

A new rooftop terrace and ground-floor garden in the atrium

Lounge seating in the winter garden atrium

The bridge-like canopy in the winter garden atrium

The restored lobby of the historic Centre Block

An upper floor of the Centre Block during renovation

Downtown.
At the intersection of

The new plaza as a foreground to Erickson's glass tower

The bank entrance from the plaza

The Bank of Canada Museum entrance pavilion

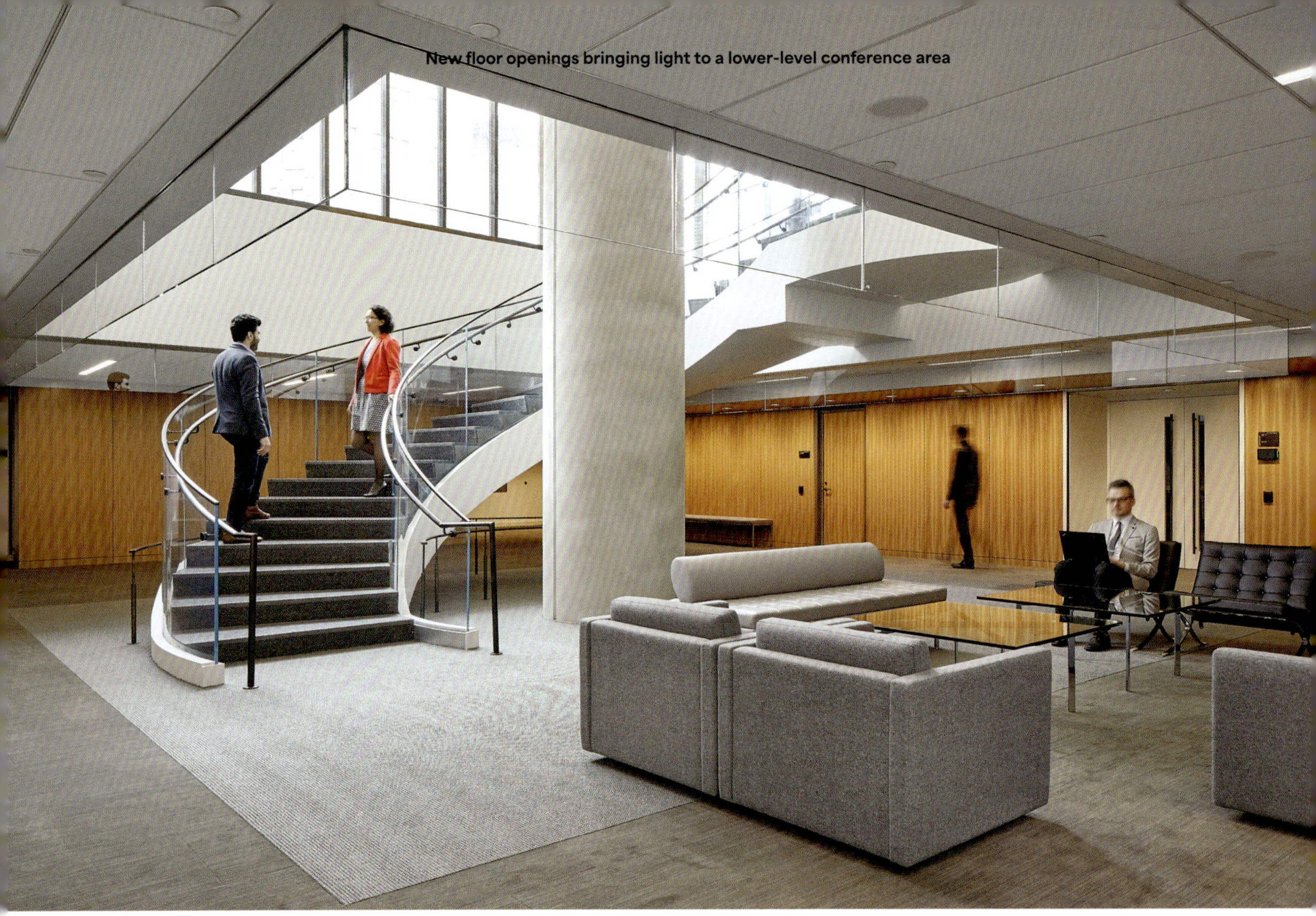

New floor openings bringing light to a lower-level conference area

Lobby of the Bank of Canada Museum

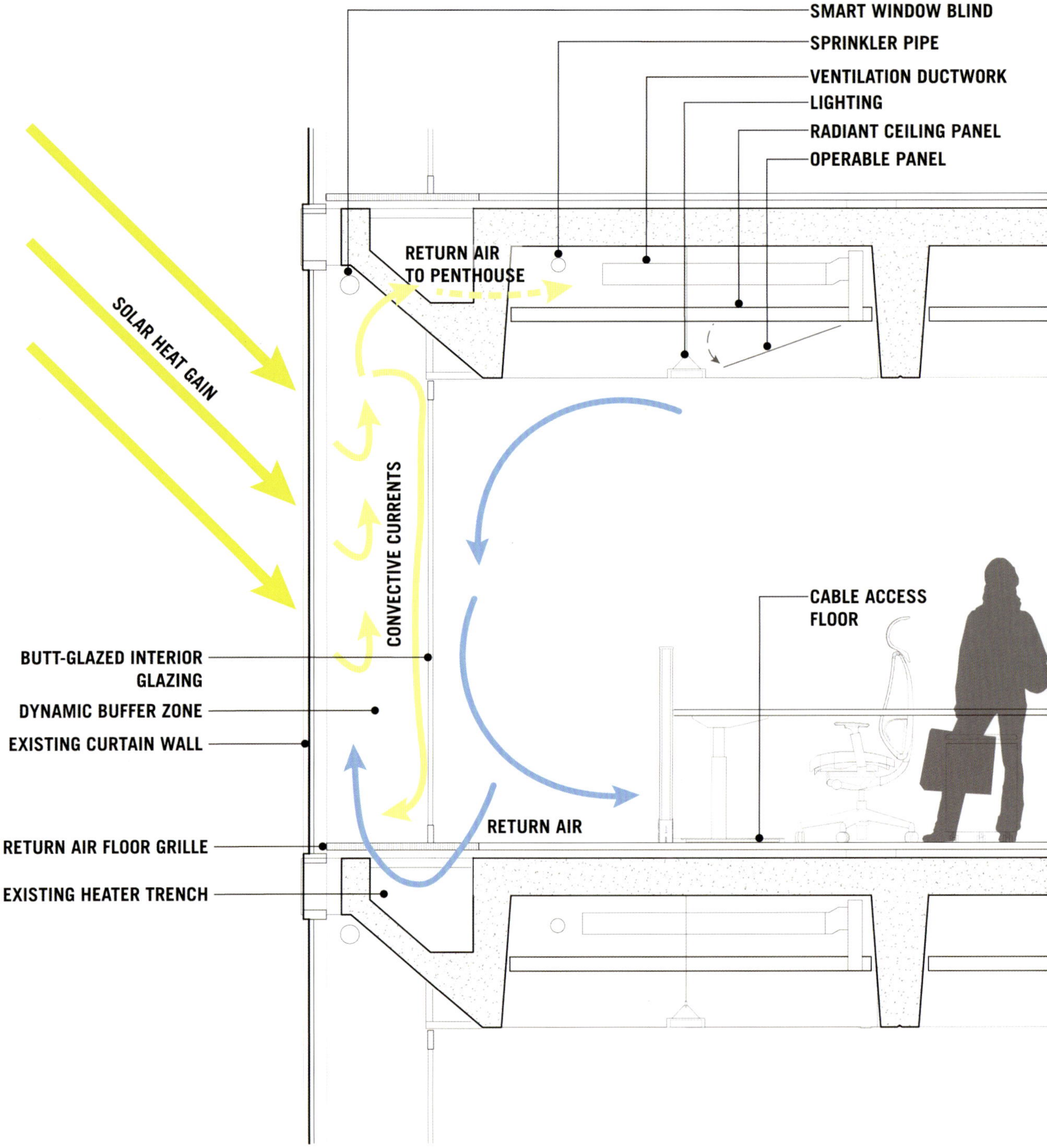

Diagram of the new dynamic buffer zone and other systems

The surgical demolition of the elevator core

Tenth-floor collaborative work area

Man-Made Lake

Meadowvale Community Centre and Library

Mississauga, Ontario 2012–2016

The boy was still there, standing at the end of the dock with his fishing rod extended over the dark green water of the man-made lake. With his back to the path and his small frame silhouetted against the water, he lent an atmosphere of the wild and exotic to what was essentially a large open storm sewer surrounded by a multi-use trail in the heart of an aging suburb. He'd been there an hour earlier, when I'd begun my tour of the lake's perimeter and his commitment suggested that nature's forces had managed to transform the engineered basin into something at least partially wild over the past 40 years.

"How's the fishing, catch anything?"

I called from the path. The boy, probably eight or nine years old, turned slowly and replied with a dispirited air.

"Yeah, I caught six, but I can't keep them. My dad says they're no good cause the lake's dirty."

I nodded and walked on. The lake was probably stocked by the municipality and the fact that the fish were not particularly palatable was not surprising. Lake Aquitaine, as the kidney-shaped reservoir was called, had been engineered in the early '70s to act as the infrastructural and recreational heart of Meadowvale, a planned community 50 kilometers west of central Toronto, in the city of Mississauga. The community featured a mix of low- and high-density housing, a local theatre, several places of worship, a large shopping centre and several mid-rise commercial office buildings, all orbiting around a park at the centre of which was Lake Aquitaine. The lake serves as the central stormwater management pond for the whole community receiving surface water from municipal catch basins and culverts at its north end, where a large weir sets the level and catches the major debris before it passes into the lake. At the south end, a second weir filters additional debris and allows the water to drop another three metres into an exit sewer that carries the water on to its point of final discharge, Lake Ontario.

An hour earlier, my colleague Phil Fenech and I had entered the site off Glen Erin Drive, parking in a badly potholed parking lot in front of an aging red brick bunker—the original Meadowvale Community Centre, and the site of what we hoped would be our next commission with the city of Mississauga. While our walk along the lakeside trail would reveal a landscape that had naturalized and matured over a 40-year period, masking its infrastructural origins beneath a deepening layer of flora, its architectural counterpart hadn't fared as well. The physical and cultural shifts of time had left the community centre in poor repair and ill-suited to the needs of its increasingly diverse community. To the arriving visitor, the building presented a set of three nested octagons clad in weathered red brick, colliding unapologetically with a rectangular box, itself partially buried in a pair of sodded berms, each topped with a trinity of blighted conifers. Presenting the worst impulses in the landscape and architectural design of its day, the community centre and grounds seemed to be simultaneously of any place and of no place. The composition was divorced from the evolving urban fabric and offered neither invitation to,

A local resident fishing on Lake Aquitaine

nor anticipation of, the verdant lakeside trails beyond it.

For no apparent reason, the community centre had been oriented at 45 degrees to the main roadway and the prevailing urban grid. Upon entering the facility, we were presented with an atmosphere of chlorine and old sneakers as well as a series of puzzling geometric shifts that seemed to have been conceived with the end of orienting us to the lake, which was vaguely discernible through a clutter of fitness equipment on several inaccessible levels. It was apparent to us that originally a two-level lobby had opened to a second entrance facing the lake, connecting the city to the park in some fashion. At some point in the building's history, the lobby had been infilled with a fitness centre, the lakeside entry permanently closed, and the building's only gesture to its context removed. The exterior experience of the community centre was similarly uninspiring. This was a building that presented an obstacle in the landscape—an obstacle to be walked around while negotiating dangerously sloped asphalt paths and the steep berms, as one blindly searched for the lake and surrounding park beyond.

If you are wondering why I am dwelling so much on the building's shortcomings, it is because the project brief called for an addition and renovation to the complex through a new library and upgrades to fitness and community spaces. My colleague and I were doubtful whether this low-ceilinged, poorly sited hulk would support any meaningful transformation, but nevertheless we endeavored to focus on the first task at hand, which as always was the invention of a winning pitch.

The dilemma faced by our young angler provided the inspiration for an attitude towards transforming the community centre and the surrounding landscape. We developed a narrative around a series of "eco-terraces" where integrated elements of landscape and architecture would support an exploration of the building program, the surrounding landscape, and a journey from "city" to "lake." Instead of an indifferent obstacle, the transformed complex would open the landscape to the community and play a part in its regeneration through a series of landscaped terraces filtering stormwater runoff from the streets and parking areas above the lake. Highly accessible and sustainable, the new architecture was to unlock the potential of the existing complex and the park while contributing to an improved water quality for Lake Aquitaine.

Our story won the day, and we were selected as the new architects of the Meadowvale Community Centre and Library, but (as is so often the case) with a caveat. Our approach had excited the selection team about the site's potential, and they began to wonder about the wisdom of retaining the existing structure. Our principal client liaison, Raj Sheth, was politically astute and knew that the local councilor was a strong advocate of adding on to the facility rather than replacing it. Her motivations were both fiscal and political, as many of her older constituents were strongly attached to the existing senior centre in the basement of the building. At some point, she had promised not to disturb their subterranean lair for, while it was damp, dark, and dingy, the space was large, and it was theirs. If the structure were to be razed, it

The existing park

The community centre before redevelopment

would not happen without a strong fiscal rationale. We were retained to develop three high-level concepts examining the potential of the existing community centre. Our options were renovation and addition; partial demolition, renovation, and addition; and complete demolition and new build. At this point, I must stress that I take no particular joy in demolishing buildings. Our practice is rooted in sustainability, and we have a deep appreciation for our built heritage. We always encourage our clients to investigate the potential of an existing structure, both for the embedded energy and effort that it represents and the cultural value it carries, but there are limits. If the restoration of a building will consume more resources than the act of demolishing and rebuilding, or if the existing structure will unduly compromise the design potential of the finished project, then we must consider the building's cultural worth. In this case, the poorly executed design by a third-rate local practice presented us with meagre sustenance in terms of heritage value, and it was clear that the exercise would focus on the design potential of each option and the money required to execute it. We set out with six weeks, a modest stipend, and what we thought was a clear agenda—until we scratched the surface.

A thorough structural analysis of the existing structure revealed major limitations with regards to both expansion and modification. The tortured maze of painted concrete block that we had navigated on our first day was in fact all load-bearing. This meant none of it could be removed without inserting steel transfer beams, which would in turn need to be supported by the expensive process of inserting micropile footings in the existing basement. In most cases, the beams would have been set too low to walk beneath due to the impoverished existing floor-to-floor heights. In short, the entire structure was so meagre, fragile, and inflexible that it could do little more than be what it had always been: a concrete-block labyrinth. The necessary mechanical and electrical upgrades similarly could not be accommodated within the existing narrow confines, and efforts to create an accessible pathway between levels proved equally impossible. The euphemism "polishing a turd" repeatedly sprang to mind as I evaluated and reevaluated the twisted path of block partitions, idiosyncratic level-changes, and inadequate dimensions of almost every space, save the cavernous senior centre, from which the clack of bocce balls and weathered peals of laughter often reached my ears during those early visits. The fact that people can find such comfort in each other's company regardless of the quality of their surroundings may be a general consolation to the human spirit, but it is cold comfort to the architect. As events would play out, our consolation was still a ways out.

There are three kinds of architects: the persistent pessimist, the blind optimist, and the manic depressive (who oscillates between the extremes of the other two). I like to partake of all three personality types as the occasion demands, and soon found myself trying them on in sequence, as I searched for ways to correct the uncorrectable, inhabit the uninhabitable, and graft life onto the trunk of a dead tree. In one of many discarded options, we enclosed the existing community centre in a cube of glass and leveraged the space in-between as the zone for all of the structural, mechanical, electrical, and mobility systems that the existing building refused to accommodate. In the end, even this approach was defeated as we succumbed to the urge to tear the back off the existing building so that we might gain a view to the lake.

Not surprisingly, the options that attempted to preserve the existing building were either spatially inadequate, grossly expensive, or both. Our rather modest proposal to demolish the existing structure and build a simple terraced complex opening to the lake was the least expensive by a margin of 10 percent and accommodated the site and program with relative grace and ease. At the end of the six-week period, we packaged our three options into a slim folio and presented them to Raj, who was given the unenviable task of bringing the options forward to Mississauga City Council in our absence.

I have attended countless municipal council meetings. Whether in the tiniest hamlet or the largest city in the country, the sensation is always the same—an almost insufferable nervous energy brought on by the combination of crushing boredom and profound anxiety as you attempt to follow the fate of your project through the perilous waters of the democratic process. You sit watching as the hours grind by, knowing that at any moment a councilor may bring forward an ingenious motion, which can be seconded and for which a vote can be passed. And then, in an instant, your treasured commission, rather than having its budget approved, simply disappears. Yes, it really is high theatre, but it is a bad place for architects (who like to imagine that they can control the order of things). When Raj called us to a meeting with the local councilor the day after his presentation, I knew that I had missed one of those special motions. Raj bowed slightly and turned to face said councilor.

"The councilor has developed a fourth option, which I think you are going to find really interesting. It's sort of the best of both worlds... Or rather, all three worlds."

While she had eventually relented in the face of undeniable fiscal evidence, giving up the coveted senior's grotto, our local councilor was convinced that something of the original Meadowvale Community Centre could be saved. We were informed, in no uncertain terms, that the existing swimming pool tank, cast in concrete in the basement of the complex, was to be retained, and graciously integrated into an otherwise new complex as a testimony to ingenuity, tradition, and fiscal prudence. Whether the good councilor realized it or not, she had, through her motion, committed our team to a set of very exacting design parameters. Swimming pools are tied to set of planning logistics that serve public health, security, modesty, and accessibility. Where the pool sits in the plan of a recreation complex will govern the arrangement of the entire complex and its relationship to the site. Our pool sat in the very centre of the buildable site area, which was heavily constrained by steep slopes and a large flood plain set back from the lake. The old pool tank was in the basement and would stay there. The tank's geometry was set at a 45-degree angle to the city grid and would assert an undeniable influence on the orientation of the whole complex. It seemed as if the

A sketch generated for the client pitch meeting

A study of the community centre terracing down from the city to the lakefront

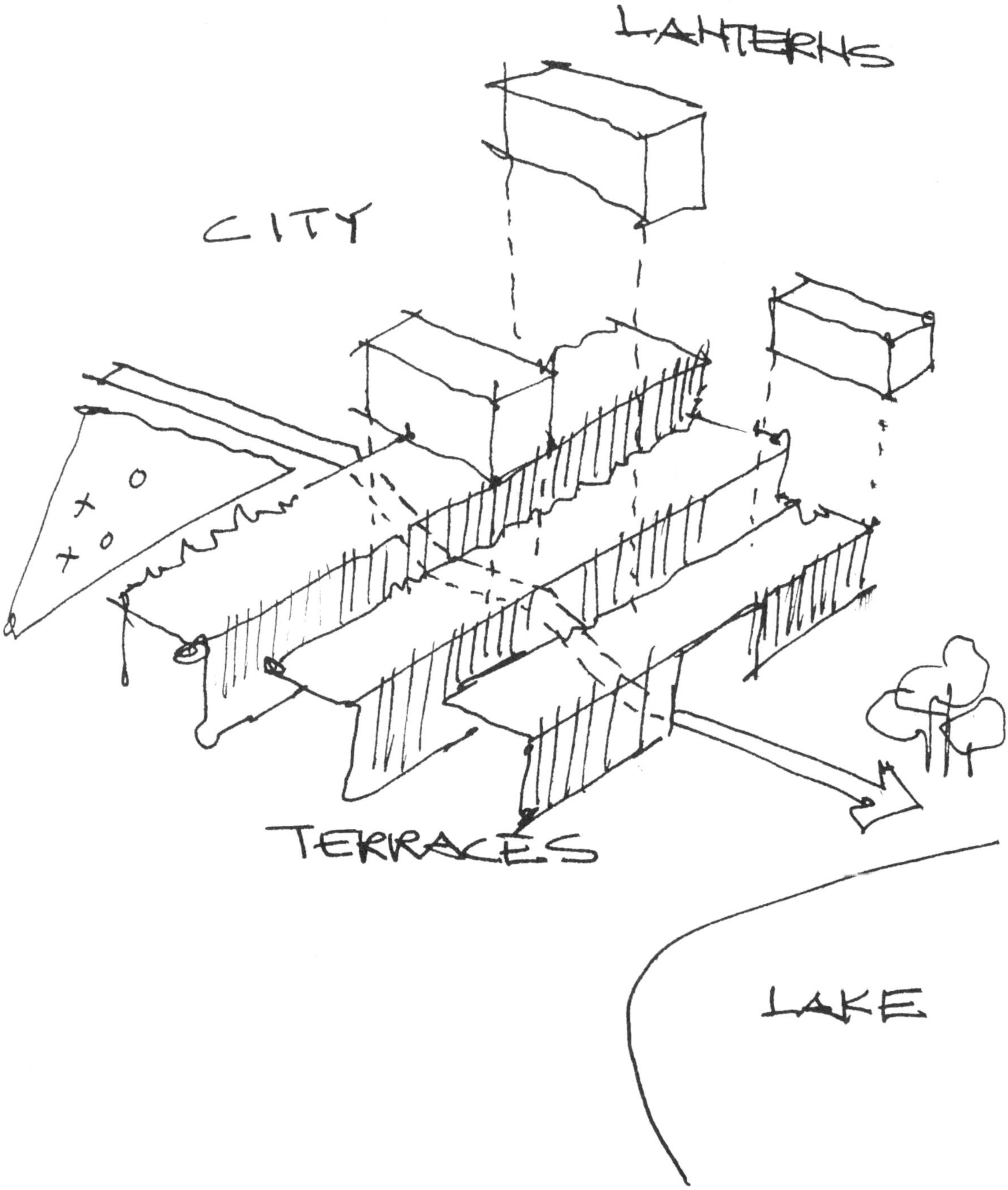

A sketch showing key elements of the design: plaza, terraces, and lanterns ghost of the old community centre was intent on haunting us with a tenacity that could only be embraced. So embrace it we did. Eventually.

I cannot tell you how hard it is for an architect of my generation to accept the planimetric conceit of the 45-degree angle. For a brief period, my objection to the influence of the angled pool basin constituted the greatest threat to the project's progress. Early in the concept phase, I had developed the notion of a set of programmatic terraces that would negotiate the site's topography and bring the building users in contact with the lake and parkland through a series of integrated indoor and outdoor spaces. I could not reconcile myself to the confusion that the pool basin presented in the heart of the composition. I recall presenting my despair to my colleague Jon Loewen (then a young intern). I had saddled him with trying to unravel the Gordian knot of planning while I tended to other projects and at the week's end we sat down to appraise the progress. By both of our assessments, it was dismal, and I doodled the parti of the parallel terraces once again.

"Imagine that each terrace is a kind of ecological filter, conditioning water, people's minds (through the library), and their bodies (through the recreational programs). They descend from the city to the lake and they reconnect with nature, knowledge, their community—it's so clear and it's so out of reach!"

I had drawn the parti over a printout of the site plan, placing it as I thought it should be, ignoring the thick black outline of the pool tank jutting incongruously into my parallel pen strokes.

"Well that's a concept, why don't we just do that?"

Jon replied, shifting the sketch paper until the terraces aligned with the tank and the whole complex sat at an aggressive 45-degree angle to the main road, to the city, and to all of the compositional baggage I had been carrying around.

I had to admit that the rotation, though outrageous, unlocked the potential to pursue our conceptual and poetic inclinations. I instructed Jon to build a sketch model over the remainder of the day, and if I could stomach the shift in the morning, we would continue into uncharted territory.

In the light of the next day, the little cardboard model offered a new perspective on our ambition to connect city and lake. The sharp orientation of the three simple bars away from the city grid created what can only be described as a disruption in the otherwise predictable suburban fabric . We quickly set to exploring the potential of a triangular plaza that would draw the city into the site and create a direct pedestrian connection to the front door. This strong oblique access would create a sectional cut through three programmatic terraces, opening the major program areas to view and allowing a powerful visual connection to the lake. In the midst of this terraced composition, the existing pool basin would sit comfortably lit from above and overlooked by the gymnasium as part of a layered composition of active programs. By letting the plan be what it needed to be, we had liberated the section to tell the story we needed to tell. Over the coming months, our primary tasks, from a design perspective, would

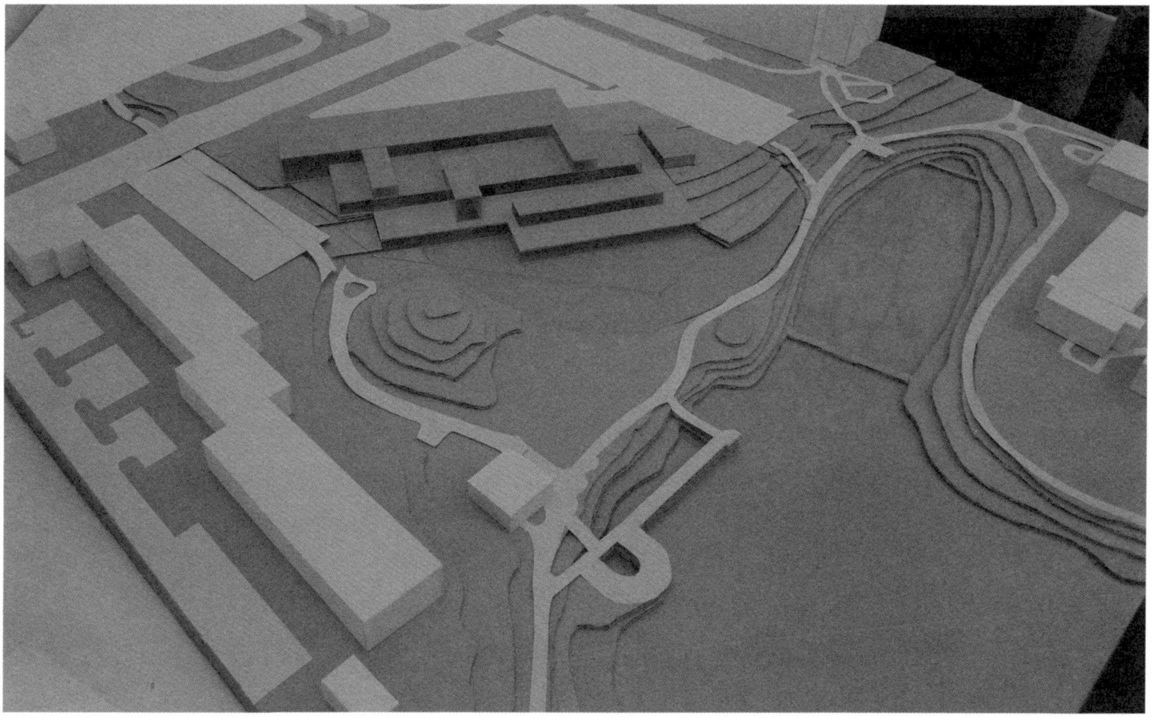

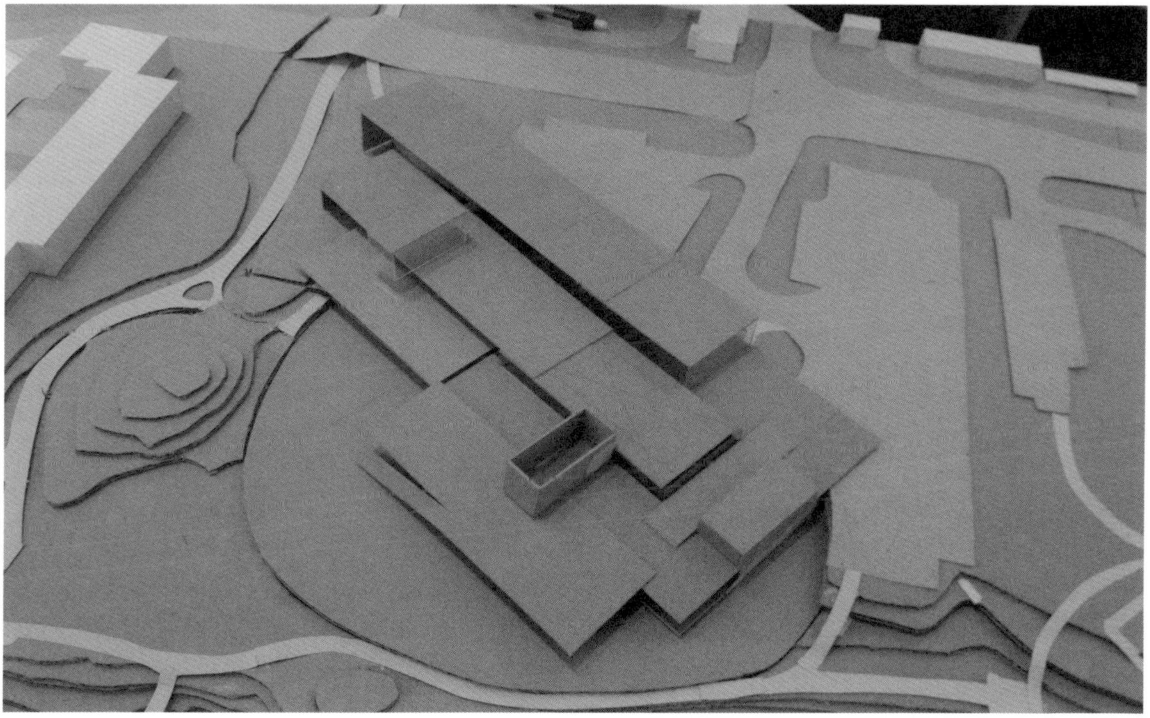

A sketch model exploring a difficult building orientation

A sketch study of the centre's volumetric expression from the lakeside

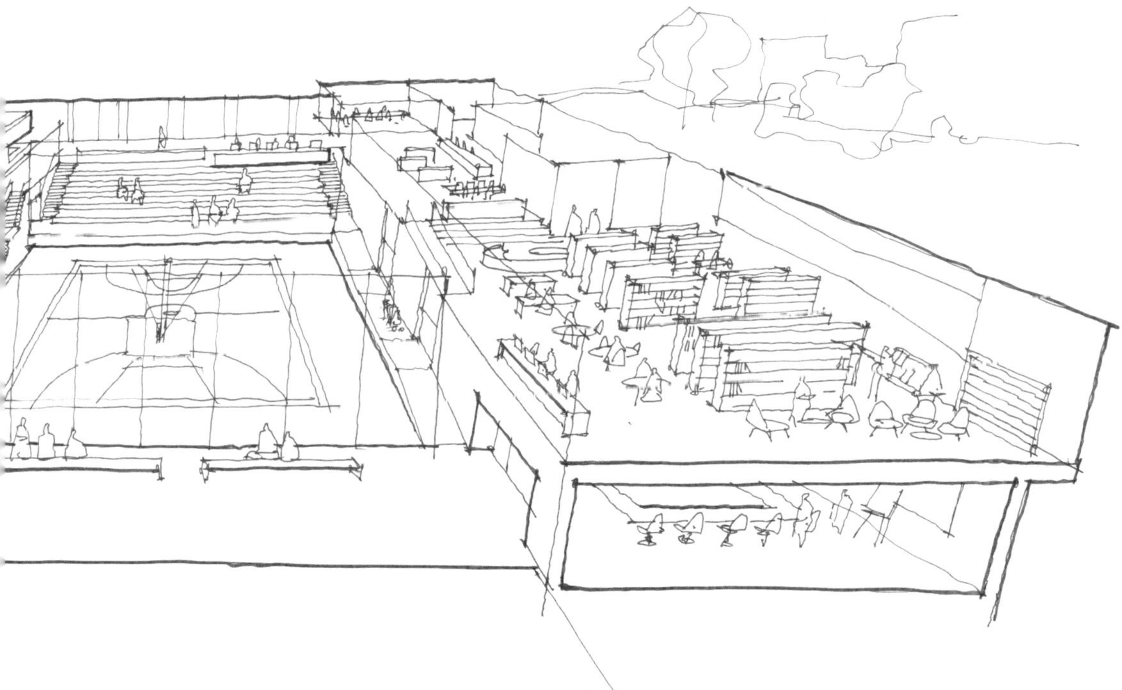

An early and rather inefficient concept for engaging the sloping site

revolve around integrating an increasing number of technical and practical considerations into the building's diagrammatic section and principal narrative—a terraced union of program and landscape that would not tolerate extraneous elements.

In the case of Meadowvale Community Centre and Library, the way forward seemed always to come by letting the building be what it needed to be—a process of divination rather than manifestation, served best by mindful listening rather than prepared postulations. The initial spark had come from a very young fisherman, and the building's programmatic connection to its landscape would be refined by a heated conversation with its most senior patrons. The frequenters of Meadowvale's senior centre, hearing of the building's imminent demolition, quickly mobilized their elected official, who wasted no time in bringing us before the crowd of disgruntled octogenarians. There is something very humbling about being told that you are robbing your elders of one of the few things that they have left to cherish—their community. Perhaps such humility is a prerequisite for any sincere consideration of how the practice of design can really serve people's needs and, in this way, it may be the grandmother of invention. Sitting in the low windowless basement room, we heard a candid testimonial, and I responded candidly with a vision for what the gathered elders could expect in the new complex. Drawing on mega Post-it Notes taped to the cinder-block walls, Phil and I described the potential for a vista to the lake, a shaded terrace, and a relationship to the outdoors that would connect them to others in the community.

While the design concept had been growing its roots for a while, this meeting is the first time that I recall directly connecting it to the people who would use it. It proved to be inspirational as we pushed the concept of the terraces forward. As we explore a concept in greater detail, we need the human connection to give it life. After all, the modernist cannon is replete with empty terraces and forgotten landscapes in the sky. As we dove deeper into the details of the design, our investigations were increasingly fueled by the people who would engage the new landscape we were creating. Over a year of design development, the terraces would take on very specific characters tied to real programming. The fitness centre would open onto a basketball courtyard and the library onto an elevated reading deck overlooking the lake and the senior terrace below. This was no accident, as the exhaustive nature of the user engagement was demanded by the local councilor and facilitated by Raj and his staff. A passionate and engaged client always means more work for the architect, but it leads to better architecture.

Viewed from its urban context, the most striking aspect of the Meadowvale Community Centre is its polychrome brise-soleil, which veers away from the streetscape at an abrupt angle, adding to the sense of a disruption in the normal course of events for this leafy suburb. In our efforts to create a clear sectional diagram, we had been architecturally reductive. Each terrace was simply articulated as a white horizontal fascia, floating above a ribbon of glass and resting on white masonry piers at each end, its top surface planted or decked, and its underside a continuous plane of fine-grained cedar slats within which structure, lighting, and mechanical systems were concealed. The alignment of the building with the existing pool tank had opened many opportunities but also positioned the long sides of our terraced composition almost exactly east to west, presenting challenges with regard to the control of low sun angles and undesirable glare and heat gain at the beginning and end of each day. The design solution to this dilemma was inspired by an evolving narrative around the theme of filtration, originally tied to water and the landscape, but then adapted to the management of light.

While our team had been building the architectural language of the complex, our landscape architect Brad Fleischer had been developing an integrated approach to storm water management on the site. The triangular forecourt leading to the building entrance was designed with a range of porous materials including planted beds, permeable pavers, and fine granite screenings. The large surface parking lot adjacent had a mandate to withstand the harsh routine of winter snow and ice removal and its gently sloping asphalt surface was interrupted with a set of bioswales collecting groundwater and filtering it of salt, rubber, and oil before it descended into the stormwater system and eventually to Lake Aquitaine. The vertical steel teeth of the stormwater weir, which had set the theme of filtration in play at the outset of the design, provided the compositional model for the last major design challenge: the solar "filters" that characterize Meadowvale's principal interface with both the City and the Lake. These brise-soleils, composed of angled aluminum extrusions, use colour to create a contrast with the unrelenting palette of red and brown brick that characterizes the surrounding fabric. Four discrete colours (pink-purple, blue, green, and yellow) are arranged in a mixed graduation that creates a sense of movement from south to north and from warm to cool, with the intent of evoking the lakeside park and the passage of the sun.

A similarly "attentive" approach proved useful in finalizing our concept for the building interiors. We developed a series of rendered visualizations to model the degree to which the brise-soleils would control sunlight within the major spaces. These visualizations made it clear to both our team and the client that the chromatic impact of the brise-soleils as seen through the windows would provide all of the colour that the space would need, allowing us to continue with a very reductive and elemental approach to our interior language. White masonry walls, wood ceilings, and dark porcelain floors established a clear reading of elements and acted as a frame for the ribbons of graduated colour beyond the windows. In the end, this elemental approach to the interiors would prove highly effective in supporting a wayfinding strategy for the visually and cognitively impaired, opening indoor programs and landscape elements to the broadest possible demographic.

It is always deeply satisfying when a building is finally complete and the public moves in and makes the space their own. At the reopening of Meadowvale, I recall an acute sense of communal excitement as people not only discovered new spaces, but rediscovered a landscape that they had always known and was now opened to them in new ways. People swarmed up, over, and through the building, finding spots to engage with the architecture and the site. Some weeks later, on a sunny October day, I brought clients from the Toronto Public Library to see the new branch within the Meadowvale building and to tour the complex in general. After an hour of fielding detailed questions and explaining all the building's attributes and flaws, I thanked our hosts and we began to organize ourselves to carpool back to the city. As so often happens when leading a tour of people whose passion is the construction and operation of public buildings, a couple of them had wandered off and "gotten lost." Given the splendid afternoon and unseasonably warm temperatures, I had a good hunch where to find them. I walked out onto the library's lakeside terrace, and there they were, sunning themselves in a pair of blue Adirondack loungers.

"We're staying here."

They cackled almost in unison. Looking out over the tops of trees that had already begun to turn to orange, I could see the broad expanse of the lake and the little jetty where people were still fishing.

"I think I'll join you,"

I said, sinking into the curved wood back of a lounger.

"I'm sure the others will find us eventually."

Client	City of Mississauga
Location	Mississauga, Ontario
Size	81,100 gross square metres
Date	2012-2016

The brise-soleils along the centre's west façade

The triangular entrance plaza and west façade

An aerial view overlooking the centre and Lake Aquitaine

An aerial view looking back toward the city

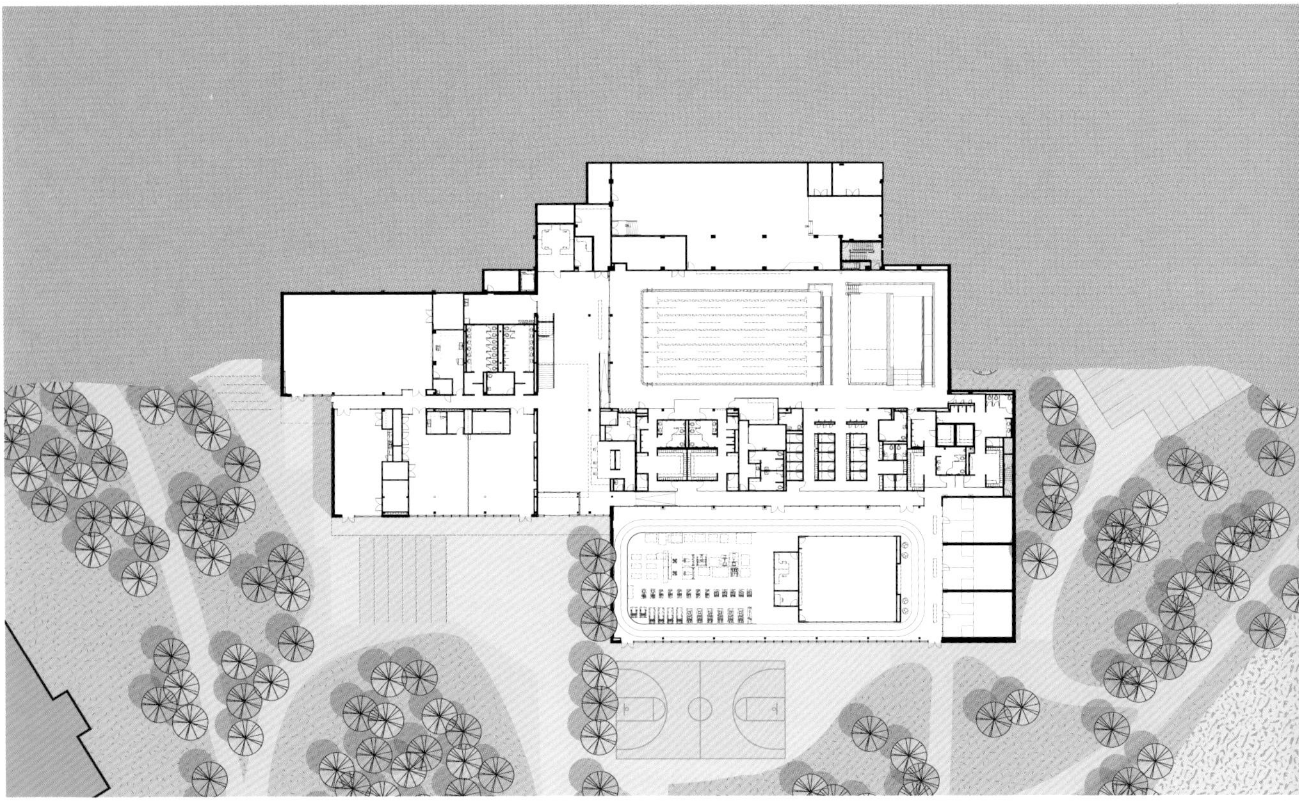

Level 01 Plan

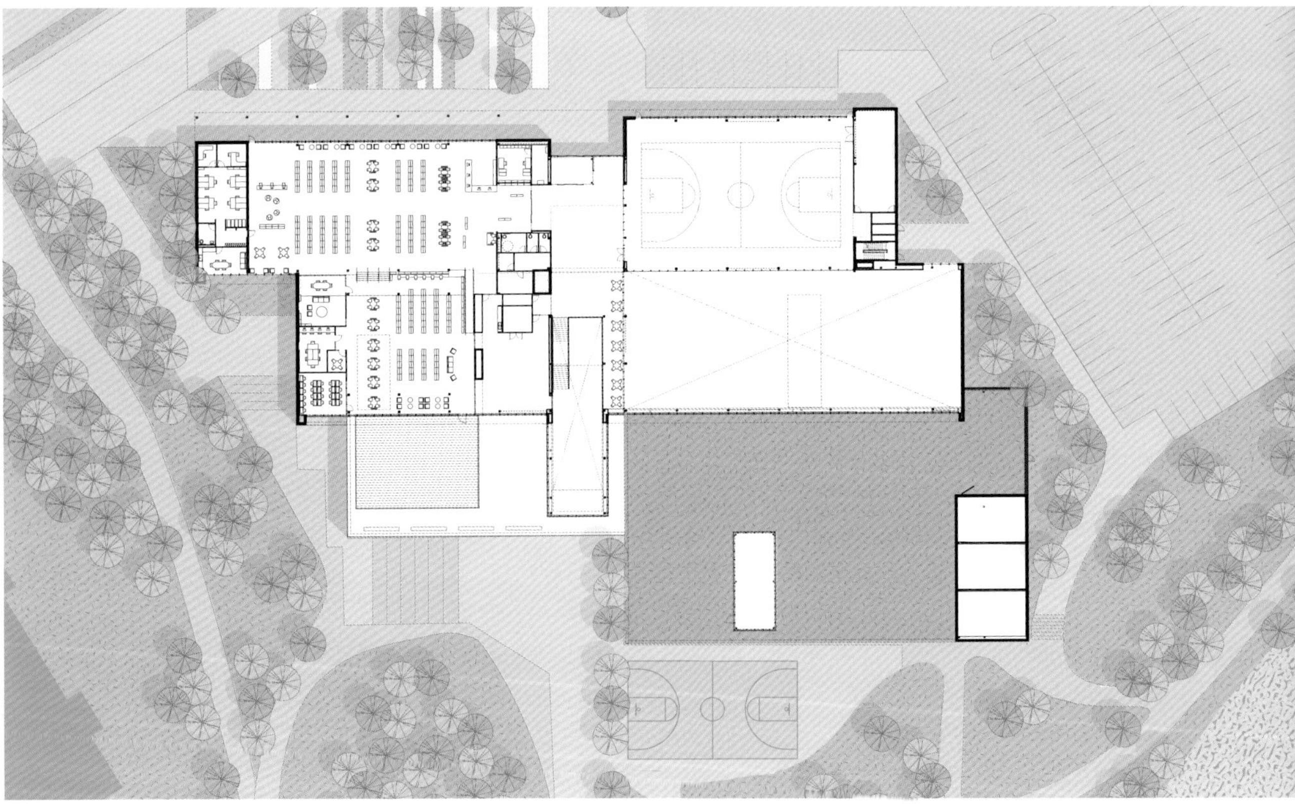

Level 02 Plan

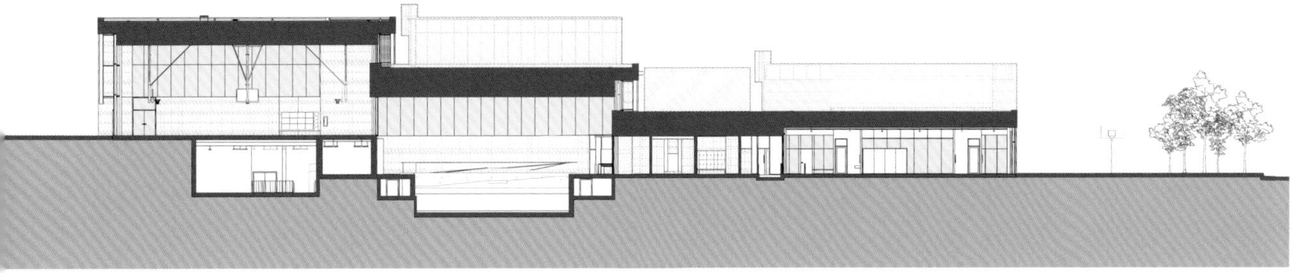

East-West Section A

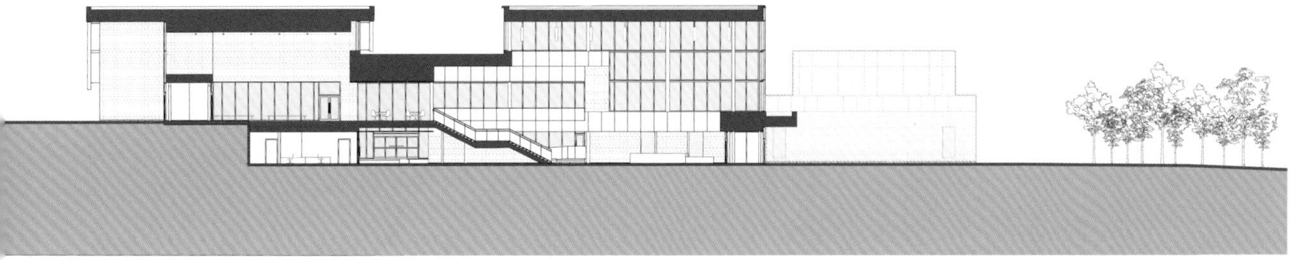

East-West Section B

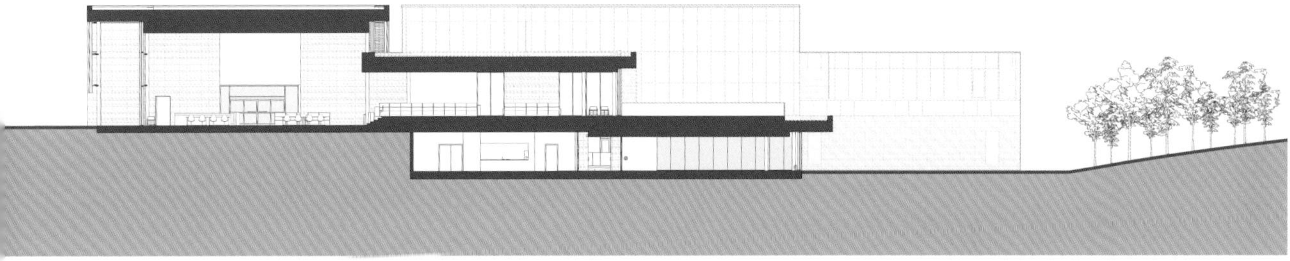

East-West Section C

Movies
05 60 Minute
30 Minute
04 60 Minute
30 Minute
12 30 Minute
Catalogue

The library main hall

The main entrance

The arcade along the west façade

The lakeside ball court and fitness area

Customer Service

The lobby connecting the city and the lake

Colour Theory

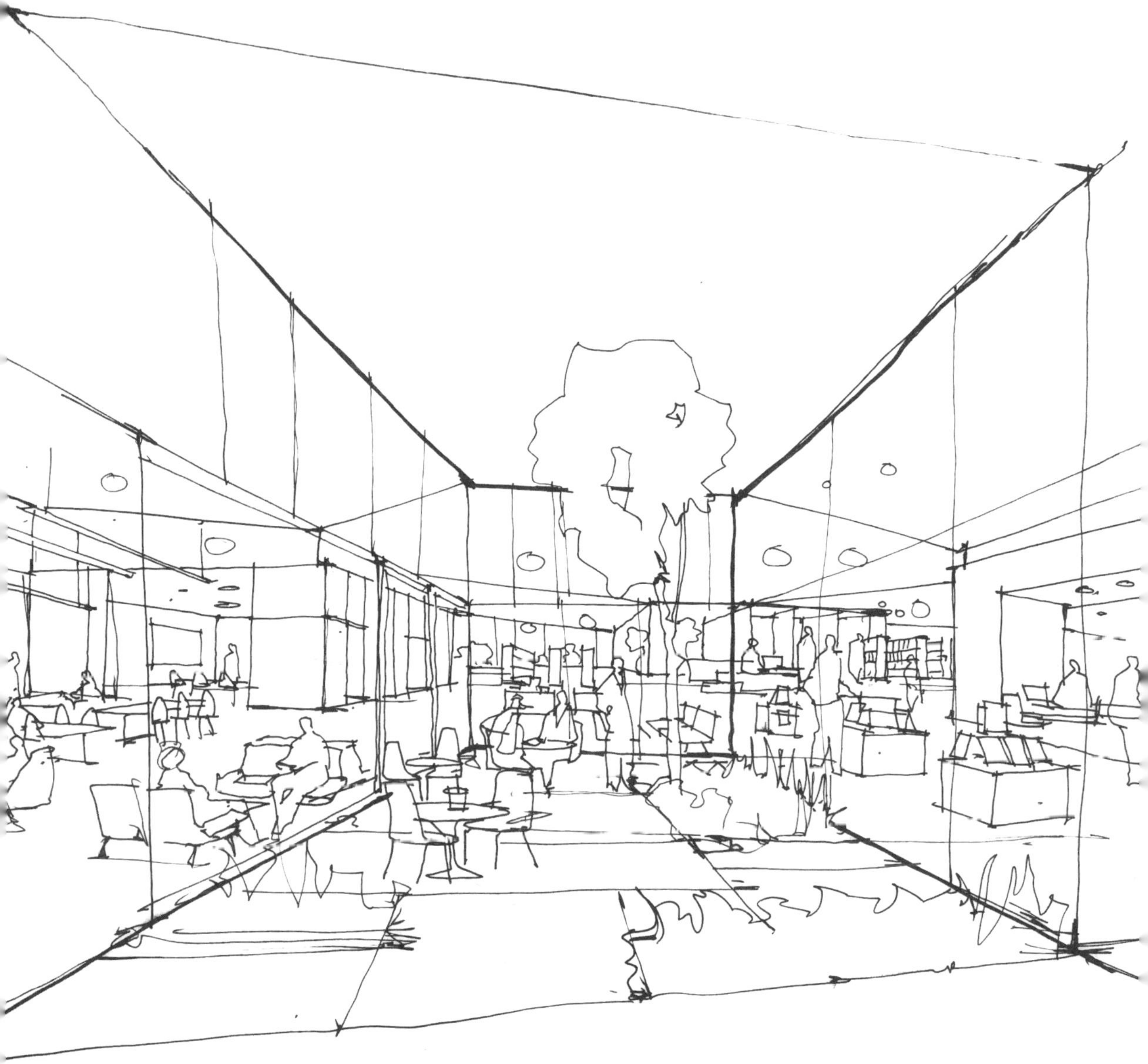

Albion Library

Toronto, Ontario 2014-2017

"The last thing I need is another white, 50-year-old male architect dressed all in black telling me about how the design for OUR library needs to be all black and white with grey thrown in for a splash of colour."

I was standing behind Anne Bailey, the director of branch libraries for Toronto Public Library. This remark and the general mirth that it had inspired amongst her colleagues were still ringing in my ears as I cleared my throat and walked around to meet her and her fellow library staffers, Gail Rankin and Susan Martin. Without missing a beat, Anne addressed me with a wry smile.

"But you aren't like that Andrew, afraid of colour?"

"Not at all,"

I replied, and really, I am not. While I was hoping that my rather bold Italian plaid sport coat would visually reinforce my conviction, it was quite clear that as an architect and a white man pushing 50 at the time, I would be guilty until proven innocent. This was my new client, an organization that I had spent the better part of a decade trying to work with, and it was run, at least at the top levels, almost entirely by women. Toronto Public Library operates a hundred branch libraries across the city, and they do it well, with a strong focus on good design and community engagement.

It was a brisk October night, and we were gathered for the first of several community consultations regarding the renewal of the Albion branch library. A very diverse and quite young crowd of about 125 people was packed into the windowless multipurpose hall of the existing library, a single-storey branch built in 1977 that we were tasked with renovating and expanding. Before putting pen to paper, we would join Anne and her staff in gaining feedback from the community on the proposed project schedule and program. Despite the relatively modest scale of the commission, I was thrilled to be adding Albion to our portfolio, as it would allow us to take "designing a library in my home city" off the proverbial bucket list.

The truth is, however, the Toronto we were gathered in that night was far removed from the leafy central neighbourhood I call home. Rexdale, the postwar suburb that Albion library serves, is a troubled neighbourhood with high incidences of unemployment and gang-related crime. Due to a concentration of low-rent, high-rise rental housing, the neighbourhood is also a point of first arrival for thousands of new immigrants to the region on an annual basis. In its Toronto Strong Neighbourhoods Strategy plan, the city had identified the Albion catchment as a neighbourhood improvement area, indicating a lack of social infrastructure, poor access to transit, limited access to green spaces and recreation, and a poor condition of the built environment.

At first glance, it really didn't look that bad. Arriving for the meeting that night, I had driven northwest on Albion Road, a busy six-lane arterial lined with an inconsistent jumble of postwar houses, strip retail buildings, and the odd three-storey brick office block. When I arrived at the library, which I nearly missed due to its battered and uninviting street presence, I found the lot full. I was later told that that has never happened before. Rumors of the branch's imminent demolition had brought its users out in force.

Abundant parking was to be found across the road, in the relentless sea of asphalt that sets the foreground for the sprawling Albion Mall. Pulling into the lot, I gazed upon the shopping mall with its endless horizon of sheet-metal–clad boxes and its cacophony of illuminated signage in every imaginable colour, font, and format. The mall, as a typology, usually offers a unifying influence, gathering together a multitude of tenants within a singular architectural order. This was not the case with the Albion Mall, which seemed to have an indeterminate and improvised exterior without the kind of hierarchy that helps one find the front door or the informality that would bestow upon it any sort of charm. There was not a blade of grass or a tree in sight over the mall's 12-acre site. Urbanistically, Albion Mall is the malignant heart of the Rexdale neighbourhood, sucking life from the street and placing the pedestrian in the most hostile of environments. But socially and economically, the mall reveals the rich ethnic and cultural diversity of the area. You have to go inside, deep inside, to experience that—as I would later do on several occasions, searching for sustenance between meetings. Canada is a fledgling society in many regards, and the immigrants' culture and experience usually don't manifest themselves in architectural terms for a couple for generations. Within the halls of the mall, the loudspeakers, retail mannequins, and Styrofoam take-out containers begin to tell a story that is absent from the grim suburban context.

Over the course of that first evening consultation, I got to know some of the neighbourhood's residents and some very passionate library users. I tried to give them a sense of who we were and, with the team from Toronto Public Library, gave a short presentation about the proposed program for the building, some of our thoughts about how libraries are evolving to meet communities' needs in the digital age, and the expected timeline for the construction. This last point drew questions and some heated discussion from the crowd. It became evident that there was a strong collective anxiety about the proposed closure of the branch for up to two years. We had already investigated the potential of leaving the branch open during construction, but the required work was too extensive, and it was the critical infrastructure that was most in need of replacement. Heating, ventilation, and washroom systems were all well past their life expectancy. Toronto Public Library had also entertained building a temporary branch in the mall, but this would ultimately slow the project down and siphon budget resources from the final product. In the mind of my client, the best move was to close and get back up and running as quickly as possible with a state-of-the-art library tailored to the community's needs.

After the formal presentation and Q and A, our team dispersed into the crowd. My colleague Aimee Drmic and I tag-teamed with library staff in a series of one-on-one conversations with library users over two hours. It was a long night fueled with strong emotions and subtle insights. I remember speaking with three teenage girls about the way they used the library to create their own cultural events, from slam poetry nights to a D.I.Y. haunted house for the community's younger children. A group of older Caribbean women spoke passionately

Inside the neighbouring Albion Centre shopping mall

The original Albion branch library (1972, above right) and adjacent apartment blocks (above left)

Inside the original Albion branch library

about the community garden plots behind the library, which they lovingly tended through the warmer months and planned together with research materials found in the library over the long winter. That night I heard many different versions of the same story, which entailed people coming together to make things and express themselves at the library.

Toronto Public Library has developed an excellent system of combining these very personal face-to-face interactions with much broader online surveys and questionnaires handed out in the library. This three-pronged approach captures live input, broad demographic information, and the sentiments of people while they are using the existing library. In the weeks following the public consultation we developed a composite portrait of the library's users, and their needs and wants.

One thing became abundantly clear: In the eyes of the community, the library provided a series of essential services that could not be interrupted. The library was neutral turf where teens could come to avoid the stresses of a gang-dominated youth culture. It was a place for new immigrants to orient themselves into Canadian society, learn to navigate the city, and find critical resources. It was a place that many people ran small businesses out of, and it was a place where people could create and express themselves in ways that were not supported by their homes or the physical space of the city around them. One impassioned survey respondent put it in simple terms:

"Leave it alone, do nothing, but don't close it—even for a day."

The various forms of engagement also revealed aspirations about what a renewed library might offer for the community. Consistent themes emerged in response to the deficiencies of the existing building and the urban context in general. Nature, garden, oasis, green, bright, sunlight, warmth, colour, safe, and escape were the words that appeared most consistently in the survey responses.

We put aside our investigations of renewing and adding to the existing structure and began to strategize a plan that would allow the existing structure to operate as it was while a new building was constructed on the adjacent parking lot. With this new approach, the library would close for only the two weeks necessary to move its collection over to the new building. This would be marginally more costly, but it met the community's expressed needs while opening up some compelling design challenges and opportunities.

Once we had taken into account the required municipal setbacks and ongoing fire-truck access to the existing library, we were left with an almost perfectly square area in which to plan and build. The theme of the library as a garden oasis inspired an arrangement of three small courtyards that would bring light and life deep into the building, offering protected and curated versions of nature. This arrangement would support outdoor programming and provide an appropriate level of privacy along the site's south edge, which directly abutted the backyards of a row of postwar bungalows. Using a series of simple cardboard models, we explored the way that the building's roofline could accentuate the entrance and key program areas, and also direct rainwater runoff into the courtyards.

In tandem, we engaged our landscape architect, John Hillier of DTAH, to imagine an integrated public realm with a unique landscape character not only for the courtyards, but also for a community plaza in the place of the old library. Having conceptually replaced a hundred-car asphalt surface lot with an urban oasis, it seemed a crime to reintroduce that same lot in the place of the old structure.

The community had articulated the desire for a greened site and public gathering spaces, but the city's planning division was pressing us to meet a minimum parking capacity based on a zoning bylaw that had remained unchanged since the 1980s. During the course of the design and approvals process, we would often run into mixed messaging from the city.

While the transportation division viewed the Albion site as part of a car-dominated community, which it certainly was, the planning division consistently advocated for New Urbanist principles whereby a building's front door should face the street in the centre of the façade. In the end, we successfully advocated for a corner entry facing both the street and a new multi-purpose public landscape—a hybrid plaza that could support markets and performance events, yet accommodate parking when needed.

The key to this design approach was an aggressive greening strategy, permeable hardscapes, and a reduced parking count. In support, the library rapidly mobilized a survey of their users, which demonstrated that most patrons arrive at the library by foot or public transit, the majority not even owning cars. The city officials were convinced, and our public realm strategy began to take shape.

Aimee and I finessed the plan and built form of the library for several weeks, until our client grew impatient waiting for the image of the library to appear. The basic form, the site-phasing strategy, the multi-use plaza, and the internal courtyards had all come into being quite quickly, having been directly inspired by the community consultation. But the next level of architectural expression seemed to elude us, as if without the community's explicit direction, we were lost. When we did finally bring forward some sketch renderings of a glassy pavilion with lifted corners, they were unequivocally rejected. The city librarian, Jane Pyper, who had specifically come to the meeting to see the renders, didn't mince words:

"We've seen this before. It looks suburban."

Susan Martin dealt the final blow with a reference to Ontario's newly completed rollout of roadside rest stops:

"It looks like an ONroute, sorry."

If you have read several chapters of this book, you are probably asking yourself, "Doesn't this guy ever get it right the first time?" And answering honestly, I would say I rarely do. Except in the case of a design competition, the evolution of an architectural proposal is a complex conversation involving many players and divergent viewpoints. For this architect, there is a process of slow absorption, of trying to pick up all of the nuances, prioritize them, and synthesize them. The conversations continue as the design evolves, and quite often it is the most difficult conversations that prove to be catalytic, inspiring a new avenue of investigation or a focus of creative energy. In this case, I would say we suffered a fruitful rejection.

Leaving the meeting with D'Arcy and Aimee, I began the process of self-flagellation that is an integral part of the architect's process. "What must they think of us? Suburban hacks! We've been fetishizing the plan for two months without drawing a single elevation!"

I resolved to go out to the site and stand there until I figured out what the context demanded. When I arrived, I can't say that my mood was soaring. The traffic was dense and loud, the wind was blowing grit and trash all over the place, the existing library was disintegrating before my eyes, and Albion Mall lurked like an urban black hole. When I returned to the office and sat down with our team, it was this bleak and hostile setting that started to inspire a conversation about what the exterior architecture needed to be.

If we were going to create a refuge infused with light, colour, and nature, the first step would be to create some way of filtering out the surrounding context. This couldn't just be a barrier, because the library also needed to broadcast its presence and invite people in. So we developed the notion of a permeable garden wall, something that defines a sense of enclosure but invites glimpses in. Our design's square building mass, with its lifted corner, had a pavilion-like quality, which led us to review the colourful precedents provided by the pavilions of Expo 67, the world's fair in Montreal. Looking for a durable, graffiti-resistant material that would allow us to articulate the vertical organization of our garden enclosure, we arrived at glazed terra-cotta extrusion, which also allowed us immense freedom to explore colour. When it came to colour palette, the natural direction would seem to be an evocation of nature, of the garden within the enclosure.

Rather than revealing everything through transparency, we would create a more protective, energy-efficient building envelope and develop a communicative façade language speaking to the rich variety of nature and the community. The limitless possibilities offered by the glazed terra-cotta were overwhelming at first, and we carried out endless studies to refine and organize the palette into a repetitive and therefore cost-effective module. In the end, it was the garish signage of the Albion Mall that helped us to establish a chromatic language fusing natural tones of green and warm grey with bolder yellows, blues, oranges, and purples. This act of sampling the man-made context to evoke the beauty of nature might seem contradictory, but upon reflection I think it adds depth to the metaphor of the garden. In a garden, things grow out of the decaying remnant of other things, so recycling and repurposing seem appropriate acts. While the mall is an architectural blight, it is a strong cultural container. Bringing some of its richness out into the open, and reorganizing that into an expression of the community, allows the library to engage in a different kind of contextualism. A garden is also a metaphor for a community, a complex ecosystem of diverse yet supporting entities, and so the act of bringing disparate and perhaps incongruous elements together also seems appropriate.

During the detailed development of the terra-cotta façade, we struggled

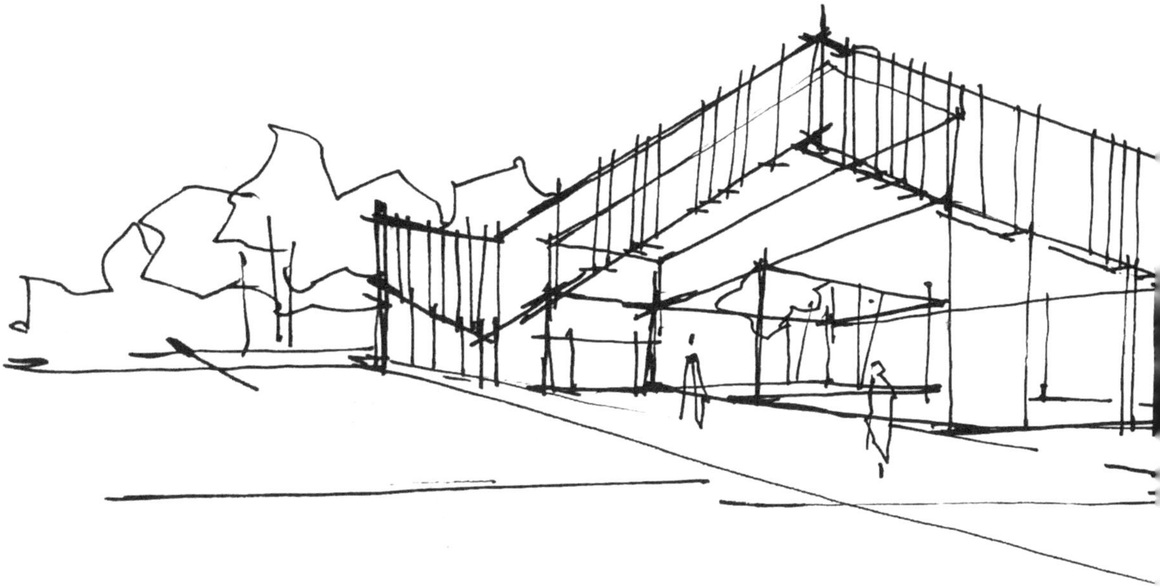

Sketch for a pavilion with lifted corners

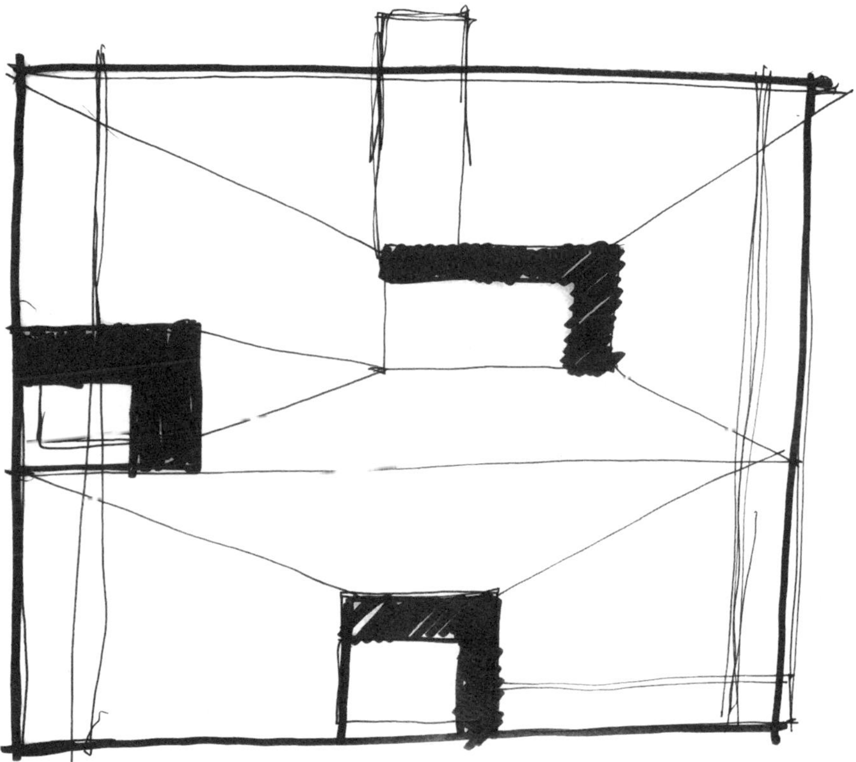

A study for a roof with courtyard openings

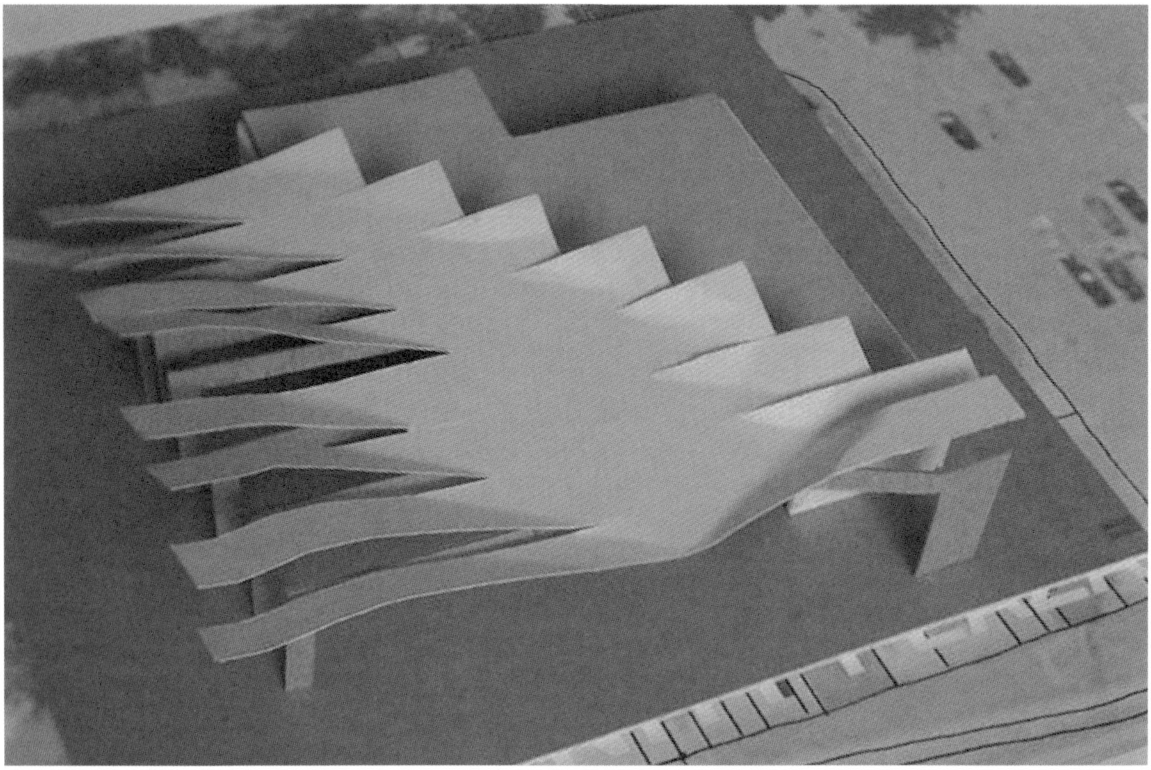

Early studies for an addition to the existing library

Concept model with inset courtyards

with finding an elegant way to extend the terra-cotta extrusions as the fence across the exterior edges of the courtyards. Terra-cotta is heavy, and a fairly robust steel frame was required to support the free-floating façade. My colleague D'Arcy Arthurs, who generally manages the office but occasionally pops his head in to offer a critique of laser precision, suggested that we line the fence with the terra-cotta extrusions on both sides, and in so doing gain multiple advantages. This is what we did. The move created a clean aesthetic where the steel was concealed, while the terra-cotta's texture and colour were made present inside the courtyards and could be seen from everywhere within the library.

John Hiller developed a landscape strategy with timber decking and benches complemented by indigenous plantings. I recall him describing the visual richness that the courtyards would provide with the textured white trunks of paper birches set off against the coloured backdrop of the terra-cotta screen. As we completed the design phase the client became thoroughly convinced of the rich layering of indoor and outdoor space. Today, in its finished state, the library is permeated with light, colour, and activity. The plaza supports concerts, food fairs, and an African market. The three courtyards are constantly programmed with an array of activities that are a testament to Toronto Public Library's ingenuity.

In the end, I think I convinced them that I'm not afraid of colour. While my whiteness, my maleness, and the indelible stamp of the architect haven't disappeared (I did hit 50 during the course of the project's execution), this project changed me. In designing the library and then seeing it used enthusiastically over the past few years, I have become acutely aware of the power of architecture to respond to communities and lift them up.

I feel humbled, empowered, and duty-bound to see that our designs help people. I like to think that the process of building and designing Albion changed the team at Toronto Public Library as well. Given all of the life and colour that the building exterior and landscape offered, they let us design a very simple interior: wood, black carpet, and white walls. Oh, and some grey thrown in for colour.

Client	Toronto Public Library
Location	Toronto, Ontario
Size	2,900 gross square metres
Date	2014-2017

The perimeter screen of extruded, glazed terra-cotta

The corner entrance addressing Albion Road and a new landscaped plaza

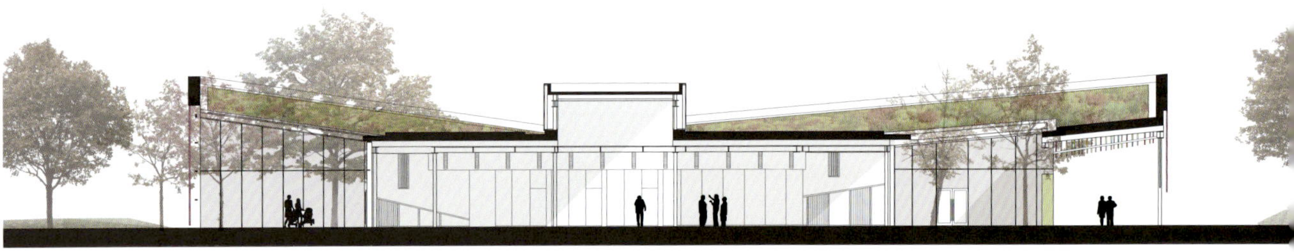

East-West Section A

North-South Section B

Bird's-eye view of the library and plaza

Site and Level 01 Plan

Site diagram for continuous operation

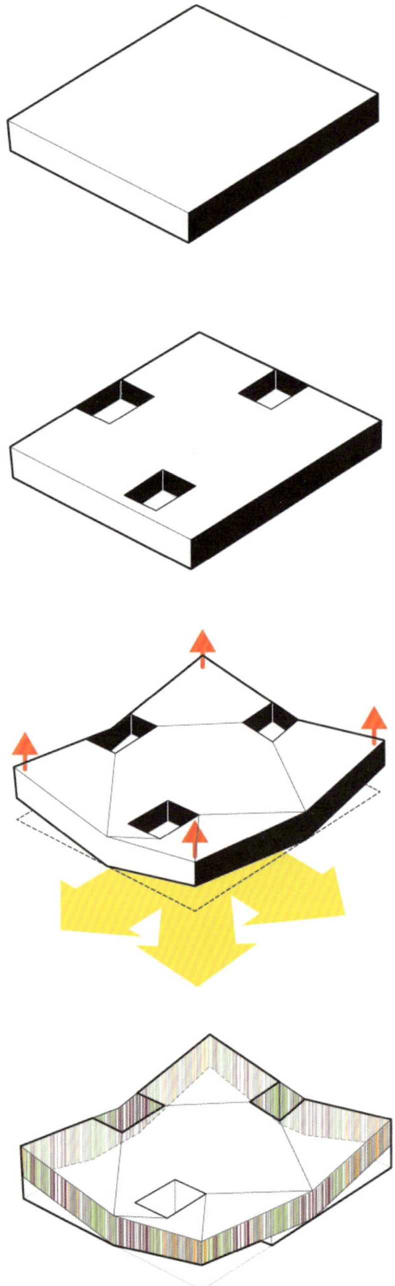

Shaping the pavilion

Looking into the children's area on the northwest corner

Community garden plots on the south side of the library

LIBRARY

The Albion Road elevation

The electronic media collection

The teen collection

Stacks and study rooms

The "Urban Living Room" and adjacent courtyard

The children's area and children's courtyard

Learning to camp in the children's courtyard

Detail of the terra-cotta scrim at the main entrance

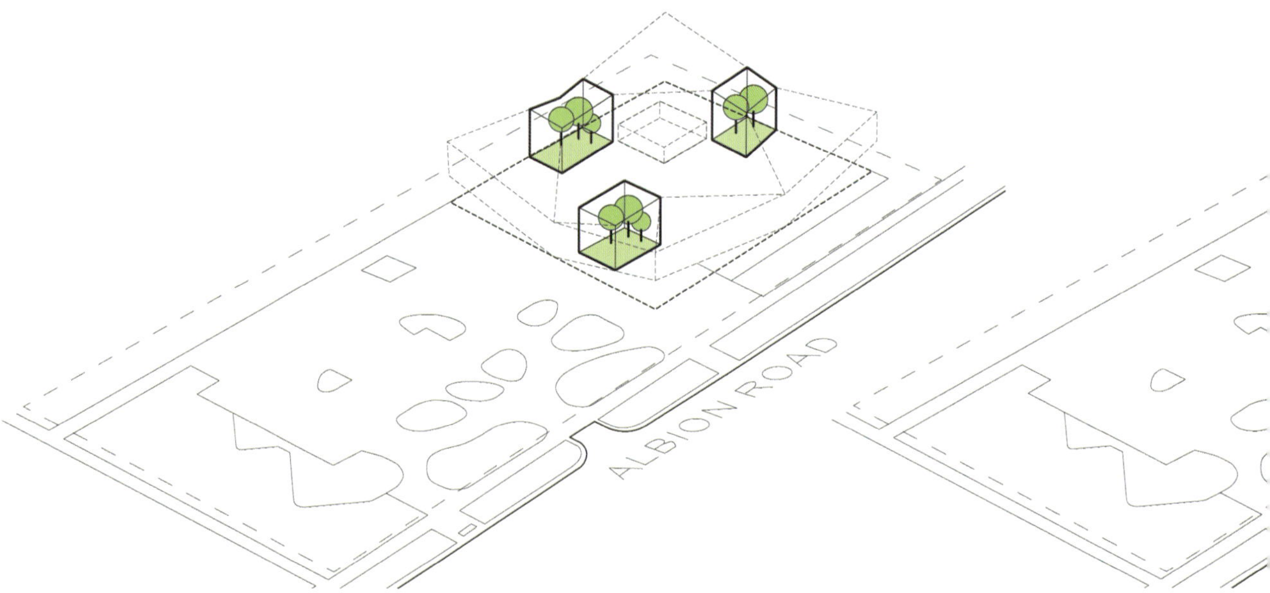

A market in the hybrid parking lot and plaza

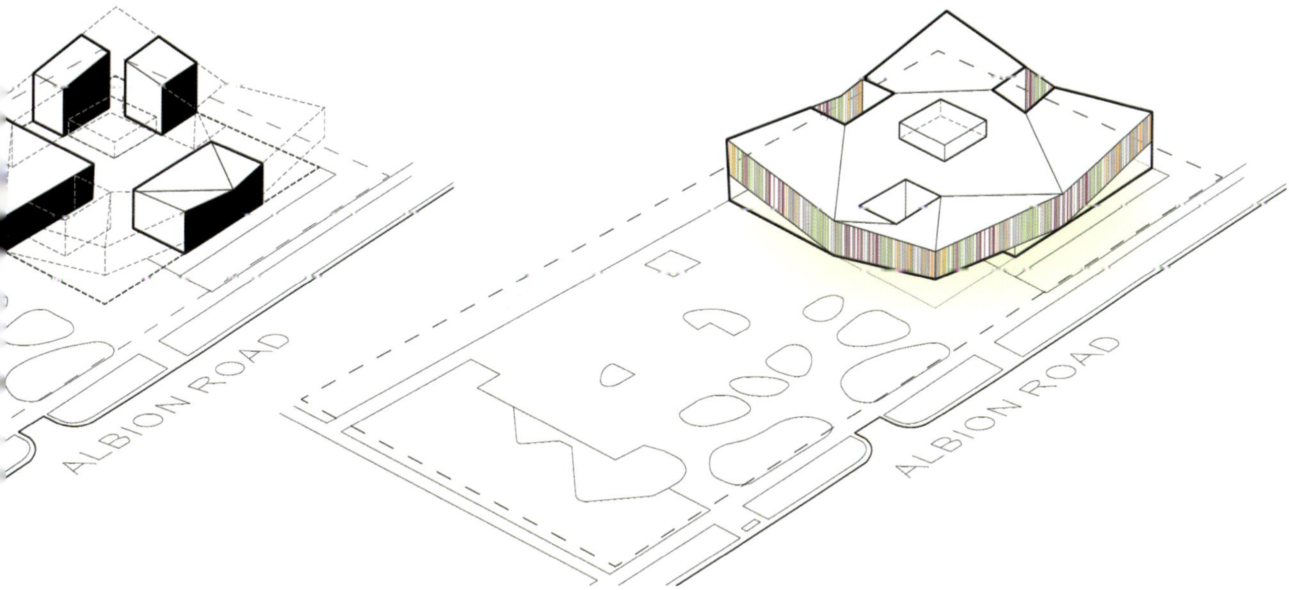

Concept diagrams of courtyards, program blocks, and the garden wall

A Bright Spot in the City

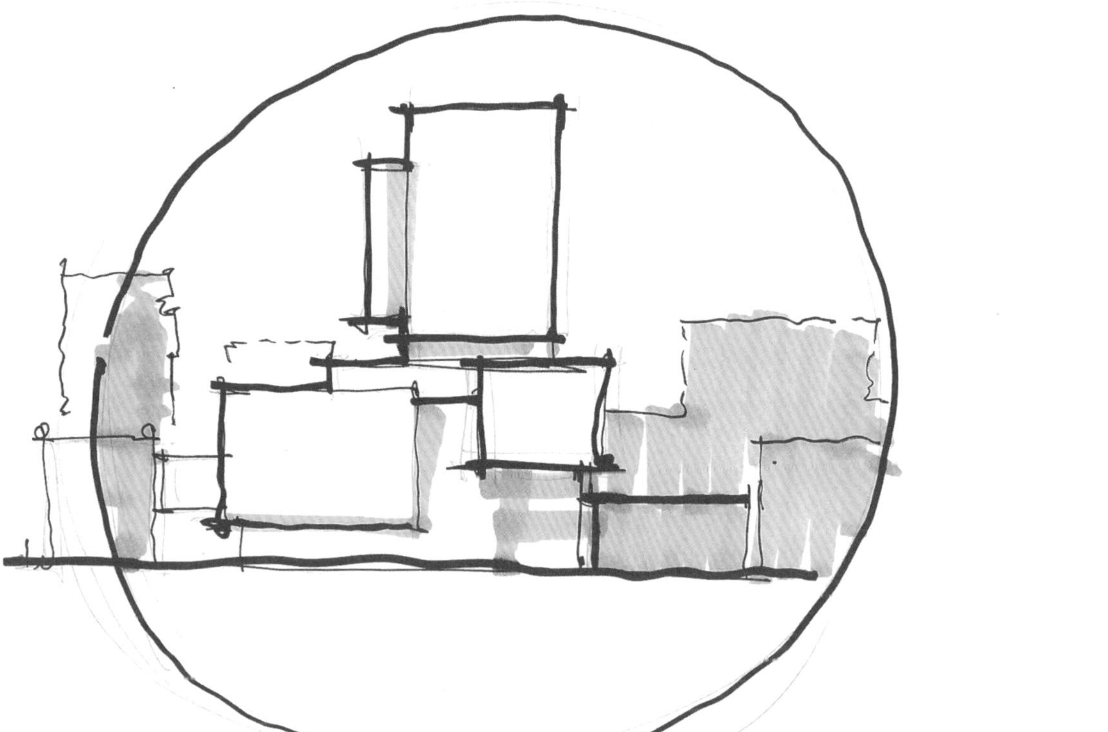

Daphne Cockwell Health Sciences Complex
Toronto Metropolitan University

Toronto, Ontario 2013–2019

We were looking out over a sea of green, occasionally interrupted by the roof line or red-brick chimney pot of a 19th-century house. This was the two- and three-storey residential fabric of Toronto, which makes up the vast majority of its developed area. From our studio on the fifth floor of the former Ford Model T assembly plant, this "city of trees" sloped gently toward Lake Ontario before abruptly ending at a wall of high-rise towers, sprinkled with nearly 100 construction cranes. This was the manifestation of Toronto's explosive speculative growth, which had distributed itself along two key axes: the lakefront and the north–south corridor of Yonge University subway line. I was standing with Elisabeth Stroback, the head of capital projects and real estate at Toronto Metropolitan University (known at the time as Ryerson University), looking to a point 7 kilometers to the southeast, trying to imagine the school's latest build, a proposed 3,000-square-metre "vertical campus," emerging from the relentless panorama of grey aluminum and glass.

"How will we stand out from all of that monotony and communicate that we are an institution , a place of learning and not just another condo tower?"

This wasn't the first time Elisabeth had asked me this question, and I had decided to stage a discussion of how to capture an institutional identity and purpose in a high-rise building in our Dupont Street studio, with its unique and uninterrupted view of the entire downtown core. We had been working with TMU for six months, refining a functional program, developing a project charter, and engaging with hundreds of students, researchers, advisors, and community members. The time had now come to speak of architectural intent and language. I taped a simple white paper silhouette onto the window and asked Elisabeth to stand at the centre of the conference-room table looking out. With the green foreground of tree-lined streets, the ragged skyline of crowded grey-glass towers, and the deep indigo of the lake beyond, the white paper abstraction of our proposed 28-storey tower shone like a beacon—a singular moment on the horizon. A little stagecraft goes a long way, and after starting with the punchline, we took our client through a series of illustrated steps as to how we would translate TMU's vision for the project and the campus into a unique architectural character.

While the design and construction of what would become the Daphne Cockwell Health Sciences Complex would pose many challenges, the client's aspirations for the project were both bold and clearly stated. TMU challenged and inspired us from the outset, as we embarked on the most complex commission in our portfolio to this point. The university's objectives for the project grew out of two key sources. The first was the 2008 master plan which TMU had commissioned to address a space crunch in the face of growing enrollment and finite land assets in the heart of the city. The second was the vision that then-President Sheldon Levy had for the university as a partner in building the city. "Ryerson The City Builder" had become Levy's battle cry as he and his capital and academic teams investigated a series of resourceful and innovative approaches to leveraging every square inch of space out of the surrounding urban context. In the lead-up to our project, TMU had redeveloped the iconic home of the Toronto Maple Leafs, Maple Leaf Gardens, in partnership with the Loblaws grocery store empire. The design effectively suspended a varsity athletics facility from the arena rafters, above a two-storey grocery store. The redevelopment opened up the rather imposing brick façades of the Gardens, bringing new life and animation to the streetscape. TMU's new business school was built around a courtyard on the fourth floor of a co-developed commercial and academic block that featured large Canadian Tire and Best Buy outlets at grade. In a testimony to the mother of invention, TMU negotiated with multiplex-giant AMC to build a cinema on top of a university parking garage, in exchange for use of the theatres as classrooms on weekdays. This last example captures the degree to which TMU was "of the city," thoroughly enmeshed within the gritty mix of buskers, cheap fashion retailers, strip clubs, and fast-food outlets that characterized the Yonge Street strip circa 2013.

The Church Street Development, as our project was initially known, was to mark the first coming together of TMU's novel co-development strategy and the master plan's recommendations for a new vertical campus building typology. Simultaneously addressing a series of pent up institutional needs, the CSD was in the first instance a form of "real estate release valve" designed to consolidate a dispersed faculty of health sciences whose individual units would then vacate a set of older spaces on campus, freeing them up for renewal or redevelopment at a higher density. At the same time, the new development was to address a chronic shortage of on-campus housing for students. A research grant from the federal government proved to be the catalyst for the university's most ambitious co-development yet, establishing the "big middle" upon which a private housing developer could build a student residence and below which a private parking provider could build a subterranean parkade. Once the real estate vision was established, the university realized that they were about to build something very unique and very visible, which would need to communicate TMU's core values as well as set a standard for the next generation of high-density learning environments. In the project brief for the Church Street Development, design excellence, advanced sustainability, and the creation of a connected and pedestrianized campus were put forth as primary objectives, along with the standard requests for functionality, fiscal prudence, and good management.

When I reflect on our pursuit of the project and the second of two interviews where we clinched the deal, I think that it was our ability to identify TMU's values as an institution and convince them that a research-based and human-centric approach to design could translate these values into a unique and highly communicative architecture. Elisabeth Stroback made it quite plain that my design portfolio was wanting in terms of complex urban buildings, but our story about what the CSD might be was compelling enough to convince TMU to take a risk on our team. I suppose that while preparing for the interview, and sensing that I didn't have the hard goods to win the day, I had shifted the emphasis to what I did have—the ingredients of a good story, which I drew from the talented team around me and the hints that TMU stakeholders had given us.

In 2013, our studio was relatively new to the Perkins&Will family, my partners and I at Shore Tilbe Irwin & Partners having joined the multinational federation only three years prior. Perkins&Will's leading commitment to sustainability and its investment into research around occupant health proved to be critical differentiators. Working with my peers Max Richter and Ryan Bragg in Perkins&Will's Vancouver studio, we were able to push narratives around a community of health-science researchers working out of a building committed to health in the broadest sense—physical, emotional, and social. For this second interview we carefully curated our Dupont Street studio as a gallery we strolled through, pausing at a series of exhibits that summarized key elements of our approach. One exhibit drew the client into Perkins&Will's Precautionary List—a research project that identified commonly used building materials that are harmful to human health. A second exhibit drew upon a collection of public spaces we had designed for a variety for academic clients and which all demonstrated techniques for bringing people together to form an active and engaged culture. Another display demonstrated the innovative approaches to building skin and materiality, which had allowed our designs for the University for Waterloo's engineering faculty to communicate an aspirational institutional message. Walking and talking, we stopped at a series of casually pinned-up sections and information graphics that told the tale of the Vancouver studio's Centre for Interactive Research on Sustainability at the University of British Columbia—a net-positive building that boldly communicates its sustainable strategies. Drawing together the threads of sustainability, occupant wellbeing, community, and public space, we drew the selection committee into our way of thinking—a balance of emotive, story-based techniques and technical rigor backed by hard research.

This was new territory for me, as I was able to harness the power of collaboration on a different scale and draw upon an incredible depth of experience and knowledge to support and amplify my own inclinations—all within the incredibly diverse framework supported by one firm. While the potential was in many ways untested, it proved convincing enough for TMU to take the plunge with us. At this early stage, before the commission was even ours, the project began to take on a persona that would gradually come into sharper focus. Our design process, with its blend of the emotional and the scientific, inevitably led us to create an architectural protagonist—the leading actor in a drama of its own making.

A project of this scale will necessarily be shaped by the voices of numerous individuals and by requirements that are so bureaucratized that they seem to be forces of nature or fate—anonymous and inevitable. If you can gather the former together in a shared purpose, it will help you weather the latter. Our first real challenge on the job was to tease out a vision that everyone involved with the project could share. I recall my first meeting with the building's intended users. It was a brilliant fall day, and the TMU campus was buzzing with the palpable energy that characterizes the advent of a new semester. Making my way through ebullient throngs of students, I approached the south end of Kerr Hall, a dour, four-storey quad complex with a symmetrical plan, dating from the 1960s, that was TMU's first academic building. Notorious for its dim maze of locker-lined corridors, the building was home to three of the four departments of the faculty of health sciences that were destined to move into the Church Street Development. The plan was to meet with the heads of nursing, nutrition, occupational and public health, and midwifery in their existing spaces to understand their current challenges and needs. It was also an ice breaker, our first personal connection to the we people were designing for. As I approached the entrance and a cluster of professorial types gathered there, I was struck by a familiar silhouette with an unruly shock of white hair. Abandoning all of the professional decorum that one usually brings to a meeting of "first impressions," I called out:

"Mary Sharpe! It's Andrew Frontini, you delivered my daughter Giuliana and my son Felix! I'm going to be your architect!"

Mary, the leading advocate for bringing midwifery under the umbrella of socialized medicine in our province, a mother of eight, and a working midwife who has tended to the birth of literally thousands of babies, somehow remembered me. I ran up the steps and we embraced as old friends. Mary chided me:

"You better design us a great space, or I'll take the children back!"

Having established that I was a human being first and architect second, I gathered my composure and introduced myself to the other department heads, and we began our tour. As we walked, listened, and observed, I couldn't help but reflect on the birth experiences of all three of my children, each of which involved a complex and sometimes strained interaction between nurses and midwives. As professionals, they were trained differently and brought different priorities to the clinical setting. Could living and learning under a shared roof shift those cultures, allow them to influence one another and perhaps converge around the best interests of the patient? As architects, could we interpret and support a new shared culture through our design? Touring Kerr Hall and then crossing the campus to see the bright, newly renovated space the midwifery department occupied, I began to see sharp differences in the levels of enthusiasm that the respective groups held for the imminent colocation. The nursing department was working in dingy, cramped, and antiquated spaces that threatened their future as an accredited professional school. The school of occupational and public health was struggling to conduct a wide range of physically based experiments in spaces that, ironically, were in contravention of the university's occupational health standards. Similarly, the school of nutrition was hampered in its clinical endeavors by inadequate ventilation and accessibility. The midwives were simply quite happy where they were.

University leadership and the dean of the faculty were optimistic about the potential synergies leading to a holistic understanding of health and wellbeing and also about the efficiencies to be found around shared resources and amenities. However, in the wake of our initial tour and meeting, it became clear that apart from nursing, the member departments were not enthusiastic about the colocation, siting nursing's scale and a perceived disproportion of influence over the design. Before design could begin in earnest, our team was charged with engaging all of the stakeholders in building a shared vision around what the facility could be, the culture it could support, and the benefits that would flow to all of its occupants.

At our first structured visioning session, we intentionally grouped members from the different departments along with students into working teams and asked them to brainstorm on the building's character, identity, and legacy. President Sheldon Levy bolstered our efforts by encouraging the participants to think of the building not only as their new home, but a home for future generations, pointing to the potential of integrated health education at TMU. In hindsight, this initial session was immensely productive. The playful nature of the exercises we provided for the participants effectively broke down some of the barriers between the four schools and proved influential in determining the architecture's final character. One group, which was obviously dominated by the irascible Mary Sharp, christened the new building " the Cauldron," suggesting the potential for an alchemical transformation. When asked to vote on images that should inspire the character of the building's public realm, all 65 participants gravitated to an image of coloured umbrellas hanging over a sun-dappled laneway. While focusing the outcome of these engagements would take time, our initial foray had been successful in suggesting that perhaps the four schools could come together around an architecture that promised transformation and a sense of playful delight.

Over the next six months, we engaged with hundreds of students, faculty, researchers, and community members, capturing a multitude of voices in conversations around health, accessibility, creativity, culture, and thought leadership. Summarizing these conversations was a complex, iterative process involving every level of faculty and campus leadership. TMU's vice president of administration and finance, Julia Hanigsberg, impressed upon us the need for clarity and brevity, requesting a vision statement that could fit on a coaster. In the end, we settled for a large cookie, with the statement printed on it in blue icing:

"Creating Connections for a Healthy City."

My colleague Jon Loewen, whose manifold contributions to the project cannot be overstated, created a series of excellent communication graphics that amplified each of the key words in the statement to convey the project's commitment to a healthy and connected urban environment. From this commitment stemmed a series of detailed guiding principles on the themes of inclusivity, sustainability, flexibility, and the public realm. Together with a detailed validation of the functional program, these statements constituted a project charter—a valuable map for navigating the seven-year journey ahead of us.

While we dove deeply into the aspirations and needs of our end users, a set of

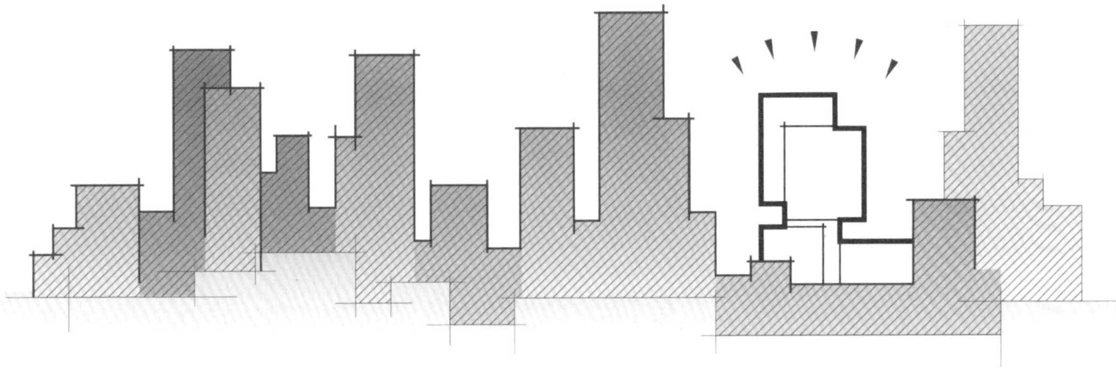

Cartooning the aspiration to build a bright spot in the city

Visioning sessions with TMU leadership, faculty, staff, and students

parallel obligations were being addressed in tandem. The building site was completely constrained, hemmed in on all sides by existing buildings and municipal infrastructure. Using a set of iterative physical and digital models, our team worked and reworked solutions attempting to balance the ideal arrangement of the building program on the site, the challenges of loading and parking access, the impact of the built form on the surrounding context, and the requirements of the city's Tall Building Design Guidelines, which would ultimately influence our ability to navigate a complex rezoning process. In the midst of this intense period, as we were coming to understand the nature of the challenge, we received a request from the office of the president. Sheldon Levy had very specific attitudes about how TMU's building should interface with the City. TMU's latest building, the Student Learning Centre, had just opened, and the president was not happy. The SLC, designed by Snøhetta, offered a bold reimagining of the academic library as a stacked series of "learning landscapes" on seven floors. With its chiseled form and graphically fritted skin, it created a striking architectural presence for TMU on Yonge Street. None of this mattered to Sheldon at the moment, as he was deeply disappointed with the way the building hit the ground. The SLC's complex section began its journey outside with a steeply terraced bleacher with interwoven ramps that brought the public to a main floor 5 metres above the street. Beneath and behind this bold gesture, a set of awkward residual spaces offered tiny retail units and glimpses down into a lower level off of Yonge Street. The design was, in the president's view, divorced from the city and not inclusive, posing a physical and psychological barrier to entry. At the outset of our project, Sheldon had stressed upon us the need to create architecture that was "different but not odd," provocative but not antisocial. To make sure that we did not repeat the mistake of the SLC, we were to arrange a tour of food-related retail spaces in the bases of tall buildings throughout the city. The goals were to arrive at a consensus on how a big building should interface with the city and to influence the new building's ground-floor café and exterior streetscape. In three separate cabs, over two hours, we struggled through Toronto's traffic-snarled streets to visit six different sites. In a particularly bad stretch of traffic between stops five and six (where a much-needed lunch break awaited us), Sheldon turned to me and said,

"You've shown me some great examples of what we don't want to do, but I already knew that. I'm hoping our last stop is something that is actually good."

Fortunately, Bar Buca, in the base of a 10-storey condo tower on Portland Street, did not disappoint. The building's setback from the street offered space for a treed boulevard and modest west-facing patio. The retail frontage featured broad expanses of glass, shaded by a lightly structured canopy. The interior of the restaurant, designed by Guido Costantino, was both refined and approachable, contrasting sophisticated metalwork, stone, and millwork against the raw found-condition of the base building. After a glass of wine and some excellent light plates, our group of six got to the bottom of what made this space work while others had fallen flat. Notwithstanding the beneficial influence of sustenance and a pause from the maddening congestion of Toronto's streets, there were some solid lessons here that would inform our thinking: the importance of the space in front of the building, protected, habitable, and human-scaled; the transparency of the façade and continuity of space between the interior and the exterior; and a purposeful and clever contrast between the scale and infrastructure of a big building and a more refined and materially engaging fit-up. All of these ingredients would plug into a public-realm strategy that was already underway, but which now had gained detailed nuance and a champion in the university's president.

During the project's early stages, our team had curated a series of public-realm workshops bringing together campus leaders and members of TMU's city-building institute, architecture science department, and planning school, as well as visitors such as noted Toronto urban designers Ken Greenberg and George Dark. The goal of these workshops was to develop priorities for the public realm in and around the building as well as to study a variety of built-form alternatives. With foam models, bits of string, tape, and icons for different urban animators such as food-and-beverage and green space, we mapped out how the new development would connect to the campus and the city. The Church Street site represented the campus's ragged south edge, where it interfaced with a part of the city where drug use, homelessness, and violent crime persisted against a wave of high-rise development. It was clear that creating safe, programmatically animated sites and public routes through and around the building would be critical to the future growth of the campus and the security of its students.

These findings began to set clear priorities for public space at grade. A through-block connection between Church Street and the heart of campus would engage the adjacent school of interior design to create an enclosed street, which would in turn connect with TMU's system of service laneways, adapting them to become safe pedestrian routes. A new widened boulevard, and activating programs such as space for dining and events, would support the public realm on Church Street. For our team, this investment could not stop at the ground floor but needed to continue vertically up the entire height of the building, connecting the various inhabitants to each other and the city.

A simple diagram of a city with its streets, parks, gardens, and other public spaces turned on end communicated the ambition of a distributed and connected system of public space working at a variety of scales. A second diagram, entitled "Public Space Rules," established the massing approach that would support this continuous public realm over both the academic and residential portions of the building. This is the kind of diagram that marks a watershed moment, where a wide range of consultations, investigations, and findings coalesce formally and conceptually: This is what it will look like and, more importantly, this is what it will do.

These ideas came at a critical time for our team, as we began to divide the labour more explicitly between our Toronto and Vancouver studios and bulk up in size. As the design leader of a large and now distributed team, I needed a tool that would do the talking for me, a kind of touchstone that we had all agreed upon that would communicate outwardly and guide us inwardly. In its childlike simplicity, colour, and playfulness, the diagram captured our earliest engagement with the client and the promise of delight and discovery offered by the laneway full of coloured umbrellas.

The diagram also concretized the notion of the building as a protagonist—a player with specific attributes that allowed it to carry and communicate stories. At the end of the detailed design phase we mounted an exhibit at TMU's Cocker Gallery entitled "Public Space Rules." For the occasion we created a 100-metre-long graphic banner that presented the Church Street Character as a comic-book hero, navigating a series of perilous trials and tribulations in the long journey from idea to reality. The banner wrapped the walls of the gallery, while the centre of the space featured several exhibits documenting the physical artifacts of our process: models, material samples, and a computer workstation loaded with the building's parametric model. In summarizing the interpretive scheme of the exhibition, I can conveniently convey to you, the reader, the key chapters of the project's evolutions:

- A vision that gathered many voices and ambitions into a simple statement dense with meaning.
- A massing that arranged a complex program around a continuous public realm connecting the building's inhabitants to each other, the campus, and the city.
- A holistic and didactic approach to sustainability that combines the health and wellbeing of the occupants with that of the planet.
- A co-development strategy that attempts to allocate the costs of base building structure, systems, services, and amenities between three investing partners.
- A structural system that "invisibly" traces a complex loading pathway from a residential point tower down through long-span classrooms to a parking structure below grade.
- A two-year public consultation and approvals process that navigated input from angry neighbours and ward councilors, high-rise design guidelines, hospital helicopter flight paths, two conflicting zoning bylaws, and the campus master plan.
- A scope, budget, and schedule that were sliced and diced every which way but never quite lined up.

The "Public Space Rules" exhibit was a great success, drawing hundreds of visitors from the TMU community and beyond to a reception that was really a celebration of the work that a large team of client representatives, university leaders, designers, and consultants had accomplished to date. It gave everyone a chance to reflect on what we had collectively achieved, just as the project was breaking ground—on time, on budget, and on vision. The exhibit was intended (like this book) to be entertaining and didactic, both for the architecture students who would walk past on a daily basis, but also for the larger institution, which would, in our minds, benefit from being reminded of the enormity of the undertaking—especially if the CSD was to establish the prototype for the vertical campus. The irony in celebrating the passing of so many complex hurdles was that in many ways, the worst was yet to come.

At the time of the exhibit, Eastern Construction had recently come aboard as the construction manager for the complex build ahead. Our negotiations with the city had progressed to the point that we had achieved a notice of conditional zoning approval, and partial permits were released for the shoring and excavation of the building. The contractor had started digging while we and our consultants continued drawing the final details. This overlapping of construction activities and design poses challenges but is something that our team and the builder were well versed in, and with good communications between us, we were generally confident that the project was on track.

One fact of life that was made plain during the CSD's long gestation was the nature of decision making "on campus." A university is not a democracy. Once a project's direction has been set, it can never be changed by a grassroots movement of intended users (that is, from below), but any and all manner of changes can be initiated from above, without the least regard for cost or schedule. As architects we have been charged with delivering a fixed scope for a fixed cost within a fixed timeline. We are constantly reminded that any deviation from these fixed parameters will come at a cost to our reputation and future prospects with the institution. Not surprisingly, we are concerned about changing priorities during the course of the project's execution for a host of reasons, not the least of which is any perceived threat to the underlying vision of the project, which we have all worked so hard to protect for so long.

In November of 2015, Sheldon Levy stepped down as president to be replaced by Mohamed Lachemi, a thoughtful and compassionate leader who was happy to let our project proceed on the tracks laid by his predecessor. Within two months, the entire cast of the TMU facilities and real estate team assigned to the Daphne Cockwell Health Sciences Complex (as the project was now called) had moved on, and we were effectively without a project champion on the client side. The institutional memory for the project, while documented exhaustively in the Project Charter and Design Reports for each stage, lay with us. Binders on a shelf are just that—mute objects, unless someone brings them down, dusts them off, reads them, and interprets that reading for the application at hand. And that is what we did, time and time again as the project responded to a seemingly endless storm of challenges from within and without.

It is hard to appreciate the value that your client-side champions bring, and the degree to which they protect the project from the institution's own pathological impulses, until they are no longer there. Like any large object, the Daphne Cockwell Health Sciences Complex had a gravitational pull that attracted people and ideas to it like so much space junk falling to earth. All we could do was roll with the punches and filter the constant request for new programs, departments, and "novel ideas" through our professional gaze and the sieve that the project charter provided. Some notions were successfully deflected, such as an overwrought café design brought forward by a prospective developer for the food and beverage offering. The café, with its closely spaced archways of artificial plants, flew in the face of both the public-realm principles, which called for visual connectivity between the interior and the street, as well as the university's commitment to access and inclusion. When a donor came forward with a desire to integrate urban agriculture into the rooftop amenity space, the negotiation took a different tack. The proposed change would impact the schedule and ultimately cost more than the donor was offering, but it was aligned with the project vision, with its focus on health and connectivity. The decision, filtered in this way, lay with the client, who elected to proceed. All the while the concrete was pouring, the welders were welding, and the project was making its slow climb up the Toronto skyline.

I will be eternally grateful to my colleagues D'Arcy Arthurs and Gayle Meeks as well as Eastern's Steve Gray and TMU's Paul Chung, who weathered many storms in the off-site trailer, through what proved to be a long and challenging build. With the change in guard at the university, our teams were often forced to have difficult conversations with people we had just met, at times when the project was at its most demanding and stressful. When the project opened in the fall of 2019, it was a year behind schedule, but it was the building we had all imagined for so long. The investment we had collectively made in this architectural "persona" had paid off. By crystallizing the project's values and ambitions in such a precise way, we had created a resiliency that today shines through as a bright spot in the city.

Client	Toronto Metropolitan University
Location	Toronto, Ontario
Size	26,000 gross square metres
Date	2013-2019

A bird's eye view of the project amid central Toronto

The tower complex viewed from the heart of campus

Looking south down Church Street

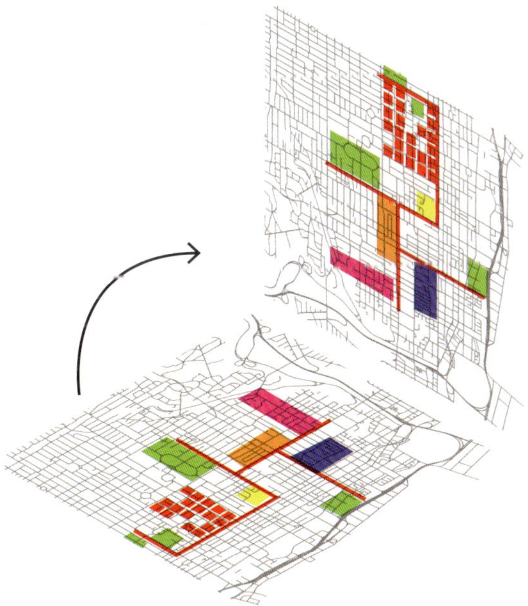

The city on its side

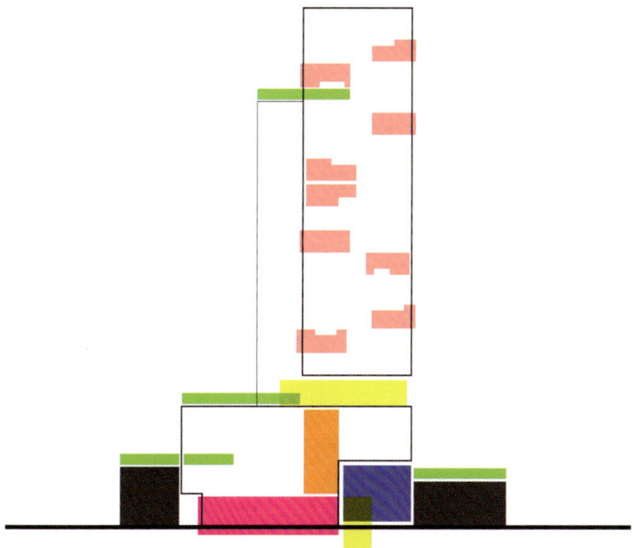

An urban paradigm for a vertical campus

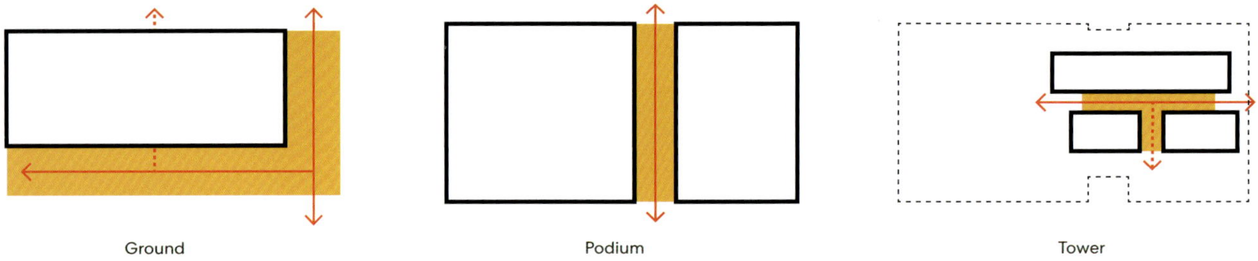

Public space distributed vertically

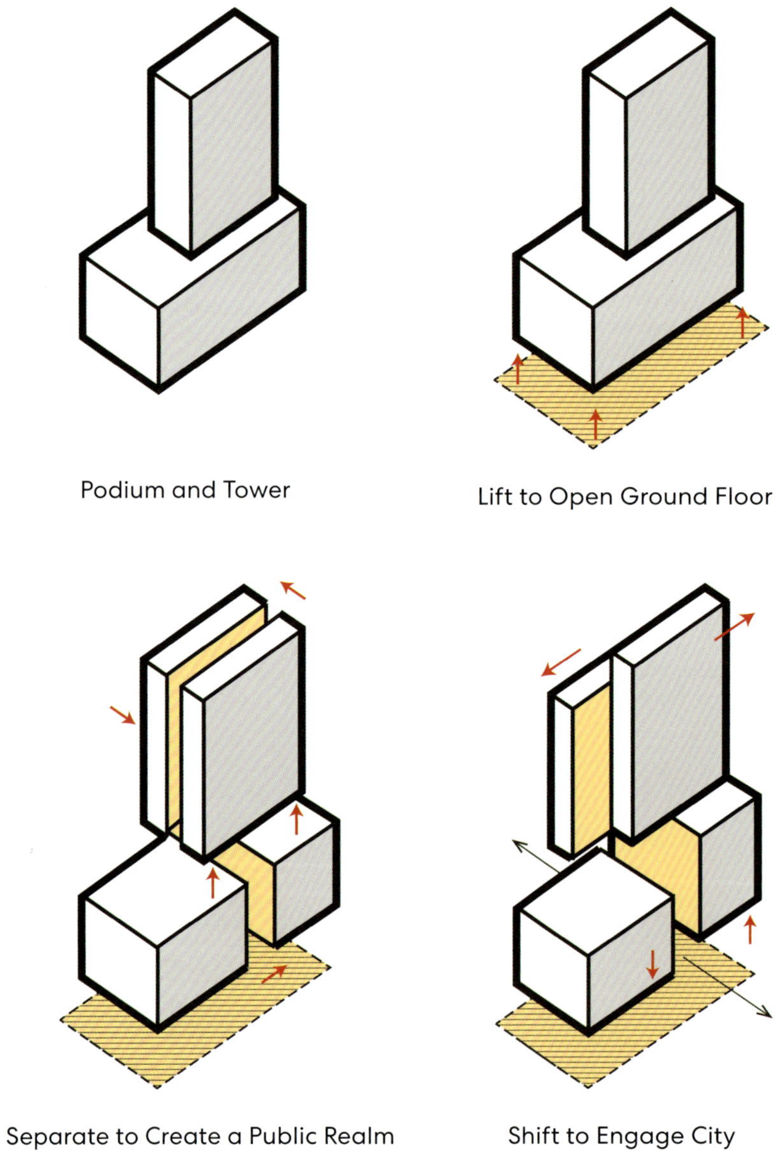

The interplay of built form and the public realm

Looking west from an adjacent tower

Detail of the east façade

The rooftop farm on Level 08

Integrating urban farming into the public realm

TESTING TESTING...

BUT HOW WOULD THESE PRINCIPLES TRANSLATE INTO ARCHITECTURAL FORM AND WHICH FORM WOULD SUPPORT THE PROGRAM?

PROGRESS SKETCHES

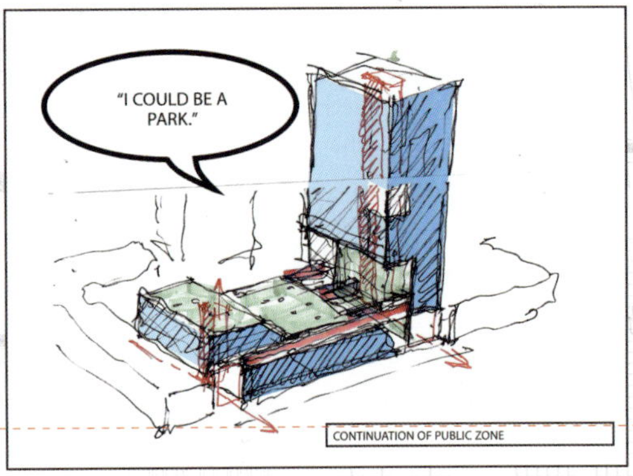

CONTINUATION OF PUBLIC ZONE

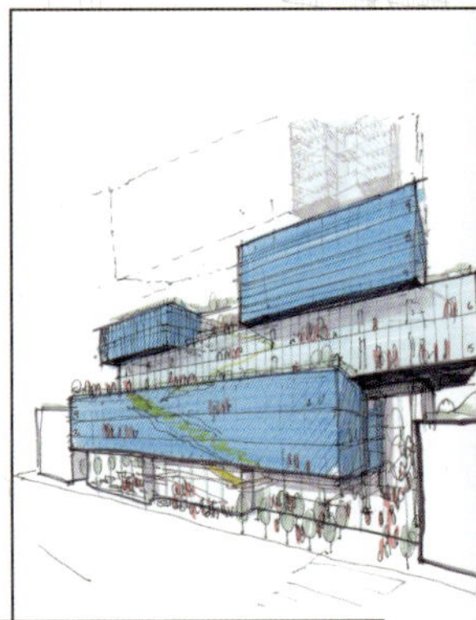

WHERE THE PUBLIC SPACE IS THE MEAT.

PRELIMINARY STACKING

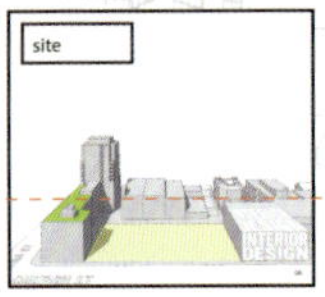

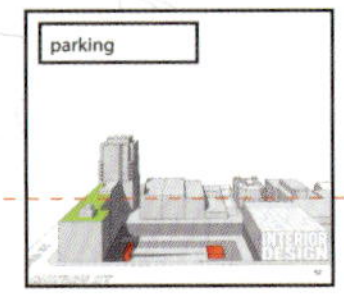

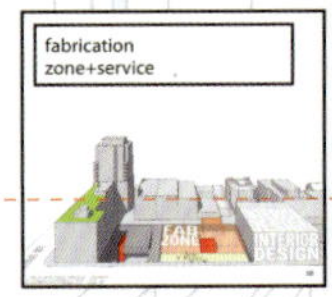

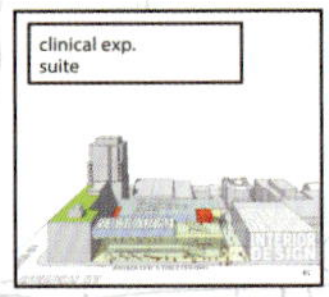

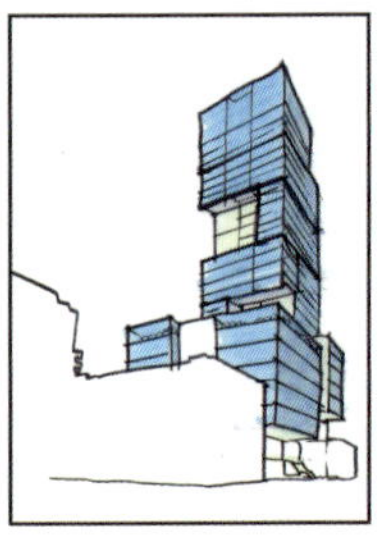

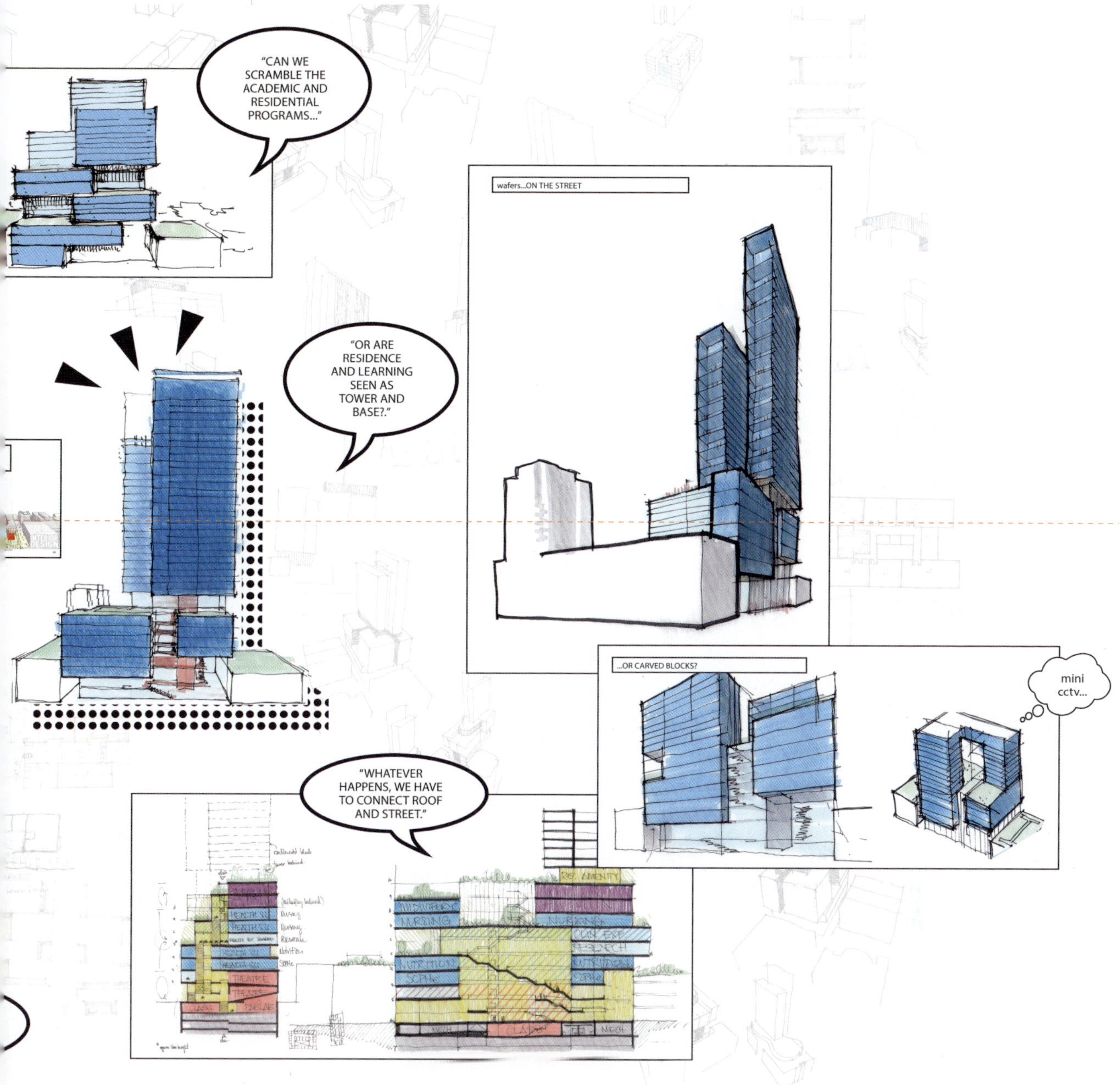

Excerpt from the exhibition "Public Space Rules," held at TMU's Paul H. Cocker Gallery in the fall of 2015

Looking across the galleria to TMU's school of interior design

The street-facing lobby on Level 01

A lecture hall on Level 02

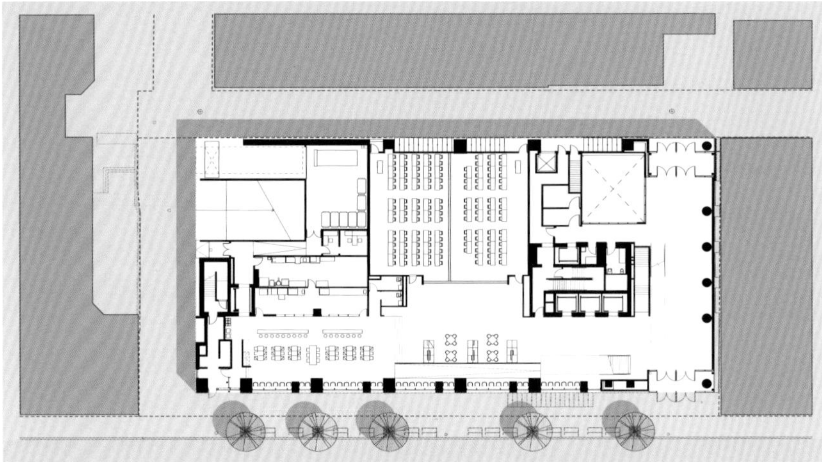

Level 01 Plan

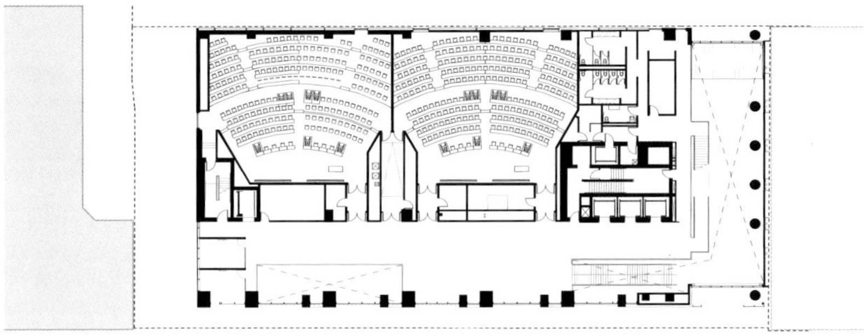

Level 02 Plan

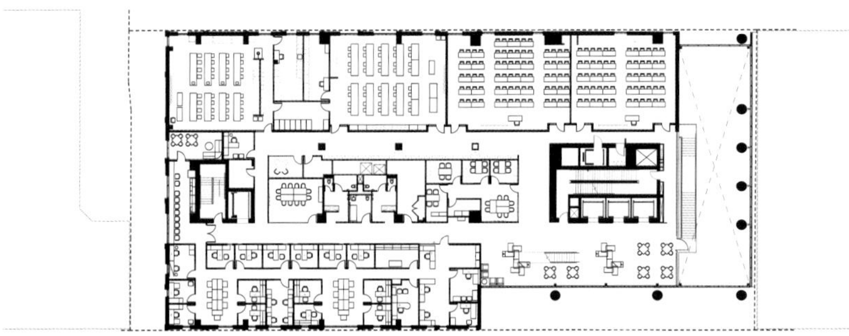

Level 03 Plan

Level 04 Plan

Level 05 Plan

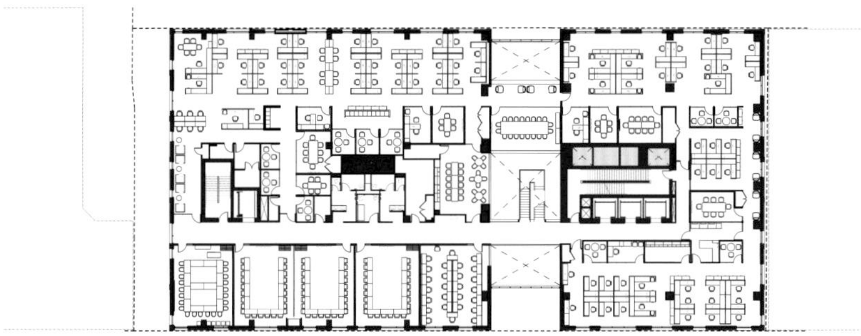

Level 07 Plan

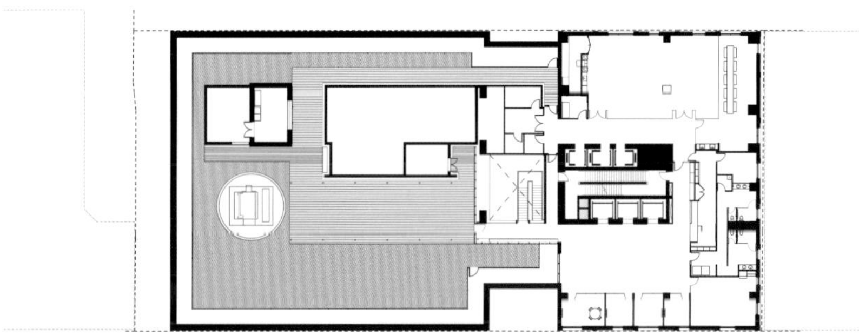

Level 08 Plan

Levels 10-28 Plan

View from the southeast

Section perspectives describing program and the public realm

The atrium, looking east

Looking towards Church Street in the galleria

Looking up in the atrium from Level 03

Sectional model demonstrating the podium's vertical public realm

Level 05 lounge

Level 03 study lounge

Nutritional-science teaching lab

Les Yeux

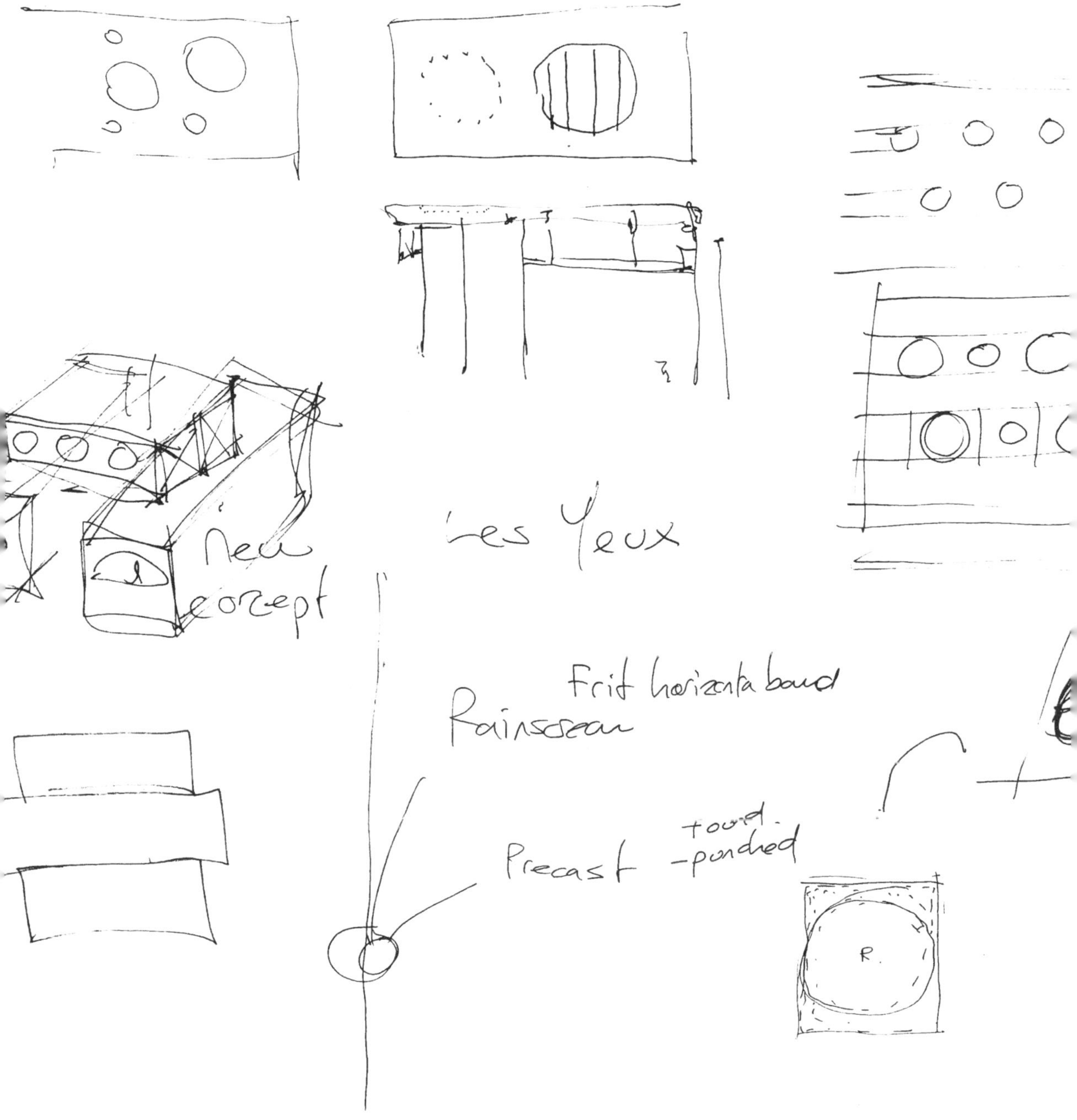

STEM Complex, University of Ottawa

Ottawa, Ontario 2016-2019

In the summer of my 13th year, my family took a four-day trip to Ottawa, our nation's capital city. I have scant recollection of the obligatory tours of our fine governmental institutions—the Parliament, the Senate, the National Library—but other aspects of the trip seem to have had a formative influence. My father always made an excellent guide, with his embellished and in some cases fabricated histories of the sites that unfolded before us. If he was interested in it, he made it memorable. As a metallurgical engineer, for instance, he had a deep appreciation for the expressive patination of the copper façade elements of Arthur Erickson's then newly completed Bank of Canada. Millions of litres of horse urine had apparently been collected and sprayed on the façade of the completed building. While factually incorrect, the underlying chemistry of his description was sound. I would learn much more about this patination technique and the Bank of Canada in the decades ahead (page 166). At the National Gallery my father, who was himself an aspiring amateur artist, drew us to the Pop and Op art floors of the gallery's interim home at the Lorne Building. Marcel Barbeau, Victor Vasarely, and Roy Lichtenstein presented to me forms of art I hadn't imagined possible, much less relevant, until that point in my young life. Leaving the museum, I recall strolling along the Rideau Canal and being struck by a set of huge eyes staring out from the blank façade of a building across the water. They were rendered in a black-and-white halftone—the dot-matrix technique that I had just been introduced to in the National Gallery. My father was at the ready with what, at the time, was a convincing narrative: The building was the seat of Canada's secret service, and the eyes were a reminder that we are all under surveillance, all the time. To this collection of holiday memories I will add a stroll along Ottawa's then newly completed and quite festive pedestrian mall, Sparks Street. From a set of blaring speakers outside a record store, I heard Dire Straits' "Sultans of Swing" for the first time—a song that would change the course of my fledgling guitar practice and set a standard for tonality dexterity and melody that I still aspire to as a player but will never attain. I did, however, get the opportunity to revisit some of the trip's more memorable sights as a mature architect—to be both inspired and challenged.

In 2016, the federal and provincial government announced a massive stimulus campaign known as the Strategic Infrastructure Fund, designed to bolster the nation's knowledge economy by targeting shovel-ready building projects at colleges and universities. The University of Ottawa was successful in obtaining funding for a new 300,000-square-foot STEM complex that would address a series of pent-up requirements involving deferred maintenance, outdated facilities, disjointed accommodations for research, and a deficit in the student-focused public realm. In addition to these drivers, the university was thinking a bit like a developer—looking for ways to free up valuable and underutilized land on a campus that sits in the middle of a fabric. "Shovel-ready" is a very open term in these contexts, and by the time our firm had gone through the competitive process to be awarded the contract, the schedule requirements imposed by the federal government left a mere 24 months to program, design, and build a research building of considerable scale and enormous complexity on a challenging site. The region's largest contractor, PCL, was brought on board as construction manager and from the outset was given considerable agency to meet the outrageous schedule requirements at seemingly any cost. Starting in the spring of 2016, our team stepped into a crucible where design, programming, construction, and approvals overlapped and often reversed their conventional orders. The jobsite trailer, where many people spent two years of their lives, had an almost hallucinatory atmosphere of stress and concentration. I won't delve into all of the challenges and opportunities this sort of intensity can create, as I touch on that in another chapter (page 126). I will, however, focus on a unique aspect of this project that became conceptually foundational, setting a project direction that I don't think the university would have dared to follow if they had had time to think about it.

On our first tour of the site, with the contractor and the university's campus architect Claudio Brun del Re, we evaluated the possible locations for the main building and quickly realized that a structure on the most likely site, MacDonald Hall, was going to throw two obstacles at our fast-moving train. It would have to be demolished using the painstakingly precise and time-intensive process of material separation required for both the new building's targeted LEED Gold standing and the safe handling of the asbestos-laden structure. The second challenge was the presence of an artwork painted directly on the stone blocks of the building's west façade, overlooking the Rideau Canal: *Les Yeux* (*The Eyes*), a large-scale halftone representation of a pair of human eyes by the deceased Canadian printmaker James Boyd. Boyd had executed the work in 1972, while serving as an instructor in the university's fine-art faculty. The administration's initial impulse was to catalogue and dismantle the work and to then deal with the issue of its artistic merit and patrimony after the dust had settled. To me this would have been the worst possible outcome. The work had made an indelible impression on Ottawa's cultural landscape and had, I argued, a new potential relevance.

Claudio was a cautious individual and the contractor was already beating the drum faster and faster—schedule, schedule, schedule. The shared anxiety around the project timeline proved to be an ally in reconsidering Boyd's work. As Macdonald Hall occupied nearly half of the available site, PCL suggested that we build in phases, with early foundations and structure beginning on the north while the painstaking disassembly of MacDonald Hall progressed to the south. This approach inspired a massing with two discreet blocks to be built sequentially. A buffer zone was necessary to separate the demolition and construction activities, and we conceived it as an atrium between the two blocks, setting up a public-space system that would integrate multiple levels and activities in a complex journey through the world of STEM. With the contractor enthusiastically endorsing this time-saving approach, the presence of two squarely proportioned block ends facing the canal was assured. I then proposed that the two blocks could act as canvases for the recreation of *Les Yeux*. To demonstrate that this was an appropriate approach we drew upon an interview conducted with André Lalonde, the former dean of science who had sponsored the complete restoration of *Les Yeux* only three years earlier. Lalonde is quoted as saying,

"I interpreted [the eyes] as symbolizing scientific curiosity. We can interpret them in our own personal way."

This existing relationship between the artwork and the faculty of science inspired the design team to develop a conceptual proposition that acknowledged the single point in space, which is the building block of Boyd's artwork, as the universal starting point for all art, mathematics, and science. The human gaze upon a point or set of points is the basis of our perceived reality. Claudio, himself an artist, was intellectually engaged by this proposition and saw it as a way out of his growing anxiety regarding the fate of the artwork, which was starting to be questioned in the press and on social media. With no time to waste, Claudio engaged the university's legal department and James Boyd's estate to seek consent for the reproduction of *Les Yeux* using digital technology and the more permanent medium of ceramic ink bonded on glass (commonly known as "frit").

After a brief discussion and presentation of the design approach, Steven Boyd, the artist's son and an artist in his own right, granted permission for the one-time use of the image as an integrated artwork. Ottawa is a political town, and an abundance of caution surrounds all decisions and actions. Anxious not to offend the capital's artistic community by having an architect as the sole interpreter of an existing artwork, Claudio and the university issued a call for proposals for a Canadian artist to supervise the recreation. Established Calgarian artist Derek Besant was eventually selected, validating the process from the university's perspective and providing me with a valuable sounding board and creative ally. Derek's practice is primarily concerned with the human gaze in the space of the city. His works bring ephemeral images of the human form rendered at a massive scale to engage with the infrastructure of highway overpasses, transit systems, and office towers. The idea of the lens that conditions perception is a constant in his work and fueled many energizing conversations on the degree to which we would reinterpret or recreate Boyd's work.

My colleague and primary design collaborator on this project, Dan McTavish, provided the following workflow that summarizes how the existing artwork was documented before its demolition and then transformed into a new digital artwork at twice the original scale.

1. PCL surveyed the entire artwork and each piece of painted stone with a drone, in order to create a composite image of the existing artwork in situ.
2. An image of each "eye" (each half of the artwork) was analyzed by a Grasshopper script within the modelling program Rhino. The script did the following:
    a. Allowed us to input the overall boundary of the new façade at 1:1.
    b. Created two subdivisions of the overall boundary to establish a series of offset points on a staggered grid.

    i The first grid established the points as a series of white dots to reproduce the artwork.
    ii The second grid established offset points for a fine black frit that was uniform across the entire façade.
  c There were parameters to control the size of the grids and the radii of the two different dots.
  d A graphic input (an image mapper) allowed for the analysis of dark and light areas in a raster image to be mapped onto the points of the subdivided boundary. Areas of white were assigned a white dot, while areas of black were left empty.
  e Window panelization from glazing shop drawings was overlaid and the vector reproduction was "baked."
  f Individual panels were exported to Illustrator, where the graphics were cleaned up. Panels were organized into perimeter panels and interior panels. In total, 267 unique panels were created, with each receiving a unique identifier based on a number/letter grid.
3 Individual panels were reproduced on glass using digitally printed ceramic frit.

It is noteworthy that through this translation only four panels were printed incorrectly. In the end, the process generated a faithful reproduction of Boyd's original work. But what is perhaps most interesting is not the degree to which we influenced *Les Yeux*, but the degree to which it influenced us. The eyes and the dot-matrix technique became a team obsession. Dan McTavish says he "saw dots everywhere," and I rewarded him for his obsession with the gift of a *Les Yeux* halftone-rendered onesie for his infant son.

Due to the aggressiveness of the schedule and the pending demolition of the artwork, the detailed analysis and documentation described above was happening while the vast majority of the building's architectural surfaces remained unmapped. The façades were blank canvases waiting for an idea. The creation of a file that rendered the entire west façade as a dot-matrix grid was an integral step in recreating *Les Yeux*, and it also inspired the team to imagine the possibilities of a façade language for the rest of the building.

We imagined that the dot matrix would have the ability to loosen in density and create openings or apertures in the building's skin, in much the same way that Boyd's original halftone graphic expanded and contracted to create areas of light and shadow. The apertures became a series of lenses, in our conception, evoking the gaze of scientific research, with varying radii and densities at different locations on the façade. Perhaps more discerning than the fixed gaze of *Les Yeux*, these apertures presented edited views of the surrounding context and controlled the degree to which light and solar heat gain entered the building. We ran several factors—desirability of views, potential for solar heat gain, and required privacy—through a Grasshopper script and assigned one of four aperture typologies to each window location. The result is a façade whose modulated abstraction suggests a responsive membrane, with circular windows contracting and expanding in response to

James Boyd's *Les Yeux* (*The Eyes*), on the canal-side façade of the now-demolished MacDonald Hall

On-site mock-ups of the "apertures," insulated-glass units with graduated ceramic frit

In the studio, full-scale mock-ups on acetate of the fritted glass their varied surroundings. At times, this level of abstraction appears in contrast to Boyd's representational imagery, and at other times the play of light dissolves the explicit imagery of *Les Yeux* and a continuous reading of taut glass and metal panels dominates our perception. Within the building, the various treatments of the fritted windows animate the laboratories' perimeter corridors with a varied play of light that tracks the sun's slow arc.

In the end, the STEM Complex is a building about seeing. The stacking of the program and the public realm's journey through seven storeys reveal a layering of space and use that challenges viewers to speculate on the vast potential of interdisciplinary research. The central atrium is a kind of panopticon, superimposing one experience upon another as we move through the complex. In the skylights, the rubber flooring, and the office privacy film, the recurring motif of the circular lens reminds us of the primacy of vision—and that we are all made of millions of points in space.

The original artifact of *Les Yeux* is now dismantled, numerically catalogued, and stacked in an archival-storage facility on campus, but its image and conception have been transformed and magnified in reproduction to engage at a truly urban scale. A long-standing urban myth surrounding the original artwork is that Boyd modelled the fixed gaze of *Les Yeux* after a photograph of one of Prime Minister Pierre Trudeau's mistresses. The notion that the work's fixed gaze is not merely the byproduct of a static medium, but is perhaps the representation of a lover searching for the soul of another, adds a further dimension to the recreated work. The obsessive passion that dominates the most extreme of human experiences and achievements is captured as the common ground of love and science. Physics, mathematics, and chemistry become universally relatable as by-products of the restless human spirit—communicated through *Les Yeux*.

Client	University of Ottawa
Location	Ottawa, Ontario
Size	26,480 gross square metres
Date	2016-2019

Detail of the frit glass on the south corner

The STEM Complex and *Les Yeux* seen from across Rideau Canal

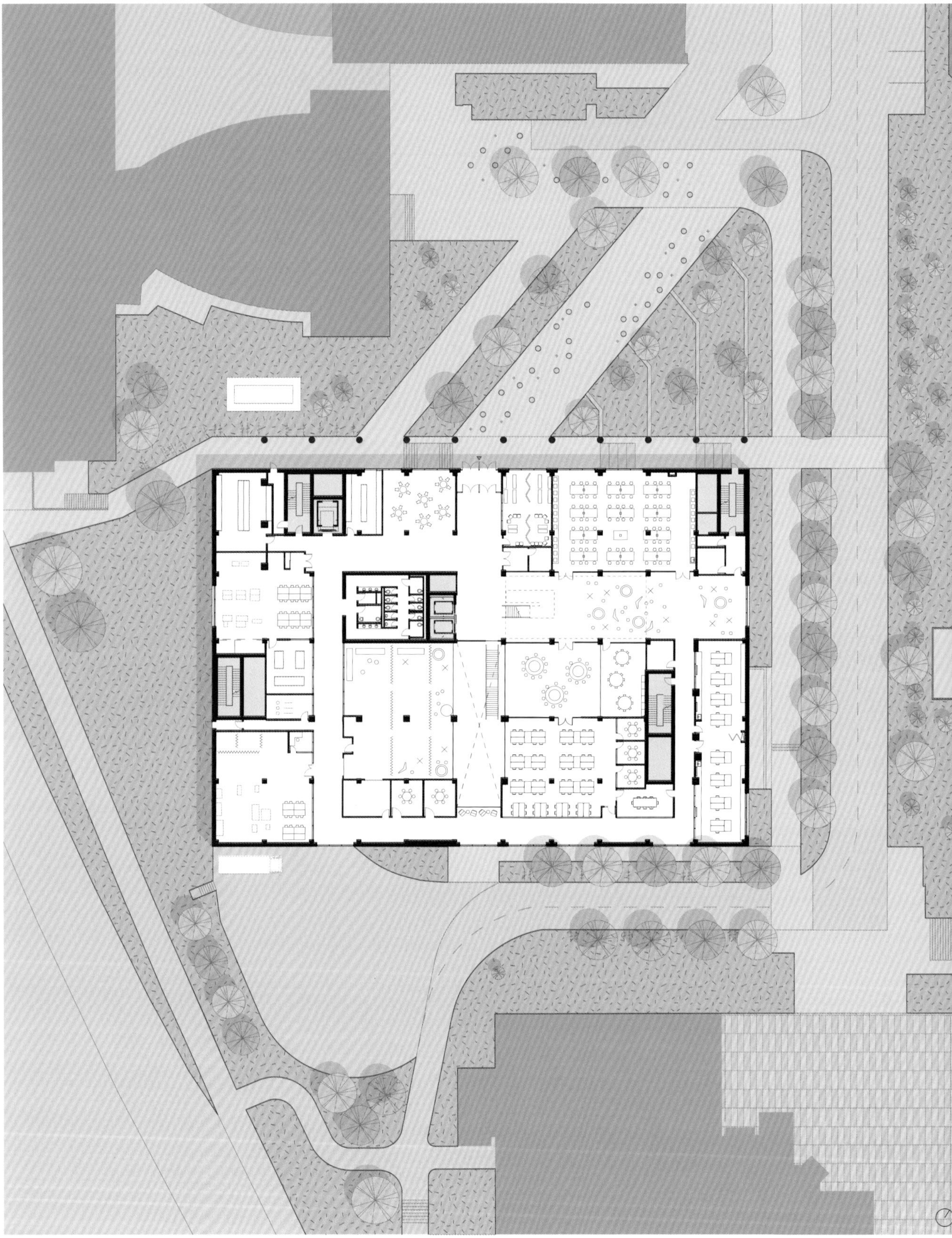

Site and Level 01 Plan

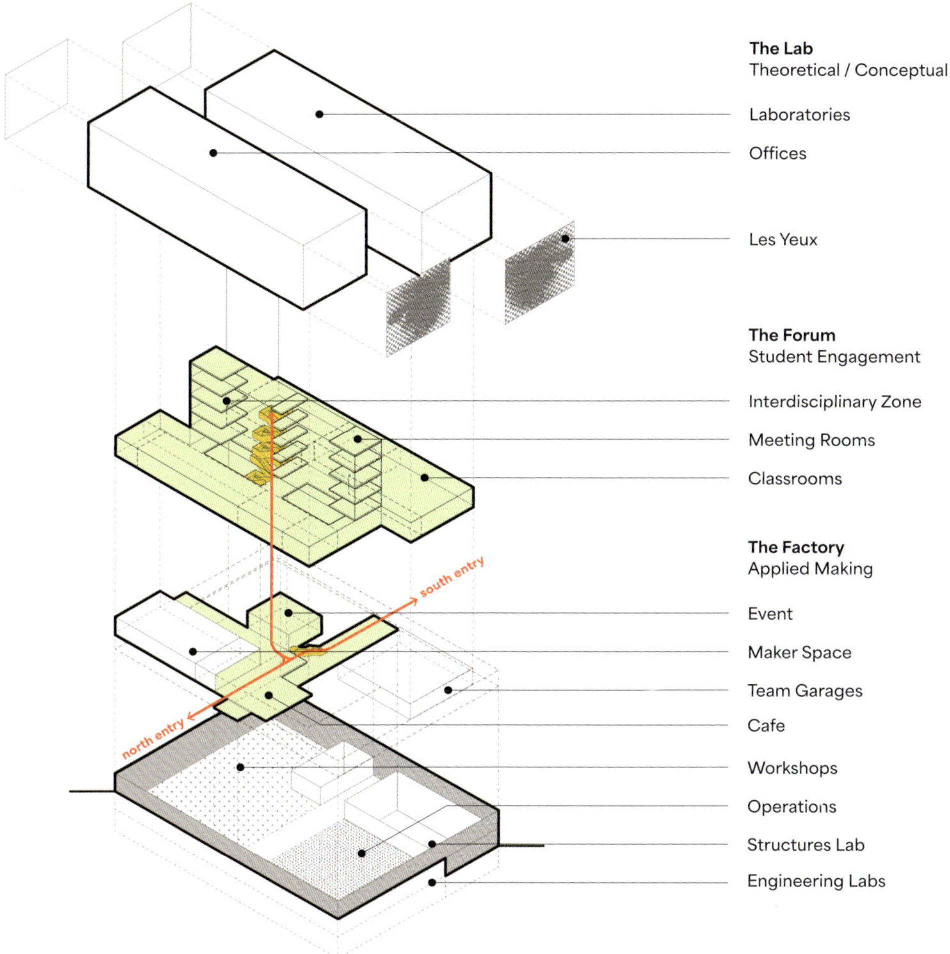

Diagram of the constituent elements

Early sketch exploration of the section

Complexe
STEM
uOttawa

Skaters on the Rideau Canal

Les Yeux viewed from an apartment in central Ottawa

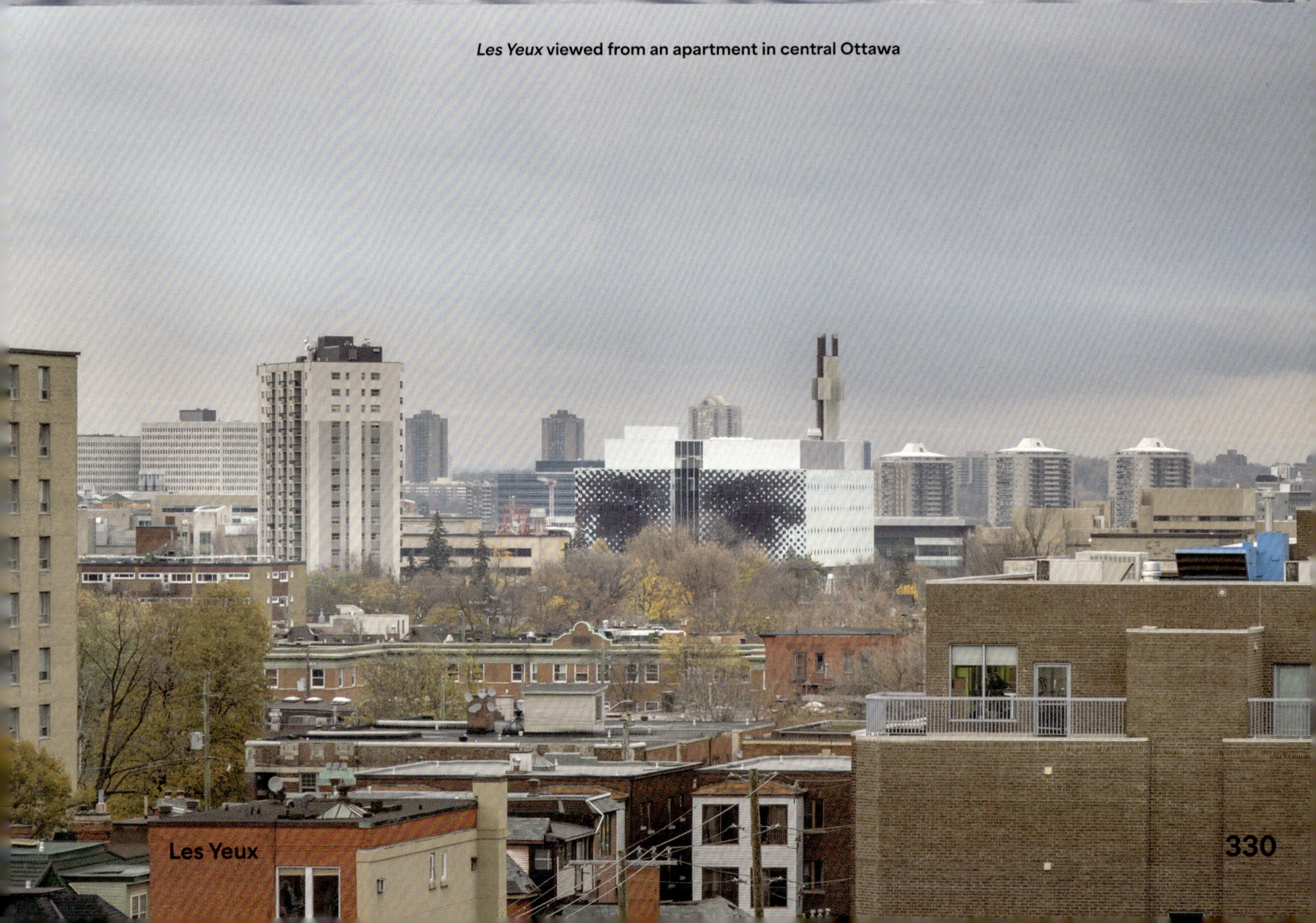

Aerial view of the building and its context

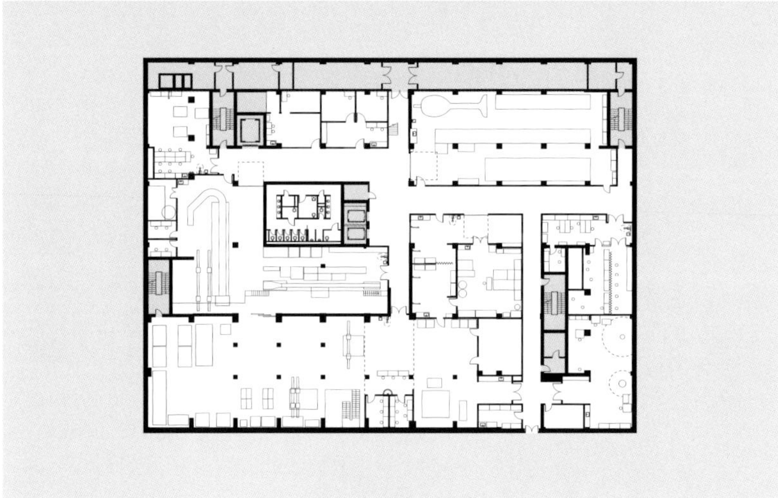

Level -01 Plan

Level 01 Plan

Level 02 Plan

Level 03 Plan

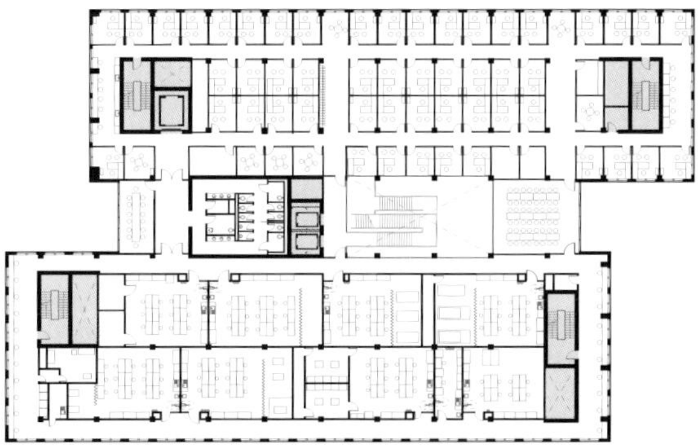

Level 04 Plan

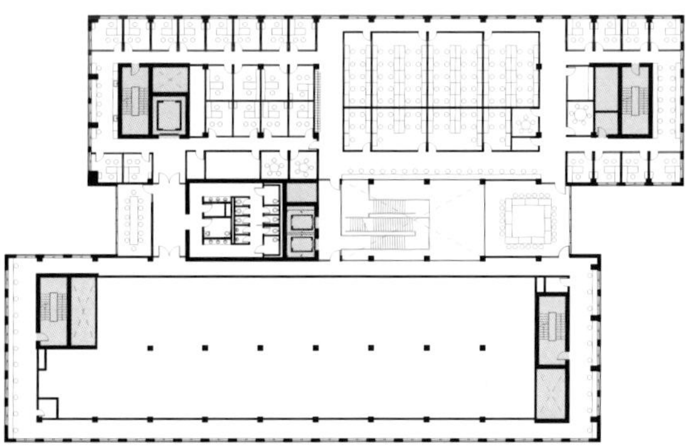

Level 06 Plan

Southeast corner façade detail

Perimeter corridor and study lounge

Concept for an interdisciplinary lounge, with the atrium beyond

Level 04 research labs overlooking the atrium

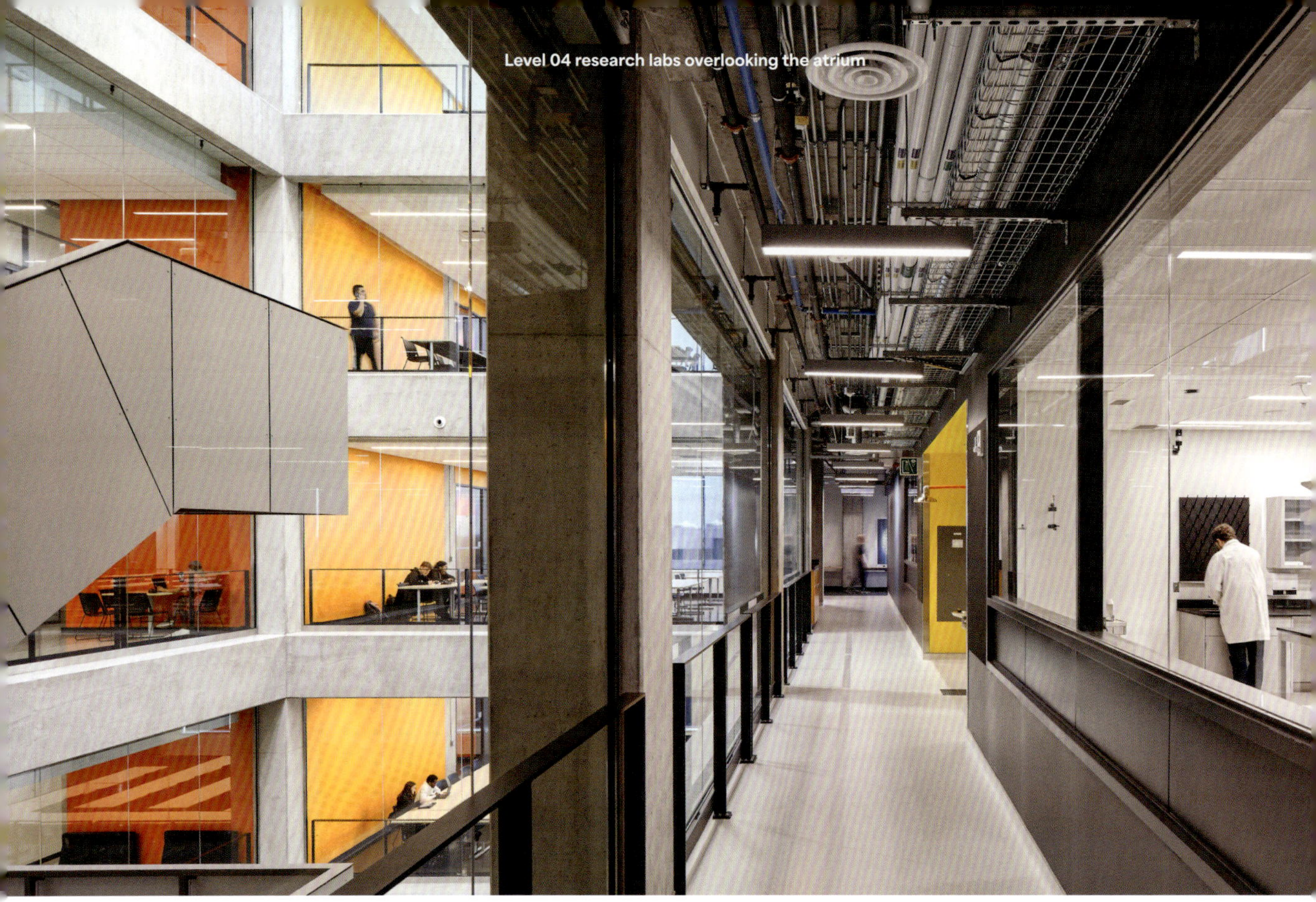

Sketch concept for the atrium

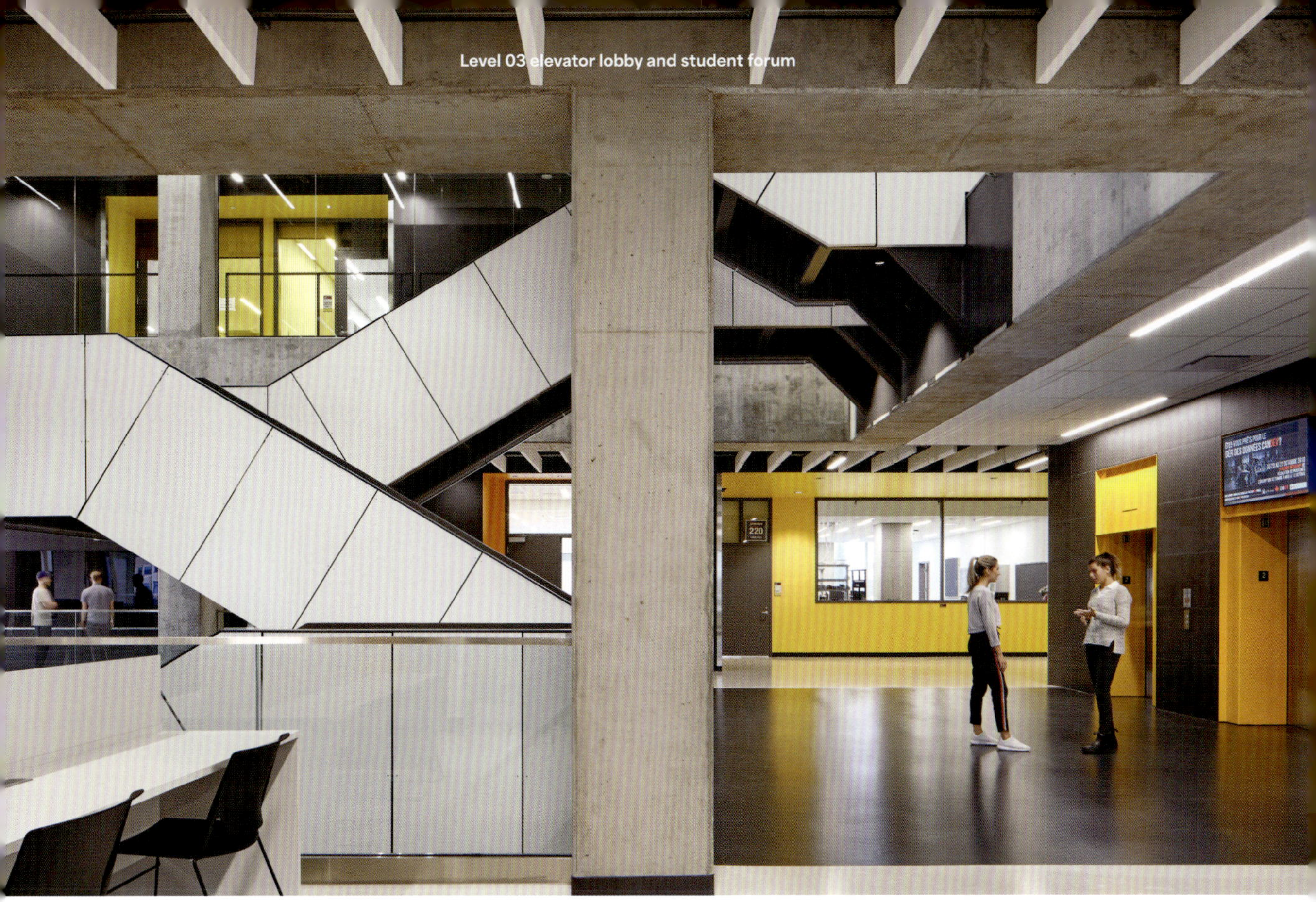

Level 03 elevator lobby and student forum

Sketch concept for the south entrance

The STEM atrium

Maker space and event space viewed across the south entrance

The atrium skylights

James Gillies St

Plot Twist

School of Continuing Studies, York University

Toronto, Ontario 2018-2022

I had a dream that I was visiting one of our completed projects for the first time. I was with my colleagues Jon Loewen and Dan McTavish and we were wearing suits, so I assume the occasion was a grand opening. As we approached the building on foot, navigating the congested sidewalks of some great metropolis, the building's form and materiality were revealed to us in a series of tightly cropped vignettes. It was something otherworldly: a series of convex protrusions pushing out of a twisted metallic surface that deformed at its centre to create a cave-like maw. The three of us kept remarking at how strange it was, how ambitious and how unfamiliar. We had taken our ideas to another level, but had we gone too far? The building kept changing before our eyes, its protruding volumes growing in depth and developing domes with oculi at their tips. A polished stainless-steel anemone.

If you have flipped through the other stories in this collection, you will know that there is nothing like this in our practice. And of course, the project that the dream was about, the York University, School of Continuing Studies, isn't nearly so ambitious or bizarre in reality. But the dream (as dreams are want to do) presented an interesting combination of my own obvious anxieties about the project as well as a set of less obvious or latent anxieties and hopes that have been my constant companion over several years. These concerns could be broadly lumped into the category of "practice evolution" or "what comes next?"

During the construction phase of the SCS, visits by the design team would trigger alternating tsunamis of excitement about the building's sculptural presence and anguish about the myriad sacrifices that might have been made to achieve that form. Our practice has consistently generated buildings where the shape is intentionally and obviously in service of a public-realm strategy that connects people to each other, to ideas, and to a place. In my work, I would say that I have intentionally steered away from formal excess in favour of a well-crafted container or containers defining a dramatic public realm. This approach has been successful, aligning with the limitations of what Canadian clients are willing to invest in architecture and focusing on what I feel we need most as a society—public space that supports community and culture. We are a young nation and generally lack the sophistication and resources to do extravagance well. Regardless of how firmly I might hold these convictions, we are in the business of architecture. We need to win commissions and to do that we need to excite and inspire our prospective clients. My colleague Safdar Abidi, the principal-in-charge on the York pursuit, was close with the university's campus architect Patrick Saavedra, and in their casual interactions Patrick had often chaffed Safdar about the studio's "boxy" architecture. What we proudly viewed as a body of work that consistently grappled with a set of core ideas was, to Patrick's eyes, indicative of a lack of imagination or perhaps even complacency. I initially resisted this critique, as I felt that Patrick, as revealed in the commissions that York had most recently awarded, tended to be seduced by a superficial brand of formalism—buildings that look interesting at first glance but lack consistency in their spatial proposition or technical execution.

An engineering building full of boxy spaces that attempts to look like a cloud but fails, because, well, its full of boxes. A student centre that spent so much on cantilevers that its interior, where the students spend all their time, was utterly impoverished. When the competition brief came out for the School of Continuing Studies, it was clear that my opinions on York's recent crop of buildings were beside the point. If we were to stand a chance, Safdar convinced me, we would have to generate an architectural solution that, to the client, seemed a departure from our past work.

York organized a competition among a limited shortlist of three prequalifying firms. We were up against HOK and Henning Larsen. An ambitious brief asked for an "iconic" gateway building targeting net-zero energy (as demonstrated by a full energy model), a conceptual-level costing report, and design briefs for all of our subconsultant disciplines. The competition guideline was issued on December 14 and was due January 24. Effectively a five-week burn over Christmas. As with any design competition, it was critical for the conceptual work to occur up front so that our extended team could contribute their insights into something of a fledgling idea. Before the holiday break, we barely had time to read the brief, put together a team, and discuss the broadest strokes of a strategy. Safdar, whose insights are always laser-focused on mirroring the client's values and culture, kept the pressure on the designers to defy expectations (whatever that might mean), and I continued to chafe, feeling that an obligation to formal frippery was being imposed upon us. Before we could really get much done, Christmas was upon us and the team was obliged to disperse at least for a few days. Due to the looming and inconvenient deadline, I had pulled out the stops and managed to snag two of our studio's most gifted and industrious designers, Dan McTavish and Jon Loewen. I had hired, mentored, and worked with them on numerous projects, but I had never worked with both of them on the same project and was not certain as to how the dynamic would function under my leadership, or whether my leadership could even contain the ensuing reactive output. While the "lads," as I call them, are always deferential and respectful, there was a heightened sense of competitive ambition with York, intensified by the demand to do something quite different from what we had done in the recent past. I made it clear that I would lead them, but that I had no idea where we were going. I was going to need a lot of conceptual and moral support.

I tend to lead design as conversation, positing ideas to others, eliciting a response, and building on that response. The degree to which I generate the ideas is irrelevant and varies according to who is around the table. It's my job to edit and synthesize the elements of the conversation with the conviction that the best ideas are in, wherever they come from. These conversations vary in scale, sometimes with dozens or even hundreds of participants pitching ideas into the mix. That Christmas of the York competition, there were just three of us, calling in daily from our various locations to exchange sketches, precedents, and bits of writing. On the third of January, I was in Miami participating in Perkins&Wills' annual design review, looking at hundreds of projects from around our firm. I spent three days looking over a wide range of projects, critiquing their conception, execution, and beauty (or lack thereof), all the while, aware that we had yet to land on a direction for the design that was to due in four weeks' time. On the flight back to Toronto, I began to diagram the only thing I was sure of—that this notion of a campus gateway and home for York's continuing education faculty would need to begin with a proposition for public space.

On January the 5th, the three of us met in the otherwise empty Dupont Street studio to compare initial thoughts. We had all been grappling with the same key drivers: York had provided the competitors with a set of simple diagrams that organized the program of teaching spaces, student engagement spaces, and offices into a five-storey rectangular box that took up most of the available site. In large part, the program suggested a generic academic building, but the brief's narrative stressed the need to achieve the extraordinary out of the ordinary. Words like "iconic" and "landmark" revealed the expectations of the campus architect but didn't provide us much fuel for inspiration. Instead, we looked to an integrated approach to sustainability that would dovetail with the context and the culture we were being asked to interpret. We started with the missions of two schools who were to share the building and the circumstances that they were currently operating under. The school of continuing studies focuses on providing a wide range of academic upgrades to working graduates, largely of the millennial generation. These students, by and large, commute to York to attend classes in the evening and on weekends. The English Language Institute focuses on providing English instruction to foreign students who hope to attend York but lack the language skills. These students are recent high school graduates, mostly Asian, who come to take an intensive session over several months, staying just off campus in York's nearby development lands. While the two schools serve very different cohorts, at the time of the competition they shared several key characteristics that had led York's administration to collocate them. Both groups were outsiders, coming to campus during off-hours and not integrating into its community or culture. Both programs are strong revenue-generators for York but despite this, were using dispersed, improvised accommodations that included a set of portable classrooms. The design process, we determined, was about making a home.

York University presents some unique challenges from a campus-planning perspective. In its original conception, the campus consisted of residential and special-purpose buildings orbiting a brutalist megacomplex containing the core academic functions. This ensemble sat within a grassy parkland encircled by a perimeter access road. Over time this green has been filled in with a gridwork of roads and new buildings. Awkward conditions abound as these two planning philosophies rub up against each other. This crisis of spatial identity is most pronounced in the vicinity of the megacomplex (a.k.a. the Ross Building) and at the edges of the campus. The proposed site of the project exemplified the challenges of many of these perimeter plots. To the north was a four-storey structured parking garage. To the west, a satellite campus for Seneca

Polytechnic. To the east, a bus turn-around and remnant woodlot. The Pond Road marked the southern boundary of both the site and the campus, dividing the university proper from land controlled by its subsidiary development corporation. The development property presented us with a patchwork of grass fields and speculative student housing. The notion that our building would somehow form a gateway was puzzling. We couldn't help but ask ourselves, "A gateway to what, from what?" The architecture needed to make a place, a point of reference to anchor so many disparate elements.

When the three of us laid our doodles on the table we had between ourselves touched on all these issues, but no one had been able to solve the puzzle. Jon had sketched a series of façades that sought to define the edge of the campus as an ordered architectural threshold. Dan had made a series of observations about the patterns of movement. I brought my airplane doodle. With no sense of what the architectural form would be, I had looked at establishing some sense of place in concert with surrounding structures. I had taken a cue from the Seneca Polytechnic building, which with its angled front façade formed a triangular forecourt at the intersection of The Pond Road and Ian McDonald Boulevard, a modest service road that fortuitously would lead to a future (now complete) subway station by Foster+Partners. I had also wanted to address the fact that many students would be dropped off at the eastern edge of the site. In response, I had turned the rectangular parcel from the brief into a rotated parallelogram that released two triangular parcels of open space. One at the southwest corner would work in tandem with the Seneca Polytechnic building's forecourt to define a gateway plaza at Ian McDonald Boulevard. The other would allow a discrete drop-off point and entrance at the northeast corner of the site. While I hadn't been able to go beyond this simple site parti, the diagram sparked an immediate creative response in the others. Jon snapped his sketchbook closed:

"Well, let's forget about all of this drivel and look at that!"

We moved into a boardroom with a large-format LCD on which we could live-edit a three-dimensional model.

The movement of people between the two entry zones created a strong diagonal gesture counter to the parallelogram, and this suggested a rotational force, which ultimately led us to take the box that York had given us and twist it. That first afternoon Jon quickly modelled a series of floor plates rotating off one another, akin to a fanning deck of cards. While this established the basic gesture, I was concerned about the complexity of the twisting ziggurat-like composition, which with its many roofs and soffits threatened to be both ungainly and technically challenging. In the end, Henning Larsen developed a competition scheme which was virtually identical to this iteration. I suppose they stopped there, whereas we kept moving.

The next approach we took was to pleat or fold the façade, first once and then several times. This resulted in a very graphic composition with alternating slashes of glass and solid on either side of each fold line. A compelling image, but not the way forward for a building with a

Studies for the modular construction of the façade with compound curvature

Study model of the structural framing

The structural frame twists around fixed stair and elevator cores

The shifting the of frame against the rectilinear cores creates changes in plan from floor to floor

Plan view of the structural framing model with the floors rotating around a centroid

D
C
B
A

targeted energy-use intensity of under 100 kilowatt-hours per square metre per year. We were committed to creating a highly sustainable and comfortable building, and the massive ribbons of south-facing glass would work against this. Nonetheless, we all felt we were on to something. The twisted object showed promise sculpturally when viewed in motion as one approached the campus. And importantly to me, that form was rooted in the creation of public spaces and the movement of people. Yes it would be an object—but a place-making object. After stumbling about in isolation, we had made considerable progress in only one day together, debating ideas, critiquing and iterating in a rapid-volley creative exchange that I like to call "conversational design."

We parted ways and Dan went home to test how we could integrate a finer grain of fenestration into the pleated façade. Those explorations were utterly unsuccessful, but he must have stumbled upon his copy of the *Atlas of Novel Tectonics* by Jesse Reiser and Nanako Umemoto. This compelling little volume posits that the diagrid is the most versatile architectural system at our disposal today. (Remind me to return Dan's copy.) In the morning, Dan came back with a systematic solution to our dilemma: a creased surface of small triangular panels that would enclose the rotating fan of floor plates. Our explorations were shifted out of SketchUp and into the more geometrically precise Rhino. From that point on, we split into three streams of activity. I focused on writing the design narrative and sketching diagrams that would illustrate the proposal's urbanistic, social, and sustainable-design drivers. Jon developed a series of interior spaces that would complement the larger landscape moves and support a shared culture of occupation for the two schools. And Dan articulated the geometry with Miesian rigor, right through to completion.

With the basic form and layout in place, our extended team was able to dive into the fray and help us forge a credible narrative around operational and embodied energy and carbon. The basic geometric proposition begins with rectangular floor plates rotating about a centroid. The biaxially symmetrical composition would be structured with a series of angled heavy-timber frames supporting nail-laminated-timber composite decks.

Max Richter from Perkins&Will's Vancouver studio joined us as a sustainable-design advisor and helped to craft an embodied-carbon strategy that was rooted in the timber structure. The goal was to lower operational carbon and energy-use intensity through three key strategies: passive design, electrically based energy-efficient systems, and renewable-energy generation. The result, we hoped, was a building that was net-zero for energy and operational carbon. We wanted to demonstrate that the building's unique form was integral to achieving these sustainability targets. If we were going to make a sculptural form, it was going to be intentional and integral to the project's manifold ambitions.

The twisted box created some interesting spatial conditions on the ground plane as the building alternately leaned over to create a sense of enclosed urban space or canted away to open views to the sky. This condition also affected light conditions along the south façade, making it shadier on one end and sunnier on the other. The diagrid had resolved the building's skin into a series of triangular panels of consistent size but subtly varying angles. We began to think of these panels performatively. We proposed three types of panels, each doing something different: triple-glazed "vision" panels for light and views, aluminum-clad insulated panels, and building-integrated photovoltaic panels that would capture the sun's energy. We modelled the solar exposure against the building's south façade and mapped that against the internal workings of the building. Programmatically it made sense to have larger concentrations of glazing in open spaces and more discrete windows in smaller enclosed spaces. Photovoltaics would be most efficient where the building form would angle them upward toward the sun. Occupant comfort and the functionality of the classrooms would intersect with opportunities for sun and shade to influence a compositional strategy or pattern language across the twisting façades.

The occupation of the building would similarly be influenced by the twisting geometry. As previously described, the centre of the building was fixed, and with it the continuous vertical elements such as elevator shafts, exit stairs, and service runs, as well as the primary planning blocks. On each of the upper floors, the programmatic elements occupied the centre of the plan in one of two offset containers, while the space of circulation and communal interaction would occur in a perimeter zone that varied as the building twisted. This design marked a new formal approach for our group and also offered an inversion of our usual approach to public space and program. Buildings like Toronto Metropolitan University's Daphne Cockwell Health Sciences Complex (page 278) or the University of Waterloo's Engineering 5 and 7 (page 126) place the programmatic elements in architectural containers between which the public life of the building occurs in a daylit void space.

At York, the containers would sit within the architectural gesture and the public life would occur at the building perimeter, in constant dialogue with the exterior and the building's geometrical order. The twisting geometry meant that the public zones would change in size from floor to floor. Spaces to gather or move between floors were distributed in a diagonal movement both horizontally and vertically, recalling our first impulse to organize the site. Resultant pockets of public space at the southeast and northwest corners of the building created opportunities to engage unique aspects of the surrounding context, such as the woodlot and the arrival plaza we were proposing. Once again, our conviction was that the twisting geometry was to be rooted in a fundamental public-space gesture and offer unique experiences and benefits to the building users.

As I reflect on the genesis of this design, I can see both the anxiety and self-criticism that came with embarking in a new direction. The highly collaborative nature of a design process involving three unique perspectives in constant dialogue acted alternately as a creative generator and a paranoia filter. We would go new places but always chart our course. If we were going to twist, it would be a deep twist.

As you will have gathered from the supporting imagery, we did win the competition. Safdar and I—along with Max Richter; Steve Kemp, our envelope and energy consultant from RDH; and Kevin Farbridge, our mechanical designer from Smith + Anderson—shared speaking roles in a half-hour interview that built the rationale for our twisted box. We meant the scheme to appear as an inevitable outcome, with every consideration of occupant well-being, environmental benefit, and campus identity and culture met through a holistically considered gesture. Two weeks after the interview, we received a call from the campus architect informing us that we had won, and we went to York to meet with Patrick and his boss, Richard Francki, Vice President of Campus Services and Business Operations. Our initial elation was short-lived, as we soon began to sense that something wasn't quite right. Patrick had alluded to some possible "further explorations" and "interesting ideas." We made our way to the north end of the city and the farthest corners of the York Campus where the wholly uninspiring Physical Resources Building serves as base for the procurement and management of all architectural projects. We entered the complex's windowless boardroom and sat down for our debrief. Patrick, a generous and gregarious spirit, congratulated us warmly and spoke enthusiastically, if a bit nervously, about some interesting ideas that the group had regarding our design. Richard arrived late and slapped a binder on the table, tucked a tie with sailboats printed on it into his belt, and sat down. With an air of military efficiency, he congratulated us on a solid presentation and informed us that the directors of the two academic programs were very excited about our design. He, however, had concerns. As I listened to Richard warming up to the point, I could see, out of the corner of my eye, sweat breaking out on Patrick's forehead. And then Richard, with a completely straight face, asked the kind of question that architects' nightmares are made of:

"So gentlemen, what I need to know is, how much money would we save if we got rid of the twist?"

Client	York University
Location	Toronto, Ontario
Size	9,750 gross square metres
Date	2018-2022

Detail of the façade panels

Approaching from the east on The Pond Road

Aerial view of the building in context

The east façade under construction

View of the west entrance from the Seneca Polytechnic building

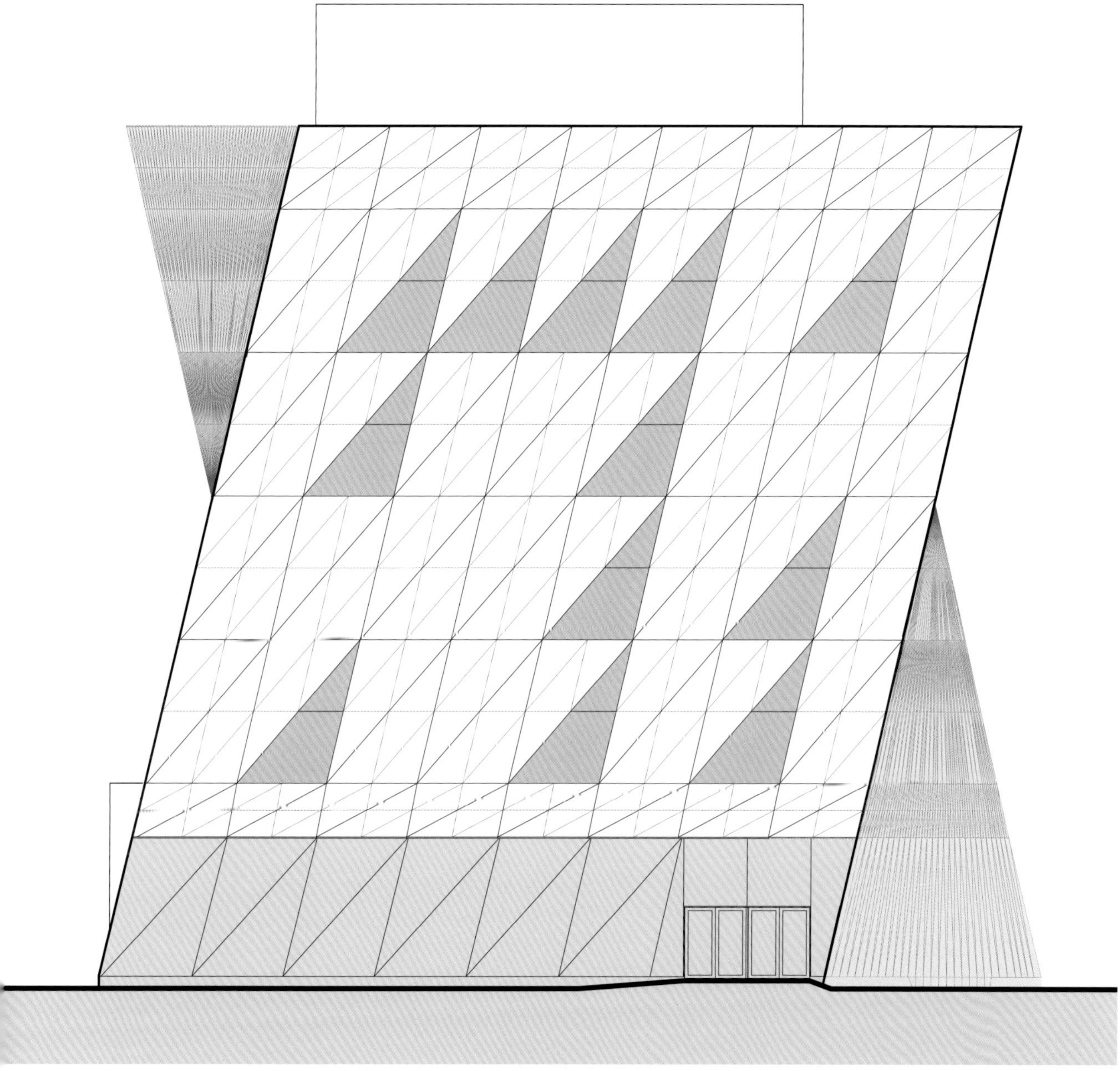

The west elevation

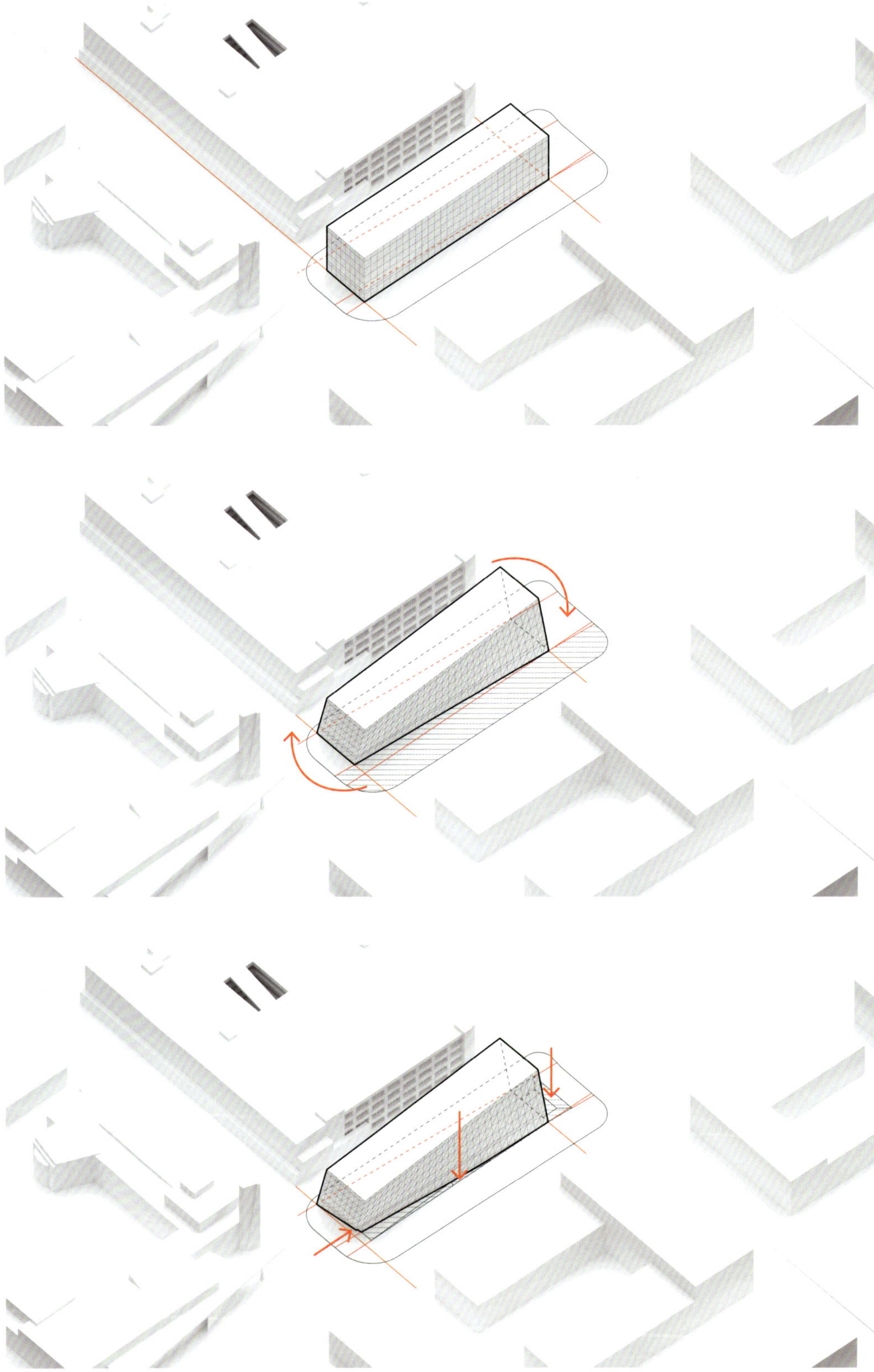

Diagram showing the box twisted and then sunk

The south façade, looking west along The Pond Road

The south façade, looking east along The Pond Road

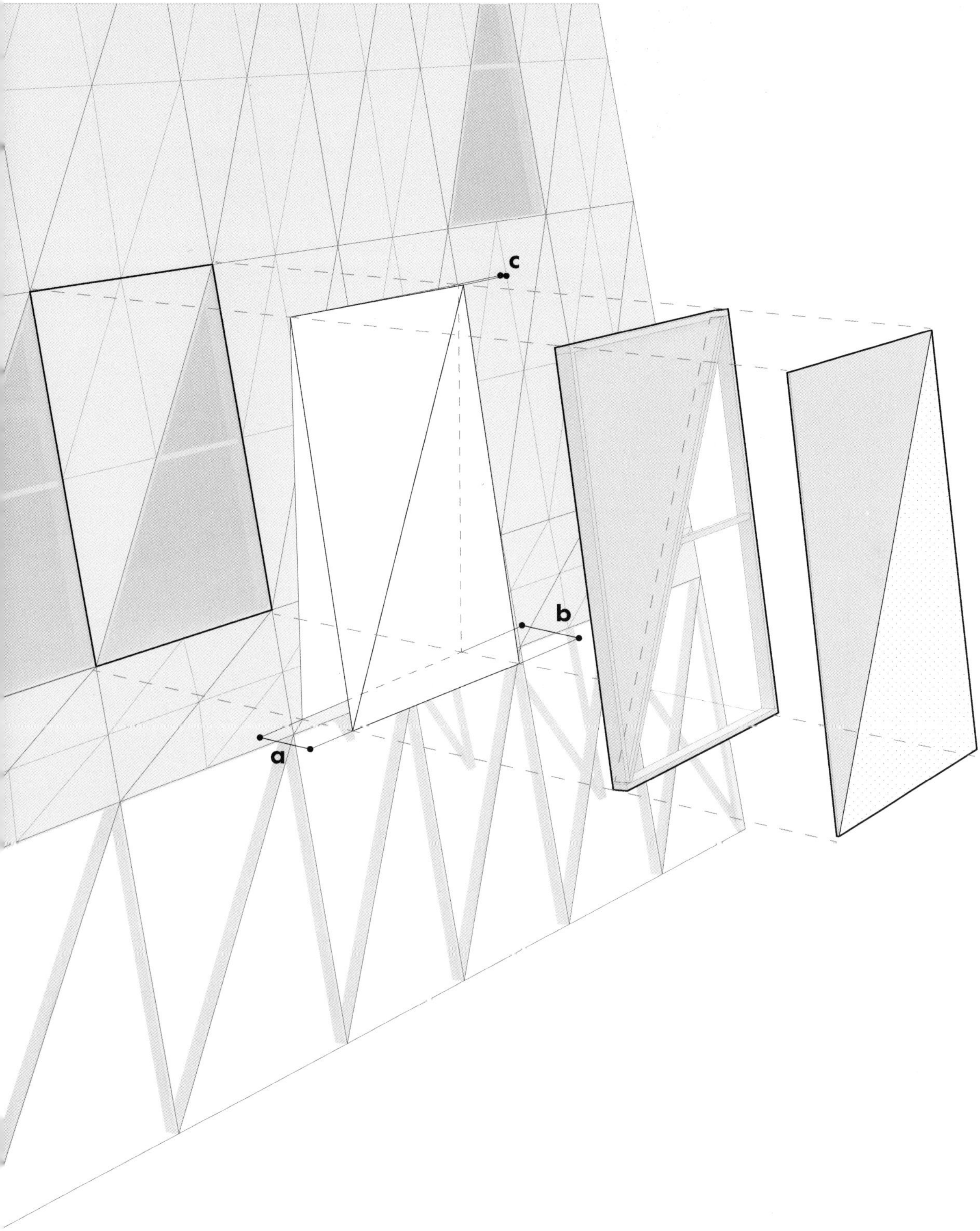

The creased elements of a modular façade

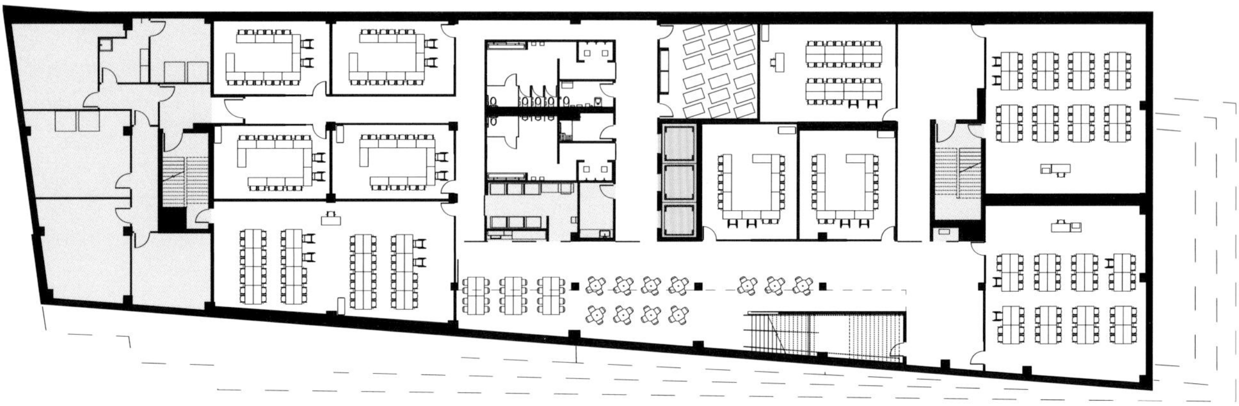

Level -01 Plan

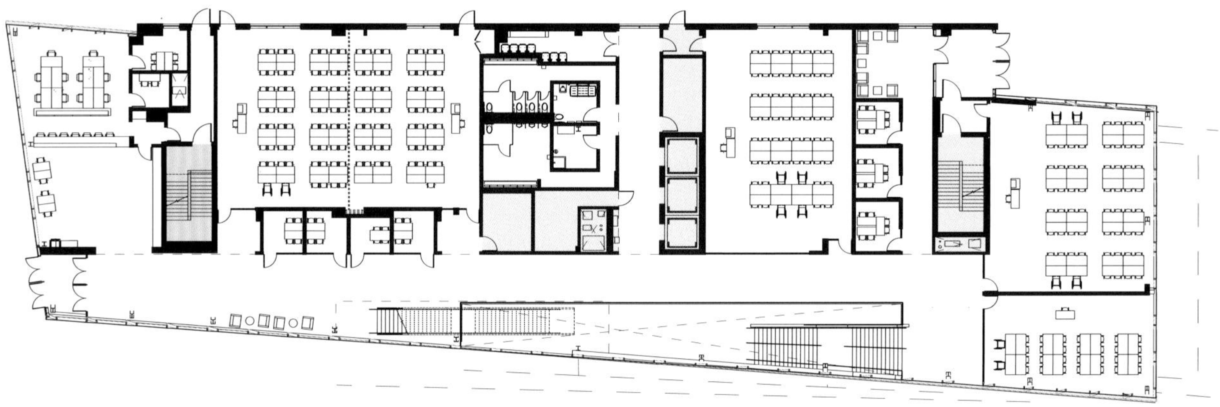

Level 01 Plan

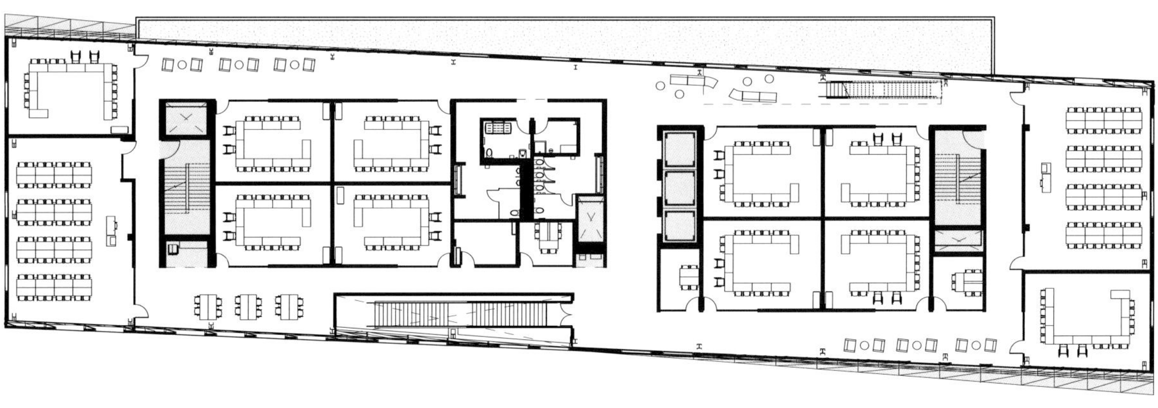

Level 02 Plan

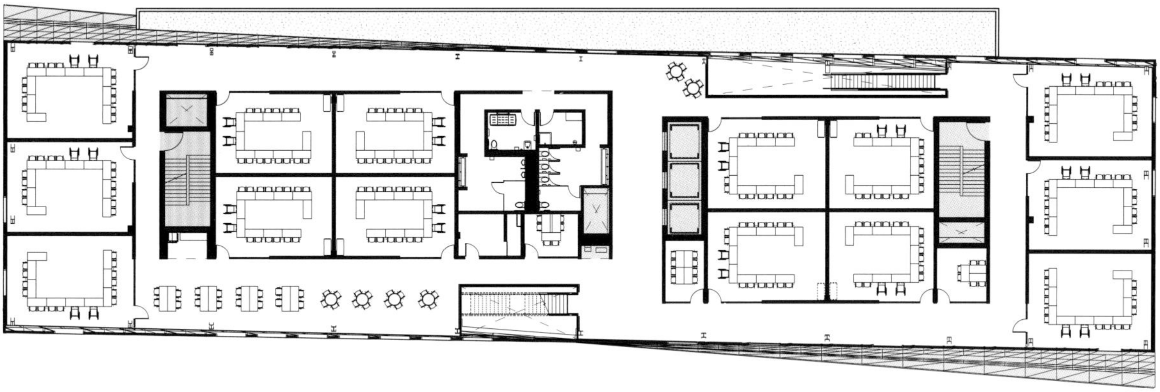

Level 03 Plan

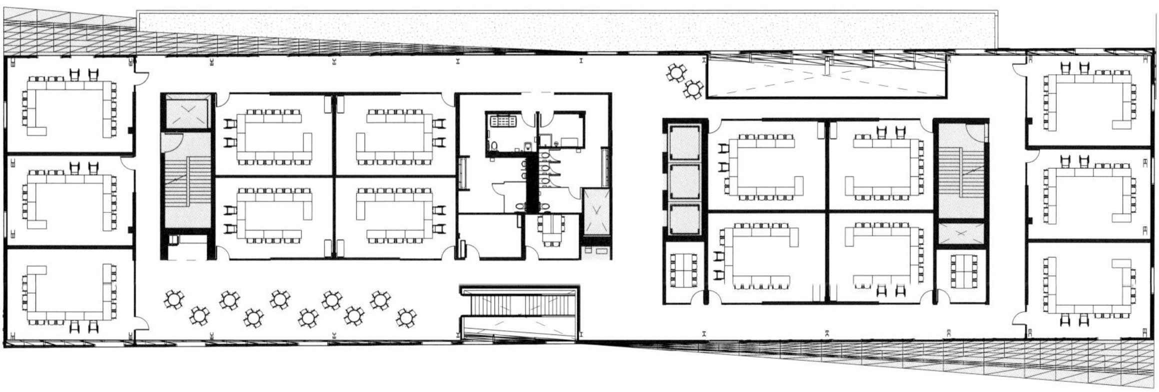

Level 04 Plan

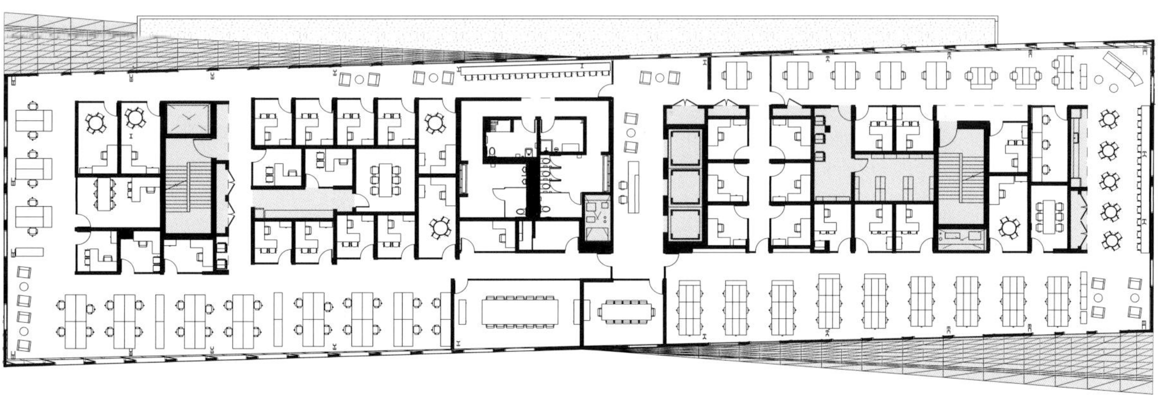

Level 05 Plan

View from the southeast

Staircase along the building's south face

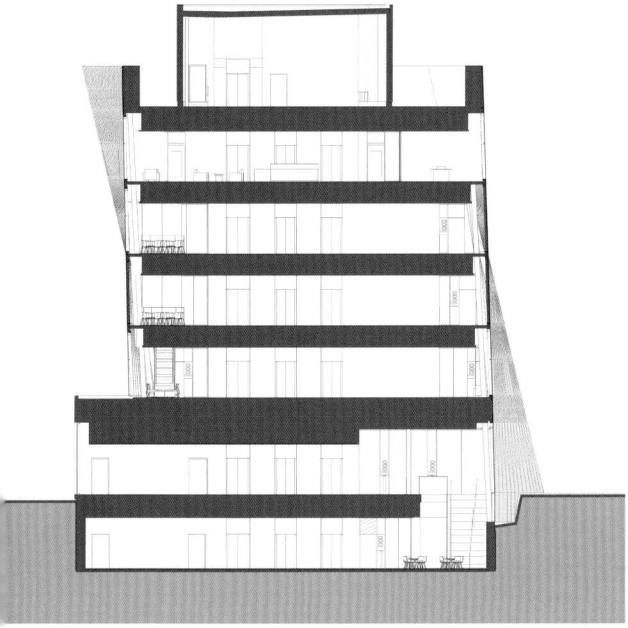

North-South Section A

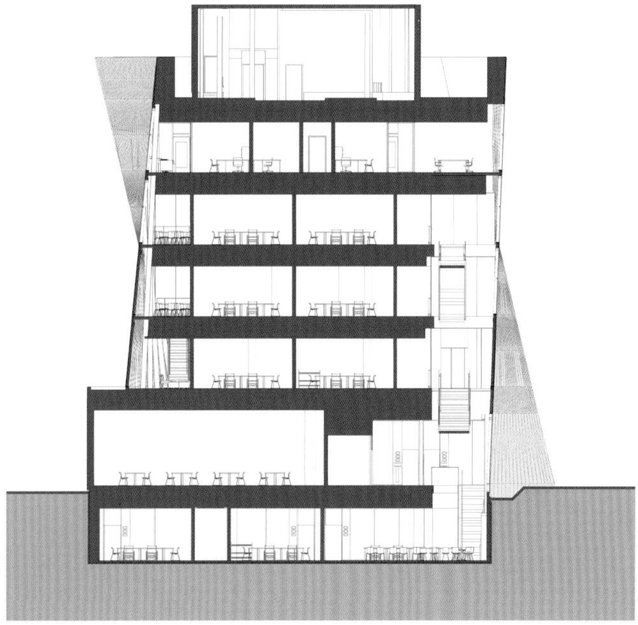

North-South Section B

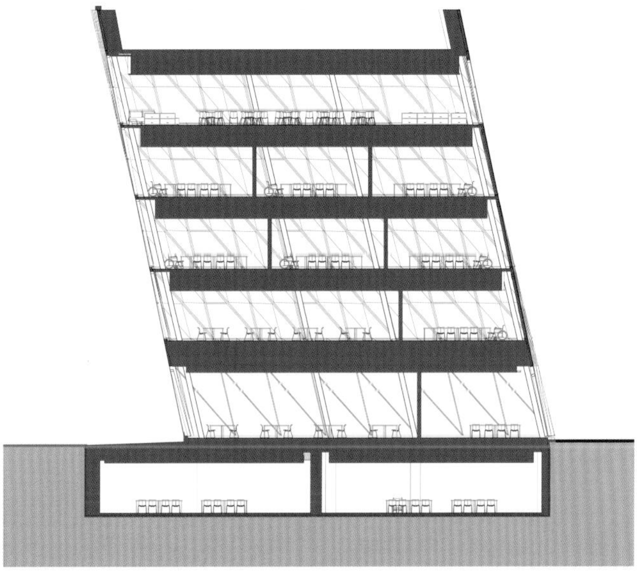

North-South Section C

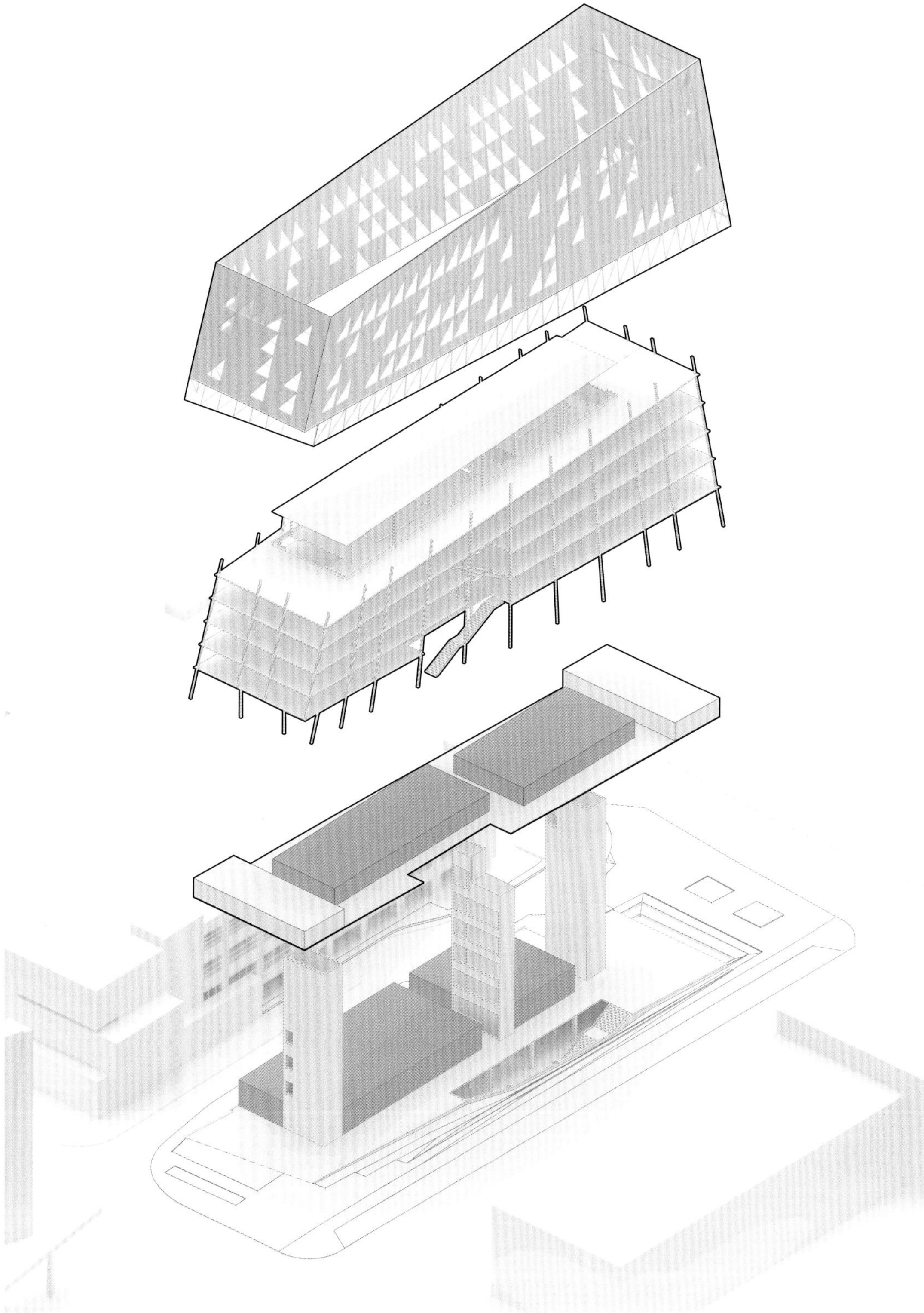

Exploded axonometric with elements of the composition

Perimeter corridor and lounge on Level 02

Student reception and registration area

Level 01 classroom

South-facing study bar

Upper-level seminar room

James Gillies

Blanket Statement

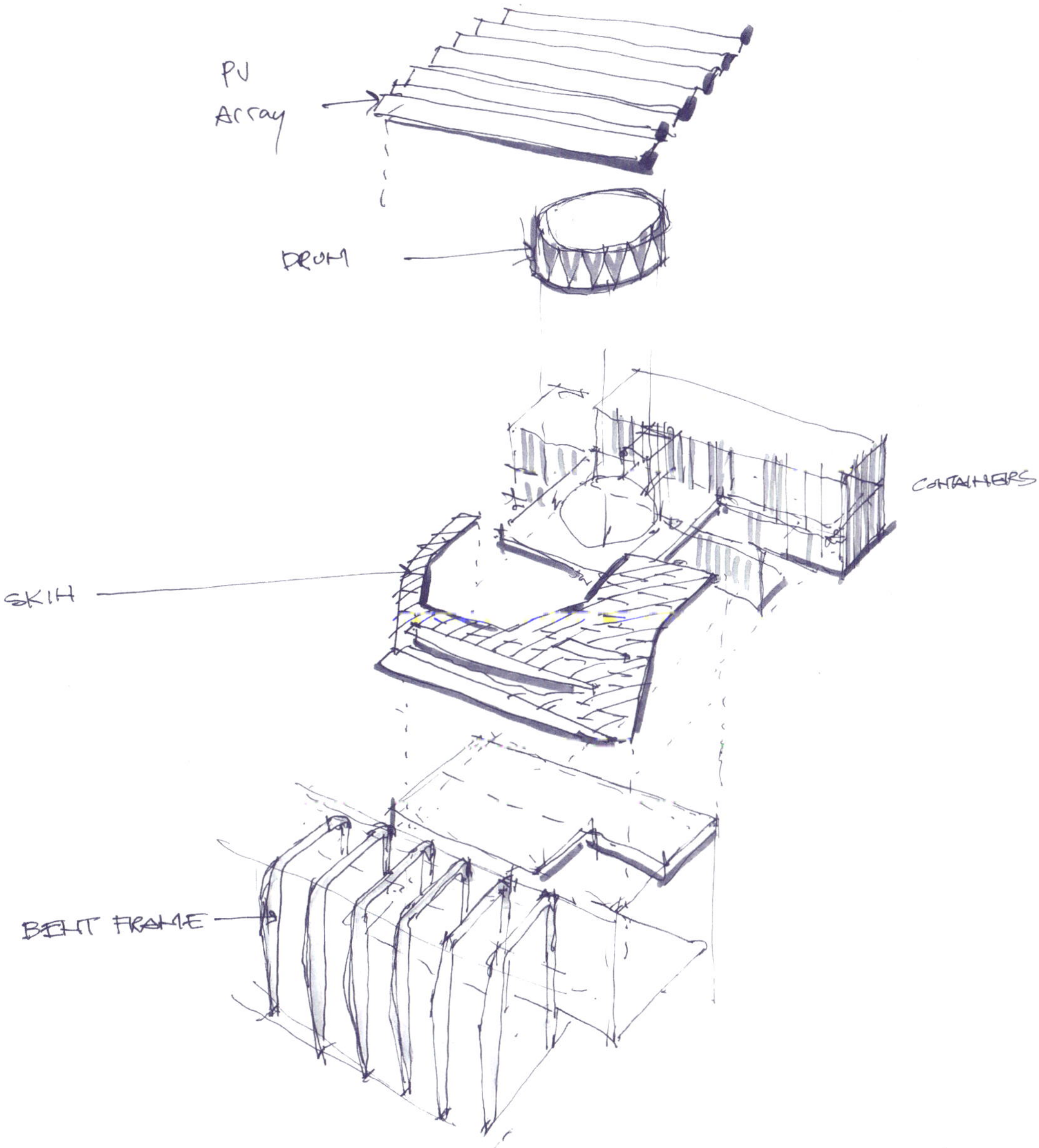

Dawes Road Library

Toronto, Ontario 2021-2026

In June of 2021, Canada was forced to hear an undeniable call to collective action. The discovery of the bodies of 215 Indigenous children, buried in unmarked graves on the grounds of a residential school on Tk'emlúps te Secwépemc First Nation land in Kamloops, British Columbia, had finally placed an international spotlight on the legacy of genocide that is inextricably woven into the birth of our nation. This call to action was magnified less than a month later by the discovery of 182 unmarked graves at the former Kootenay Indian Residential School in Cranbrook, British Columbia. There are currently 21 active investigations into similar mass graves across Canada, and the results will only solidify what has been known for a long time, but seldom has been articulated on a national or international stage. It is time for all Canadians to recognize that their country was never an empty wilderness. There were people here, and they were systematically displaced, starved, and murdered to make way for the Crown corporations, and then the nation state. The fact that, for generations, this genocide was subcontracted to the Church doesn't change the ultimate responsibility that our government, and we as citizens, must face.

But this knowledge is not new. What is perhaps most disturbing is how widely and deeply investigated and documented the genocide of Canada's Indigenous peoples has been over the past 150 years. The stories have been discovered and told time and again by well-meaning agents of the Church, the Federal Government, and the mainstream media, and of course by Indigenous artists, writers, and activists, who are creating powerful new cultural forms that address the loss and reimagining of their cultures. In 2015, the federal government published the recommendations of the Truth and Reconciliation Commission. The commission comprised Indigenous and non-Indigenous academics, legal experts, historians, and artists, who worked for the better part of a decade to plot a path forward for our nation. A path that would, in theory, reveal the totality of the loss to every Canadian and then piece by piece begin to redress the many wrongs. The task is so overwhelming as to seem impossible, and for many years it would seem that a collective inertia and ambivalence prevented any meaningful progress. Today, however, as working architects, we are starting to see something happen. While systematic injustice toward Indigenous people is lamentably alive and kicking, there is a parallel lifting up of Indigenous cultural values and practices, which is beginning to have a profound effect on the way that we think about and inhabit space in this country. It seems that we are at the cusp of a new era of architectural thought in Canada that is following directly on the recommendations and interpretation of the TRC. For our studio, the design of a small branch library in the East End of Toronto provided the first tangible lessons as to what this new paradigm might look like.

In August 2021, the discovery of unmarked graves at the former Kootenay Indian Residential School was still dominating the press and social media discourse. I was working in my small urban backyard when the dog began barking with a volume and urgency that could suggest but two things: Either a family of raccoons was taunting her from the overhead power lines that traverse our property, or the mailman had dared to set foot on our stoop. It turned out to be the latter, and when I walked around the side of the house to the front door, I discovered two FedEx packages—each containing a roll of industrial felt, one 10-ounce and the other 12-ounce. I lugged the rolls to the backyard, set them down, and resumed my work. I was using my cramped back patio as a workshop to construct a 1:25 scale maquette using simple hand tools, 1×1 pine, and ⅛-inch plywood sheets. The maquette represented the volumetric boundary of the Dawes Road Library, a commission we had won with Smoke Architecture for the latest Toronto Public Library branch early in the spring. That summer was part of the long tail end of the COVID pandemic. I was working in the garden in part because, after repeated shutdowns and reopenings, our team was only slowly trickling back to the studio, and because I was on a particular mission that seemed to require a bit of solitary focus. The Dawes Road project, from the outset, was intended to have a highly consultative, highly collaborative, and highly public design process. I wasn't retreating to design the project alone, but rather to speculate on a methodology that would allow the community, the client, Smoke Architecture, and ourselves to design together.

TPL had put out an RFP in April, soliciting architectural services to design a 25,000-square-foot, net-zero-carbon library and community-service hub in Toronto's East End. The brief also called for the inclusion of an Indigenous architect as an integral part of the team. This was a project that I had been waiting for, being eager to work with this progressive, design-focused client again. Realistically, there were, and still are, three Indigenous-led architecture practices serving the Toronto area. We had some experience working with Matthew Hickey and Brian Porter of Two Row and had collaborated on a design competition with Ryan Gorrie of Brook McIlroy's Indigenous Design Studio. All of them are excellent designers and wonderful collaborators. I suppose I was curious, wanting to learn more and see what Eladia Smoke and her team would bring to this equation. Several of our young intern architects were studying under Eladia at Laurentian University. Their descriptions of her place-based and story-driven design philosophy excited me, seeming to parallel my own, with a different starting place but perhaps some overlapping conclusions.

I phoned Eladia to explain why I thought she should team with us rather than a dozen other firms who would certainly be anxious to have her on board. I didn't ask for exclusivity but presented my desire to have a true design collaboration with her, one where we would both learn and grow as architects. I had seen a disconcerting trend for Indigenous architects to be involved in institutional projects with largely consultative roles and only a small and often poorly integrated piece of the project executed in their voice. The formula of a big building with a small Indigenous element was becoming more prevalent in Canadian public buildings, and I wanted to avoid the pitfall. I saw Perkins&Will's holistic "Living Design" approach to sustainability as consistent with the Indigenous traditions of building with and on the land as part of a network of living things. Our portfolio

Making a 1:25 maquette of the library in the backyard

The extensive community of stakeholders who informed the design of award-winning libraries and our successful working relationship with TPL all suggested we would be a strong contender if Eladia would bring her wisdom and unique story-telling ability to the effort. She agreed to join our team as an integral co-creator of the entire architectural proposition, whatever that might be.

Our entire pursuit preparation, interview, early consultation, and predesign phase were conducted virtually, due to COVID restrictions. Together with our respective teams, Eladia and I generated a story about how an Indigenous world view and a Living Design philosophy could come together as the spiritual and technical faces of a single solution—one that would connect the diverse demographic of Dawes Road to its pre-contact history, to nature, and to a sustainable future. Eladia shared that for the Anishinaabeg, an Indigenous group whose land the library will occupy, culture is a verb, perpetually enacted, reborn, and advanced through doing. Together we described the library as a journey connecting the city to its primordial landscape (in this context, the verdant valley of Taylor Creek). There were five of us at the virtual interview: myself, Eladia, my longtime colleague Linda Neumayer, our project architect Michael Blois, and sustainability advisor Zeina Elali. We wanted to communicate to our prospective client that we would be a thoroughly integrated team, with each of us offering a unique and indispensable attribute: a curious explorer, an interpreter, a seasoned guide, a crafter of beautiful objects, and a caretaker of living things respectively. We studied the history of the site and the nearby Taylor Creek ravine, from its role as a seasonal hunting ground, communication route, and settlement for the Haudenosaunee, Anishinaabeg, and other Indigenous peoples who regularly came to trade and access resources in the region, to its 20th-century exploitation as a clay and gravel quarry. We analyzed the demographics of the neighbourhood and described the impact that a representation of Indigenous culture could have to new Canadians and growing families. We provided a detailed analysis of how the library could achieve the Canadian Green Building Council's Zero Carbon Building certification through a combination of on-site renewables and active and passive strategies. We endeavoured to tell a story about what this uniquely ambitious project could become. The story was highly emotive yet grounded in experience and a bedrock of technical knowledge.

It was a rainy afternoon in May when Gail Rankin of TPL called to congratulate us on the project win. I was walking the dog in Trinity Bellwoods Park, "working from home," and taking a few calls on my headset at the end of the day.

"You came across as one team. If we hadn't known you, we wouldn't know where Perkins&Will ended and Smoke Architecture began."

Gayle went on to describe how that hadn't been the case with the other contestants. Apparently there had been very different approaches to the inclusion of an Indigenous designer. Our team had stood out in that we suggested a new architectural paradigm based on coming together as one team, with unique perspectives and a shared goal.

The project began in earnest in June with the consultation of Indigenous and non-Indigenous stakeholders. Eladia augmented TPL's existing collaborators to create a roster of 13 organizations that would be consulted over the life of the project. These included Aboriginal Legal Services, Anishnawbe Health Toronto, the Indigenous Story Circle, and the Toronto District School Board, among others. Eladia and her colleague Jennifer Kinnunen generally facilitated and documented these conversations while the Perkins&Will team focused on gathering the technical information surrounding the site and the zoning regulations, for which we needed to prepare an early package to test the building's proposed three-storey height with the city. For the collaboration to be successful and for us to live up to our own description of the integrated team, we each had to fit into our respective roles quickly and begin to contribute from those perspectives. When there are two mature designers on a team this can take some time, but with Eladia and I it proved quite simple. My lack of cultural literacy regarding Indigenous precedents and design elements meant that I deferred to Eladia in the arena of the project's overriding conceptual narrative. I would contribute but not lead. Conversely, since this was Eladia's first purpose-built library design, I led the programmatic, functional, and technical aspects. We would eventually come together in a rich collaboration around the form and tectonics of the building—how the building's particular story would be told through architecture.

For the first weeks of the project, the two studios worked together in highly energized fashion, meeting through Miro, an online whiteboard collaboration tool, due to lingering COVID restrictions and Smoke Architecture's location an hour away in Hamilton, Ontario. We shared the fruits of the latest consultations, visual precedents, and sketches several times a week in a spontaneous fashion. Initially the Haudenosaunee longhouse seemed an appropriate precedent with its layered platforms and communal focus, but the site just wasn't very long and the association, once distorted to fit the realities of site and program, wasn't translating. We did, however, keep the ideas of articulated frames and platforms as a way of organizing space and the proposed vertical journey from the street to a rooftop garden. Eladia brought forth the notion of the star blanket—a gift made and bestowed by the community for valuable work that benefits the community, and in other traditions as commemorating a union or coming together. The symbolism resonated with us and with TPL. The blanket would communicate the idea of a gift shared between TPL and the community members who would come to share knowledge here, the coming together of TPL and the Toronto community service hub in one building, and a high-performance envelope protecting the library from the extremes of the Canadian climate.

Eladia provided a series of conceptual sketches that showed a blanket wrapping the framed building, but I wasn't convinced—they seemed architecturally ungrounded, more evocations of an idea than indicators of an architectural strategy. I generated a series of quick model sketches, while Michael Blois developed early massing studies in Rhino and SketchUp. Eladia found these to be too rigid, as if we were shrink wrapping a box. Our preoccupations with fitting the building on the site, accommodating the program, and achieving some sort of cost-effective solution were overriding the gesture and poetry. We were both right, and we were attempting to do something that neither of us quite knew how to do. In different ways, we were, each of us, in over our heads. The methods and tools we were accustomed to using weren't serving us at this point, so we endeavored to invent a project-specific methodology, one that would lead us from blanket to building—a methodology, a translator, and a storyteller in its own right.

I began to ruminate on Eladia's initial assertion that "culture is a verb." If our design process was in some way performative, it could gain authority in all of our minds and become part of a shared project culture. After I had finished the 1:25 maquette, I transported it and the felt rolls to our studio at 110 Yonge Street, where we held a day-long charrette. Eladia and Jennifer made the drive in from Hamilton, and we all met each other in person for the first time. I encouraged people to come into the studio, hoping to create some energy around the improvisatory nature of the charrette. Over six hours we experimented with the thick felt, draping it over the wooden frame, but also ourselves, in various configurations. We began to ask questions: How does a blanket fold and drape? What is the blanket covering? And what is the gestural character we are trying to communicate? We documented each option photographically and scanned the most promising using lidar technology through a readily accessible phone app. These scans generated a digital mesh model which our team translated into Rhino. The scans were initially crude, but they served as an effective foundation for the act of translation between the sculptural object and its digital representation. We could rotate and navigate these models in the context of the project site and test the quality of urban space and the legibility of the gesture at a distance. Through this long day of iterative sculpting and documenting we arrived at what we all agreed would be the definitive gesture: a blanket wrapping the enclosed space of the library that would open to the east, displaying its contents to the street and inviting the community in.

A week later, we reenacted the highlights of the charrette and shared the documentation of both the process and our preferred option with the team from TPL, again at 110 Yonge. The TPL team immediately became engaged and Moe Hosseini-Ara, the director of branch operations, began to play, manipulating not the blanket itself but architectural elements within the enclosure. A key element of the design to date was the "roundhouse," a circular ceremonial gathering space to be located on the library's third floor. We had focused the charrette on the blanket and while the various spaces were implied in the conceptual floor plans, our maquette was still an empty frame. Moe was intent on understanding the relationship between all of the building's design elements and led the charge by lifting first a wastepaper basket (too small) and then a fabric-covered cylindrical pouf (just right) into the interior of the maquette. We were suddenly able to experience the spatial interplay between the blanket and the roundhouse at 1:25. We could see

A maquette and sketch exploring the building envelope

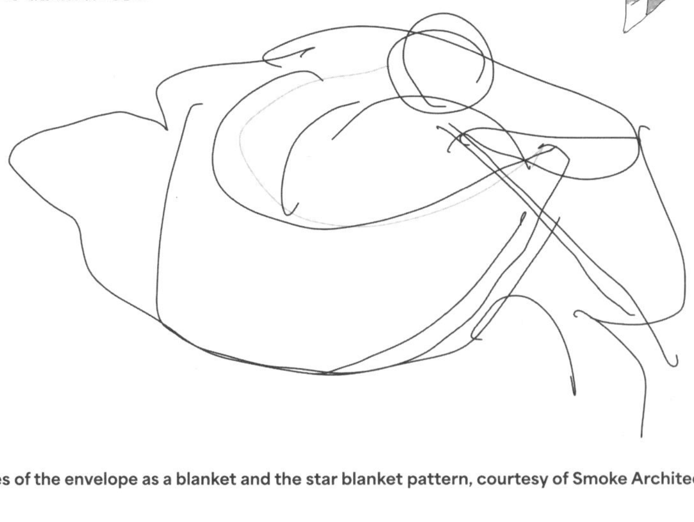

Sketches of the envelope as a blanket and the star blanket pattern, courtesy of Smoke Architecture

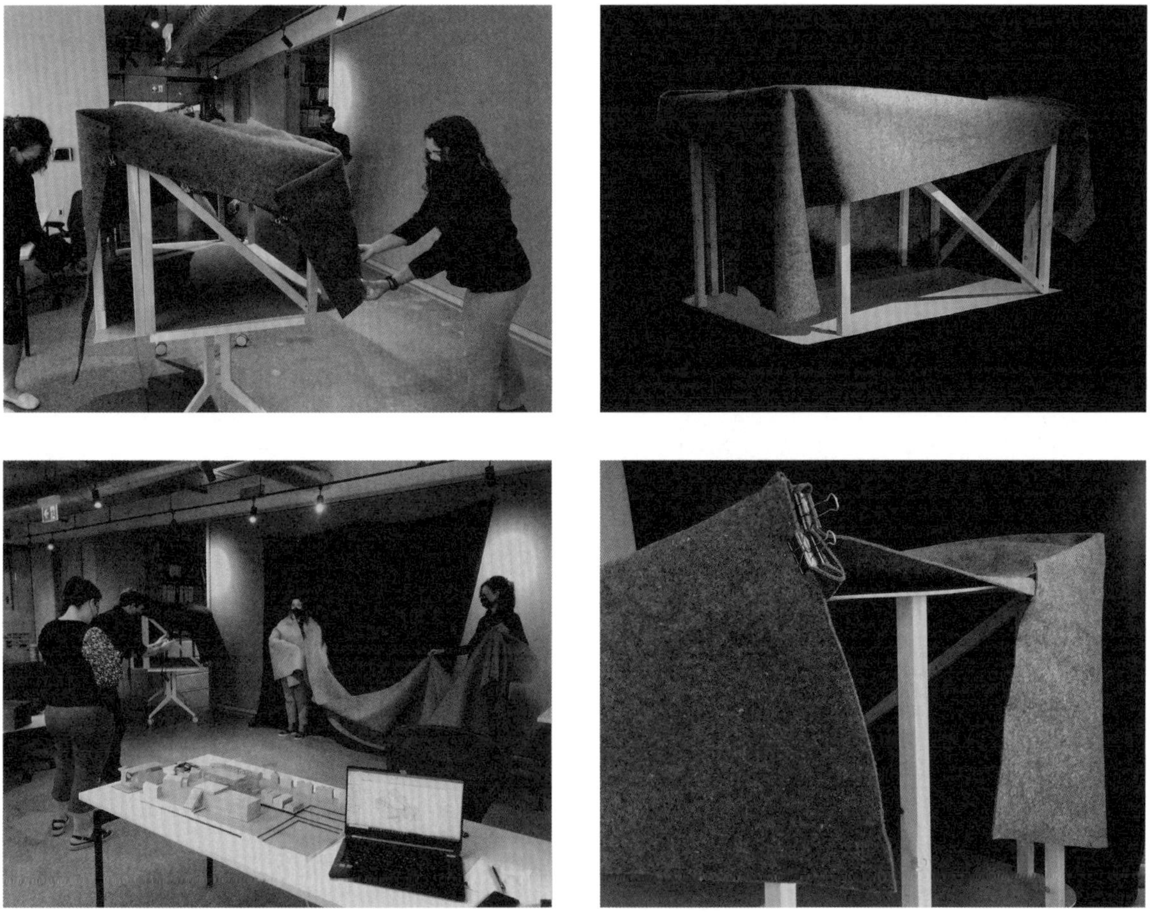

A design charrette with Smoke Architecture in the Perkins&Will Toronto studio

A meeting with the Toronto Public Library client group

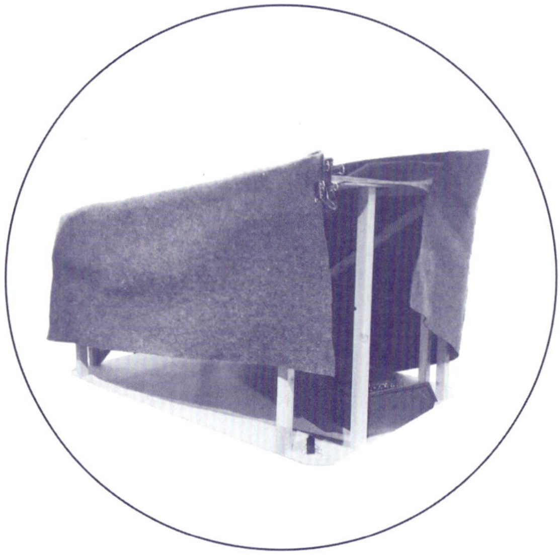

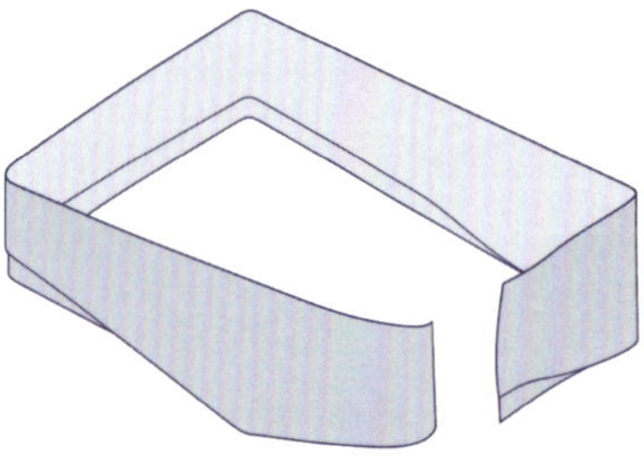

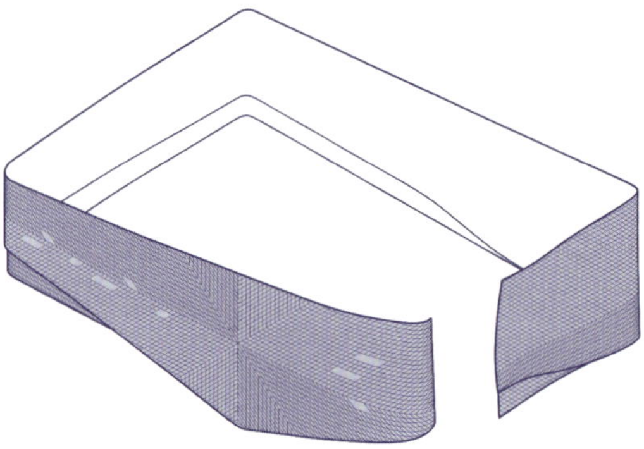

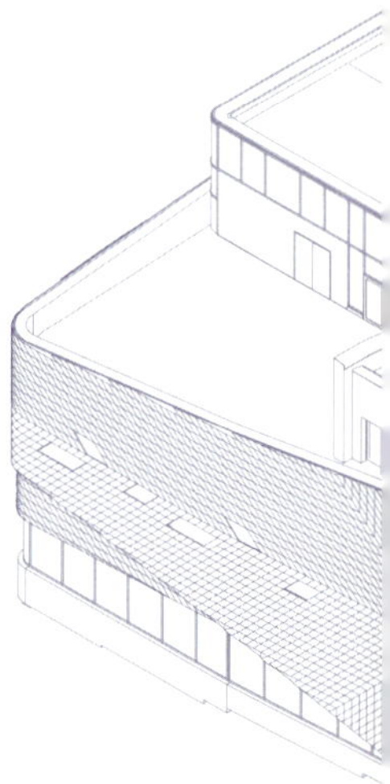

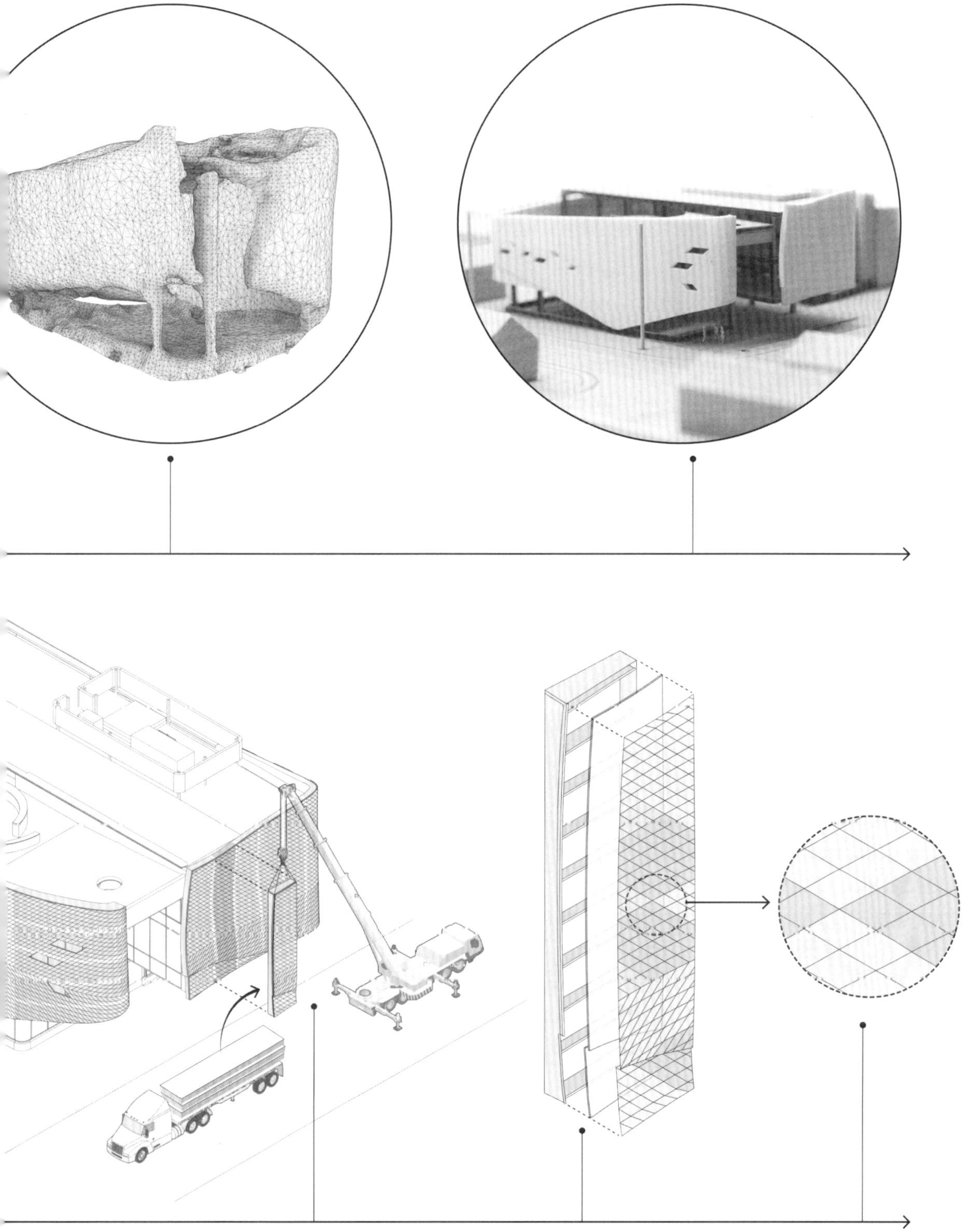

Process map: from performance to sculptural gesture, digital mapping, form evolution and modelling, optimizing the gesture, and formalizing a digital fabrication method and method of modular assembly how the roundhouse would be visible through the opening gesture to the street and how it could reveal itself from the blanket on the third floor. It was through these impromptu explorations that the team established the eventual position of the roundhouse in plan and section, concretizing the project story and spatial relationships. The charrette provided us with a means to travel from a physical gesture at the human scale (wrapping a blanket) through a series of documented steps to an architectural proposition. Along the way it had also created a game that others could play, expanding the notion of authorship beyond the design team.

Of course, the act of communal input into design is not foreign to our practice, but when we collaborate to integrate Indigenous spatial configurations, we reveal an essence of place that's previously been sublimated. Over the first year of the project, Eladia led dozens of conversations with groups and hundreds of individuals, sharing our design progress and asking for input into the project's key cultural references. Before the charrette or even the first sketch, the appropriateness of the blanket as a signifier of architectural meaning was discussed in great depth. After the charrette, the proposed position of the roundhouse was vetted with a group of Elders. When it came time to develop the blanket as a material proposition and colour palette, we again sought and responded to community input.

Eladia and Jennifer looked to the community for direct inspiration, using a collection of star blankets generated by Indigenous artists for TPL as the basis for a study of geometry and colour. In our studio, Michael had been leading designers Flora Mouchel and Shabaan Khokhar in the modelling of the blanket façade with a parallelogram shingle as the base unit of geometry. This shape was the foundation of all the star blankets we had surveyed, and it would influence both the interior and exterior panelization, giving the team ample freedom to explore the many ways that the characteristic star-blanket pattern could be expressed.

While the design conversation and the conceptual direction of the project were progressing nicely, the project was beginning to be stressed from both a technical and budgetary standpoint. Initially, moving from the original lidar scan to Rhino and then into our primary modelling software, Revit, was proving to be a multi-step, time-consuming process. The fact that we were iterating between analog explorations, fluid digital exploration, and technical documentation meant that this cumbersome translation was being carried out repeatedly, draining resources and enthusiasm along the way. At the end of the schematic design phase, our cost estimator reported that we were significantly over budget. The façade was the obvious culprit, and despite the enthusiasm for the design, our client was not prepared to go back to their board for additional funding. It was at this time that I invited a group of design leaders from other Perkins&Will offices to peer review a selection of our in-progress projects. One of the pleasures of being part of a multi-office firm is that you are never alone with a design problem. Our robust in-studio design dialogue can provide a fresh perspective at a moment's notice from any of the 30 studios around the world. Over the years, I have benefited enormously from this extended community, and for the Dawes "virtual pin-up," I decided to invite Nick Cameron, our head of digital practice, to help us navigate some of our tool-based challenges. Once we were all on the call, Nick confessed that he was surprised to be invited to a "design conversation" and wondered if had I made a mistake. I assured him that there was no mistake. The way we design and what we design are inextricably linked. I explained to the group that we were working with a new approach to consultation, a new collaboration, new cultural precedents, and new geometries. We had explored new methodologies, but our digital tools were holding us and the entire consultant team back. We were learning to think differently but we hadn't yet managed to draw differently—if drawing was what was even called for. I explained that beyond our own team, local cost estimators and the building industry didn't understand what we were trying to do. The result was a cumbersome process and an overinflated price tag.

The conversation with Nick proved to be a turning point on two fronts. He introduced us to Rhino Inside, a plug-in that allowed the team to switch at a moment's notice and as the task required between Rhino, where complex parametric geometries were best explored, and Revit, where the integrated model of a multidisciplinary team lived. We could now refine and document in the same model, at the same time. Nick also opened the door to the firm's fledgling partnership with the Kansas City–based digital fabricators Zahner, which gave us access to advanced design-assist services. The team at Zahner helped us refine and optimize our geometry so that the desired forms could be generated with a minimum of material wastage while optimizing robotic fabrication to create prefabricated façade modules. Most importantly, Zahner provided an itemized cost for our entire façade system, from the curvilinear subgirt system to the series of prepatinated zinc cladding panels that would be used to render the star-blanket pattern. It was at this point that we were able to demonstrate the viability of the design to our client and move the project forward into the detailed design phase. While many complex design challenges, convoluted municipal approvals, and long hours of stakeholder engagement lay ahead, the building's conceptual and technical foundations were now understood. In order to breath new life into time-honoured Indigenous cultural precedents, we had been forced to seek new tools and ways of making. In this case, tradition would be the mother of invention.

While Michael, Flora, and Shabaan worked their way through the building's complex geometry, Eladia and her team continued to lead the later rounds of consultation, resolving the final colouration and geometric expression of the star blanket as well as the tectonics of the roundhouse and planning of the roof garden and sacred fire. All of these elements held special significance for Indigenous stake holders and their resolution would be achieved through many long and thoughtful conversations. These conversations represented a significant shift away from the frantic tempo that has characterized most of my professional life. We were grateful to TPL for creating the space for these conversations to occur and out of them a uniquely considered architecture

The cultural precedent of the star blanket

Paper maquette describing a system of interlocking zinc shingles to evolve. But conversations take time and energy, and if the rest of the industry is pushing ahead in a mad rush to the end of civilization, meaningful dialogue can be hard to sustain across all fronts.

During the period that we were developing the detailed design and contract documents for the Dawes Road Library, Smoke Architecture grew from three people to 12 (a quantum leap for a small practice), obliging Eladia to leave her teaching position at Laurentian. The demand for Indigenous design professionals was growing month by month, but mature practitioners take decades to develop, and the pressures being placed on small practices like Smoke and Two Row seemed to many of us to be misaligned with the quest for an authentic cultural expression. Why, all of a sudden, was our society attempting to fast-track Truth and Reconciliation, or rather the image of Truth and Reconciliation as portrayed by architecture? As a white, male practitioner schooled and mentored in western traditions, I have found the process of collaborating with a committed Indigenous practitioner to be both humbling and exhilarating. Our studio and the broader practice of Perkins&Will are deeply committed to a regenerative design philosophy—one where design is used to heal neighbourhoods, communities, and ecosystems. I think we often approach this goal as an equation to be solved—its outcome a graceful technical solution. The process of collaborating on the design of Dawes Road Library taught me that there is a diversity of living cultures in this country that can adopt and spur the innovation of technical solutions to become emboldened and more broadly understood versions of themselves. Regenerative architecture can be a cultural position drawing on ancient knowledge as well as evolving science. Working together, we can perhaps imagine a new Indigenous architectural expression, unique to the peoples and geographies of this vast country. This will take new approaches to collaboration, new methodologies, and new ways of talking about building. Authorship will be imprecise as we will have to work through it together.

When I share these musings with Eladia, she is always surprisingly pragmatic:

"Architecture is about the commodification of the land, you can't get away from that."

The forces that drive production and ultimately the built environment won't stop for an unusual little library, but might they perhaps slow down and adopt different values and express different meanings? As the Dawes Road Library moves into the construction phase, it has garnered quite a bit of attention, requiring Eladia and I to dust off our old costumes and retell the story of the complementary collaboration that won us the job in the first place. Dawes Road won't be a perfect project. Sometimes it seems downright odd to me. But I love it for what it has taught me, and what it and other projects like it will be teaching many thousands of people in the years to come.

In the fall of 2023, Eladia and I traveled to Singapore to present the library at the World Architecture Festival. The day before our scheduled presentation, we sat together in the jungle-like heat and humidity of the Singapore Botanical Gardens rehearsing our densely scripted,

10-minute presentation. I had noticed that day, and in a previous presentation to a national library conference, that while I tended to tell the same story about the project and its evolutions every time we presented, Eladia kept layering on new meanings and associations, such as the significance of the clan mother bay in the roundhouse typology and the nuances of how the ceremonial fire would be used. I was a bit concerned about the timing of our script and eventually asked her about this tendency. She reminded me that our perceptions and understandings are always expanding. That we can come to know our creations as we make them and after we make them. After all, culture is a verb.

Client	Toronto Public Library
Location	Toronto, Canada
Size	2,200 gross square metres
Date	2021-2026

Rendering showing the façade's star-blanket pattern

View from the southwest

Approaching from the west

The main lobby and performance space

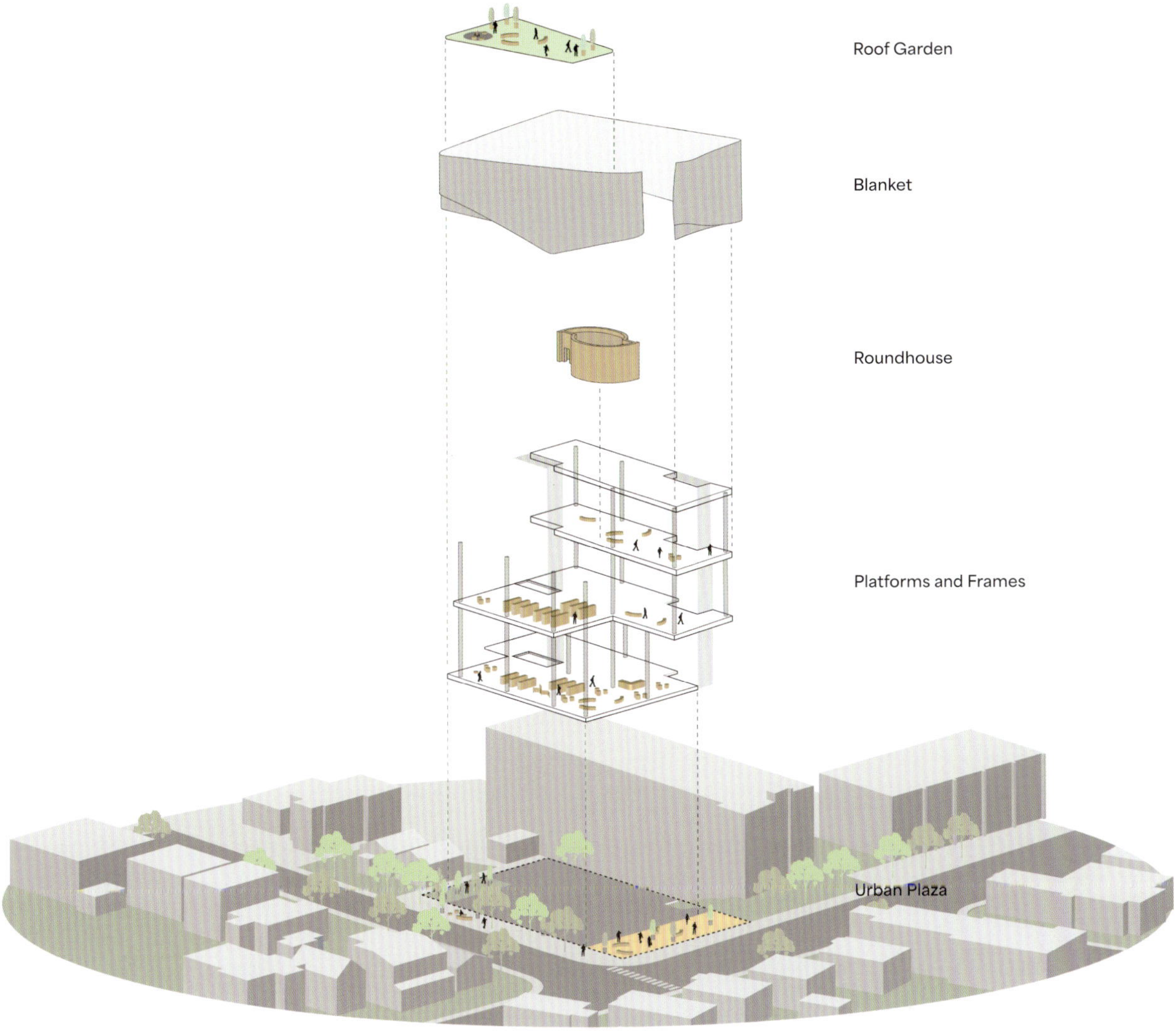

Exploded axonometric with elements of the design

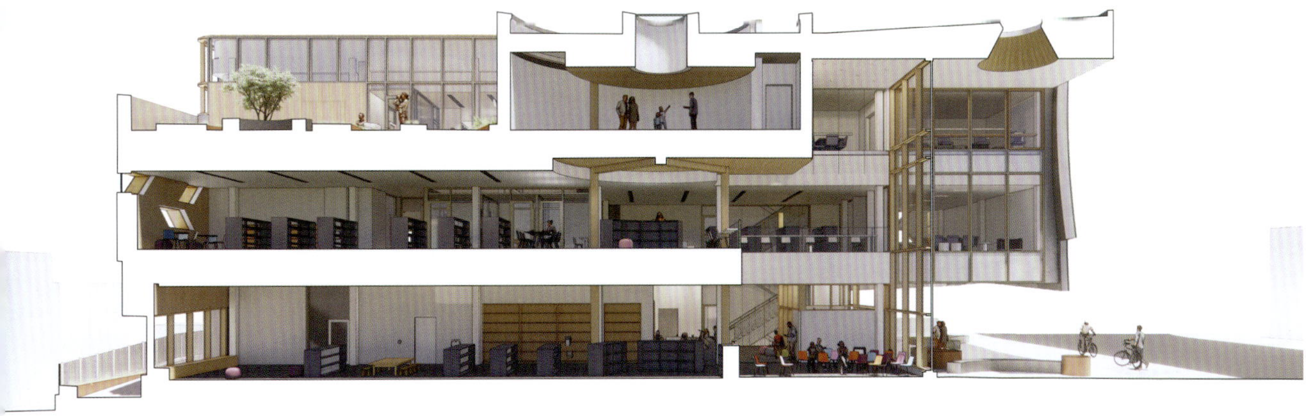

A section perspective

EOPLES COLLECTION

NATIVE PEOPLES COLLECTION

The [illegible]

Level 03 community kitchen

Site and Level 01 Plan

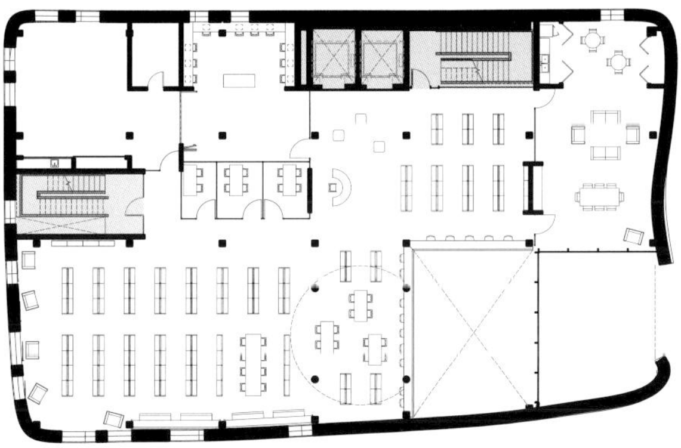

Level 02 Plan

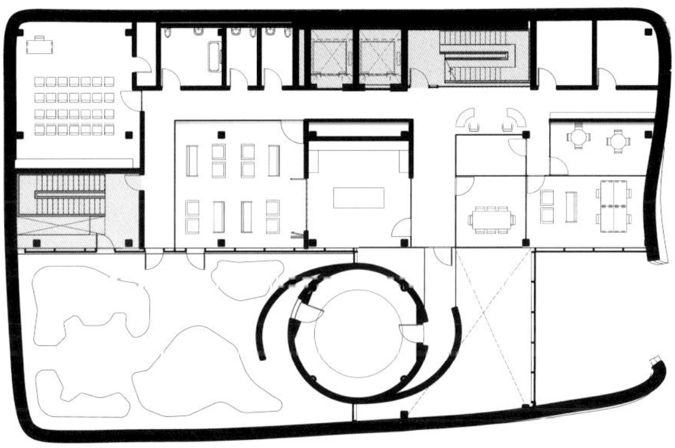

Level 03 Plan

Entrance on Dawes Road

1989
Private Residence
Stella, Ontario

1995
Laneway Studio
Toronto, Ontario

2003
Westmount Branch Library
London, Ontario

2004
Grimsby Library and Art Gallery
Grimsby, Ontario

Bruce Peninsula National Park Visitor Centre
Tobermory, Ontario

2005
Whitby Public Library and Civic Square
Whitby, Ontario

2007
Hazel McCallion Academic Learning Centre
University of Toronto
Mississauga, Ontario

2008
Holly Community Centre
Barrie, Ontario

2009
Cassie Campbell Community Centre
Brampton, Ontario

2010
Claudette McKay Lassonde Pavilion
Western University
London, Ontario

Engineering 5
University of Waterloo
Waterloo, Ontario

Brooklin Community Centre and Library
Whitby, Ontario

Stoney Creek Community Centre, YMCA & Library
London, Ontario

2011
Instruction Building
University of Toronto
Mississauga, Ontario

2012
Brant Sports Complex
Paris, Ontario

Oak Ridges Community Centre
Richmond Hill, Ontario

Orillia Public Library and Farmers' Market Square
Orillia, Ontario

2013
Roche Canada Head Office
Mississauga, Ontario

Rath Eastlink Community Centre
Truro, Nova Scotia

Darryl J. King Student Life Centre
King's University College
London, Ontario

Dining Pavilion and Student Residence
Brescia University College
London, Ontario

2014
Deerfield Hall
University of Toronto
Mississauga, Ontario

Minto Recreation Complex
Ottawa, Ontario

2015
Meadowvale Community Centre and Library
Mississauga, Ontario

2016
Nathan Phillips Square Revitalization
Toronto, Ontario

2017
Meadows Community Centre
Edmonton, Alberta

Bank of Canada Head Office Renewal
Ottawa, Ontario

Albion Library
Toronto, Ontario

2018
Amit Chakma Engineering Building
Western University
London, Ontario

Maanjiwe nendamowinan
University of Toronto
Mississauga, Ontario

Engineering 7
University of Waterloo
Waterloo, Ontario

2019
Highland Hall
University of Toronto
Scarborough, Ontario

STEM Complex
University of Ottawa
Ottawa, Ontario

Daphne Cockwell Health Sciences Complex
Toronto Metropolitan University
Toronto, Ontario

Southfields Community Centre and Library
Caledon, Ontario

Centre for Technology, Innovation and Entrepreneurship (CITE)
Seneca Polytechnic
Toronto, Ontario

2022
School of Continuing Studies
York University
Toronto, Ontario

2023
Weldon Library Revitalization
Western University
London, Ontario

2024
Multi-Use Recreation Complex
Georgina, Ontario

Ronald D. Schmeichel Building for Entrepreneurship and Innovation
Western University
London, Ontario

Whitby Public Library and Civic Square
Client: Town of Whitby and Whitby Public Library
Perkins&Will Team: D'Arcy Arthurs, Andrew Frontini, Frank Park, Dimitri Simos, Mark Downing, Lene Otbo Rozel, Liz Livingston

Sub Consultants
Structural: Meads Engineering Limited
Mechanical: Smith and Andersen Engineering Consulting
Electrical: Crossey Engineering Limited
Civil: MMM Group
Landscape: MBTW Group
Environmental Graphics: Telmut Design
General Contractor: Bondfield Construction Company

Photography
Model: Andrew Frontini
Project: Ben Rahn at A Frame

Hazel McCallion Academic Learning Centre
Client: University of Toronto at Mississauga
Perkins&Will Team: D'Arcy Arthurs, Andrew Frontini, Frank Park, Dimitri Simos, Doug Warren, Larry Silva, Linda Neumayer, Philip O'Sullivan, Marc Downing, Lene Otbo Rozel, Liz Livingston

Sub Consultants
Structural: Yolles Partnership Inc.
Mechanical: Smith and Andersen Consulting Engineering
Electrical: Mulvey & Banani
Landscape: MBTW Group
CBIP/LEED Engineer: Enermodal Engineering
General Contractor: Eastern Construction Limited

Photography
Model: Andrew Frontini
Project: Ben Rahn at A Frame

Instruction Building
Client: University of Toronto Mississauga
Perkins&Will Team: D'Arcy Arthurs, Andrew Frontini, Alan Mortsch, Michelle Sta Ana, Larry Silva, Harold Mendoza, Anne Ma, Claudia Bader, Alice Wong

Sub Consultants
Structural: EXP
Mechanical: Crossey Engineering Ltd.
Electrical: Lapas Consulting Engineers Limited
Civil: MMM Group
Landscape: Fleisher Ridout Partnership Inc.
Heritage: Eastern
Sustainability: Zon Engineering
General Contractor: Eastern Construction

Photography
Model: Andrew Frontini
Project: Ben Rahn at A Frame & James Britain

Engineering 5
Client: University of Waterloo
Perkins&Will Team: Andrew Frontini, David Mitchell, Werner Sommer, John Potter, Aimee Drmic, Larry Silva, Gavin Guthrie, Athir Jamil, Heath Churchill, Elizabeth Livingston, Cameron Turvey, Clara Shipman, Perry Edwards
Associate Architect: Joe Somfay

Sub Consultants
Structural: Read Jones Christoffersen Ltd.
Mechanical: Smith and Andersen Consulting Engineering
Electrical: Crossey Engineering Ltd.
Landscape: GSP Group
General Contractor: Bondfield Construction

Photography
Younes Bounhar at Double Space, Lisa Logan, Michael Muraz

Engineering 7
Client: University of Waterloo
Perkins&Will Team: Andrew Frontini, Linda Neumayer, Liz Tseronakis, James Mallinson, Werner Sommer, Joanne D'Silva, Anna Beznogova, Edward Lin, Alan Mortsch, Michael Blois, Will Daravong, Jared Cardiff

Sub Consultants
Structural: Read Jones Christoffersen Ltd.
Mechanical: Smith and Andersen Consulting Engineering
Electrical: Crossey Engineering Ltd.
Civil: MTE Consultants
Landscape: GSP Group
General Contractor: EllisDon

Photography
Project: Younes Bounhar at Double Space, Lisa Logan, Michael Muraz

Meadowvale Community Centre and Library
Client: City of Mississauga
Perkins&Will Team: Andrew Frontini, Phil Fenech, Douglas Warren, Aimee Drmic, Jon Loewen, Joanne D'Silva, Tamara Schmidt, Zeina Elali, Will Daravong, Jared Cardiff

Sub Consultants
Structural: Entuitive Corporation
Mechanical & Electrical: Smith and Andersen Consulting Engineering
Civil: WSP Canada Inc.
Landscape: Fleisher Ridout Partnership Inc.
General Contractor: Aquicon Construction Co. Ltd.

Photography
Model: Andrew Frontini, Jon Loewen
Site: Andrew Frontini, Phil Fenech
Project: Andrew Frontini, Lisa Logan, Rodrigo Chavez

Bank of Canada Headquarters Renewal
Client: Bank of Canada
Perkins&Will Team: Andrew Frontini, Joe Connell, D'Arcy Arthurs, Fred Vermeulen, Matt Johnston, Lara Leskaj, Jennifer Carzoli, Courtney Ruhl, Werner Sommer, Robert Van Lin, Sara Barrett, Wade Brown, Mary Anne Bull, Stan Bury, Audrey Caron, Lauren Clack, Nicholas Cross, Robert Currie, Madelyn Delgado, Ivan Desroches, Joanne D'Silva, Sara Feigl, Kat Forget, Mark Ganassin, Patrick Grzybek, Catarina Guimaraes, Gavin Guthrie, Julia Hansen, Becky Hinss, Stephen Kolacki, Adrienne Kromm, Camerson Laabs, Martin Lariviere, Bridget Lesniak, Ranee Leung, Jay Lim, Michelle Malecha, Michael Margulis, Austin Modern, Smita Modi, Alan Mortsch, Ali Navid-Bakhsh, Luc Nugent, Clayton Payer, John Pellegrino, Donald Peters, John Potter, Anthony Prince, Talayeh Rad, Shari Roberts, Nilakshi Roy, Courtney Ruhl, Murali Selvaraj, Angelo Sferrazza, Peter Shupe, Paula Swanborough, Jason Sweers, Stephen Vandeermeer, Sarah Wybenga, Debbie Young, Mathew Zelensek

Sub Consultants
Structural: Adjeleian Allen Rubeli
Mechanical & Electrical: BPA
Landscape: DTAH
Heritage: EVOQ
General Contractor: PCL Constructors Canada

Photography
Model: Andrew Frontini
Site: John Potter
Project: Younes Bounhar at Double Space, Lisa Logan

Albion Library
Client: Toronto Public Library
Perkins&Will Team: D'Arcy Arthurs, Andrew Frontini, Aimee Drmic, Jason Nelson, Stephen Vandermere, Inga Kantor, Yasmeen Bebal

Sub Consultants
Structural: Blackwell Structural Engineers
Mechanical: Hidi Rae Consulting Engineers
Electrical: Mulvey & Banani International Inc.
Civil: MMM Group
Landscape: DTAH
General Contractor: Aquicon Construction Company Ltd.

Photography
Model & Site Context: Andrew Frontini
Project: Younes Bounhar at Double Space, Toronto Public Library

Daphne Cockwell Health Science Complex
Client: Toronto Metropolitan University
Perkins&Will Team: D'Arcy Arthurs, Andrew Frontini, Ryan Bragg, Jon Loewen, Max Richter, Kimberly Baba, Yasin Visram, Gayle Meeks, Mona Lemoine, Manuela Londono Suarez, Ed Lin, James Mallinson, Dan McTavish, Alan Mortsch, Irene Neven, Elsa Snyder, Eli Wolpin

Sub Consultants
Structural: WSP Canada Inc.
Mechanical: MCW, External Link
Electrical: Crossey Engineering Ltd.
Civil: MMM Group, WSP Canada Inc.
Landscape: DTAH
Environmental/Geotechnical: SPL Consultants Ltd.
General Contractor: Eastern Construction Company Ltd.

Photography
Workshop: Yvone Bambrick
Model: Jon Loewen
Project: Tom Arban, Younes Bounhar at Double Space, Lisa Logan, Toronto Metropolitan University

STEM Complex
Client: University of Ottawa
Perkins&Will Team: Andrew Frontini, Safdar Abidi, Matt Johnston, Jan-Willem Gritters, Dan McTavish, Ali Navidbakhsh, Gary McNay, Zeina Elali, Diana Smiciklas, Luc Nugent, Lauren Clack

Sub Consultants
Structural: Cleland Jardine
Mechanical & Electrical: BPA
Civil: Novatech
Landscape: Lashley & Associates
General Contractor: PCL

Photography
Studio Mock-Up: Lisa Logan
Site Mock-Up: Andrew Frontini
Project: Younes Bounhar at Double Space, Kevin Belanger, Toronto Metropolitan University

School of Continuing Studies
Client: York University
Perkins&Will Team: Andrew Frontini, Safdar Abidi, Alan Mortsch, Dan McTavish, Jon Loewen, Gayle Meeks, Anna Beznogova, Cheney Chen, Will Daravong, Cyrille Futcha, Evgueni Litvinenko, Tsvetelina Rabashki, Paul Wong, Martha del Junco, Tarisha Dolyniuk

Sub Consultants
Structural: Entuitive Corporation
Mechanical & Electrical: Smith and Andersen Consulting Engineering
Landscape: DTAH
Building Envelope: RDH Building Science Inc.
General Contractor: Aquicon Construction

Photography
Model & Construction: Lisa Logan
Mock-up: Dan McTavish
Project: Younes Bounhar at Double Space, Tom Arban

Dawes Road Library
Client: Toronto Public Library
Perkins&Will Team: Andrew Frontini, Linda Neumayer, Michael Blois, Flora Mouchel, Shabaan Khokhar, Martha del Junco, Mikel Calleja Gonzalez
Smoke Architecture Team: Eladia Smoke, Jennifer Kinnumen, Chelsea Jacobs

Sub Consultants
Structural: Entuitive Corporation
Mechanical & Electrical: The Hidi Group
Civil: Husson Limited
Landscape: Fleisher Ridout Partnership Inc.

Photography
Backyard Maquette: Lisa Logan
Model: Andrew Frontini
Workshop & Mock-Up: Shabaan Khokhar
Star Blanket Model: Eladia Smoke

New Montreal Justice Complex
Client: Public Services and Procurement Canada (PSPC)
Perkins&Will Team: Matt Johnston, Robert Van Lin, Andrew Frontini, Samuel Houle, Danielle Leon, John Sicat, Drilla Gibney, Lindsey Furik
Joint Venture Architectural Team: A49 Bruno Verenini, Isabelle Julien, Viviane Zhang, Hugo Cloutier, Émilie Marcoux, Frédérique Fortin, Émilie Julien

Sub Consultants
Structural: WSP
Mechanical: Tetra Tech
Electrical: WSP, Tetra Tech
Civil: WSP
General Contractor: Pomerleau Inc.

Photography
Model: Shabaan Khokhar

Western Ronald Schmeichel Entrepreneurship and Innovation Complex
Client: Western University
Perkins&Will Team: Andrew Frontini, Safdar Abidi, Alan Mortsch, David D'Andrea, Aimee Drmic, Rafaela Kirloss, Martha del Junco, Anna Beznogova, Reham Jaradat, Nathanael Scheffler, John Sicat

Photography
Project: Lisa Logan

Sub Consultants
Associate Architects: Cornerstone Architects
Structural: VanBoxmeer & Stranges Engineering Ltd.
Mechanical & Electrical: Chorley & Bisset Ltd.
Civil: Development Engineering Limited
Landscape: Ron Koudys Landscape
General contractor: Hayman Construction

Highland Hall
Client: University of Toronto Scarborough
Perkins&Will Team: D'Arcy Arthurs, Andrew Frontini, Philip O'Sullivan, Ramin Rad, Damineh Dehnadfar; Hala Akkawil; Hamza Alhbian; Benjamin Gaum, Michelle Sta. Ana, Devon Miller, Adrian Worton

Sub Consultants
Structural: Entuitive Corporation
Mechanical: Crossey Engineering Ltd.
Electrical: Mulvey & Banani International Inc.
Civil: MMM Group
Landscape: Fleisher Ridout Partnership Inc.
General Contractor: Aquicon Construction

Photography
Tom Arban

Orillia Public Library and Farmers' Market Square
Client: The City of Orillia
Perkins&Will Team: D'Arcy Arthurs, Andrew Frontini, Werner Sommer, Joe Dhanjal, Michelle Sta Ana

Sub Consultants
Structural: Yolles
Mechanical: Smith and Andersen Consulting Engineering
Electrical: Mulvey & Banani International Inc.
Civil: MMM Group
Landscape: MBTW
Sustainability: Enermodal Engineering
Building Envelope: Zec Consulting
General Contractor: Aquicon Construction

Photography
Model: Andrew Frontini
Project: Ben Rahn at A Frame

Brooklin Community Centre and Library
Client: Town of Whitby
Perkins&Will Team: D'Arcy Arthurs, Andrew Frontini, Linda Neumayer, Liz Livingston, Aimee Drmic, Sarah Elliot, Gavin Guthrie, Dimitri Simos

Sub Consultants
Structural: Blackwell Bowick Partnership
Mechanical: Smith and Andersen Consulting Engineering
Electrical: Mulvey & Banani International Inc.
Civil: MMM Group
Landscape: Fleisher Ridout Partnership Inc.
General Contractor: Aquicon Construction

Photography
James Britain

Nathan Phillips Square Revitalization
Client: City of Toronto
Perkins&Will Team: D'Arcy Arthurs, Andrew Frontini, Vis Sankrithi, Joe Dhanjal, Linda Neumayer, Adrian Worton, Steven Vandermeer, Gavin Guthrie, Lia Matson, Elizabeth Tseronakis, Perry Edwards, Aaron Cheung, Aimee Drmic, Emily Maclenna, Tala Rameh
Joint Venture Architectural Team (PLANT): Chris Pommer, Lisa Rapoport, Mary Tremain, Vanessa Eickhoff, Lisa Dietrich, Eric Klaver, Elise Shelley, Lisa Moffitt, Jane Hutton, Heather Asquith, Suzanne Ernst, Jessica Craig, Jeremy McGregor, Matt Hartney, Cleo Buster, Renee Kuehnle, Oliva Mapue

Sub Consultants
Structural: Blackwell Structural Engineers
Mechanical & Electrical: Crossey Engineering Ltd.
Landscape: Hoerr Schaudt Landscape Architecture Inc.
Urban Furnishings: Adrian Blackwell Urban Projects
Heritage: Blanche Lemco Van Ginkel
Green Building System: Enermodal Engineering
General Contractor: Flynn Canada/Gardens in the Sky; PCL Constructors Canada; Four Seasons Site Development

Photography
Project: Steve Evans

Maanjiwe nendamowinan
Client: University of Toronto Mississauga
Perkins&Will Team: D'Arcy Arthurs, Andrew Frontini, Aimee Drmic, Alan Mortsch, Zeina Elali, Jon Loewen, Ramin Rezaeirad, Renee Leung, Hamza Ahlbian, Juan Portuese, Martha del Junco

Sub Consultants
Structural: Read Jones Christoffersen Ltd.
Mechanical: Integral Group
Electrical: Lapas Consulting Engineers Limited
Civil: MTE Consultants
Landscape: Fleisher Ridout Partnership
General Contractor: Stuart Olson

Photography
Lisa Logan

Centre for Innovation, Technology, and Entrepreneurship (CITE)
Client: Seneca Polytechnic
Perkins&Will Team: Andrew Frontini, Safdar Abidi, Alan Mortsch, Ramin Rad, David D'Andrea, Zeina Elali, Janine Grossmann, Tsvetelina Rabashki, Martha del Junco, Martin Lariviere, Somaye Bamati, Thea Sarkissian, Edward Lin, Will Daravong, Liz Tseronakis

Sub Consultants
Structural: Read Jones Christoffersen Ltd.
Mechanical & *Electrical:* Smith and Andersen Consulting Engineering
Civil: MMM Group
Landscape: John Quinn Design
Environmental Graphics: Bruce Mau Design
General Contractor: EllisDon

Photography
Younes Bounhar at Double Space

Additional Photography
Page 6: Lisa Samuda
Page 13: Andrew Frontini
Page 415: Lisa Logan

Acknowledgments

This book, and all the work represented and referred to within it, would not be possible without a wonderful community of colleagues, friends, and family.

First and foremost, I would like to acknowledge the comradery, support, and inspiration provided by the team at Perkins&Will Toronto/Ottawa. Without a team we are nothing. A big thank you to the entire Perkins&Will community across the globe. I am proud to be one of you. The burden of purpose is best shared.

I would like to thank my partners at the Toronto/Ottawa principals' table: Safdar Abidi, Janine Grossmann, Paul Kulig, Jon Loewen, and in particular my long-standing partners D'Arcy Arthurs, Linda Neumayer, Duff Balmer, and Phil Fenech, who turned the ship around and steered it to a new port. Thanks to Susan Gushe and Peter Busby for connecting us with Perkins&Will in the first place and to Peter for mentoring me and sharing his talent, relationships, and insights with grace and generosity. Thanks to Phil Harrison (the best boss a guy could have) for guidance, support, and friendship. To my board buddies Gina Berndt, Manuel Cadrecha, Yanel de Angel, David Dymecki, Chris Hardie, Zena Howard, Kay Kornovich, Richard Marshall, Lindsey Peckinpaugh, and Tom Reisenbichler–thank you for a masterclass in strategy! Thanks to Kristian Ahlmark, Pat Bosch, Linzi Cassels, Casey Jones, Ralph Johnson, Elif Tinaztepe, Tim Wolfe, Manuel, and Chris for creating, maintaining, and expanding a culture of design excellence.

Thanks to my family: Gianfranco and Patricia Frontini for teaching me how to spend my time, and Thomas Frontini for living the life of the artist so I didn't have to. Thanks to Lisa Logan for general tolerance, for great photography, and for reminding me to "enjoy the process" and that there is "always another way."

Thanks to Giuliana, Felix, and Zipora for growing up right in the house that architecture built. Thanks to Roisin for supporting me in the "foundation years."

Thanks to all of the builders who have tried to teach me what to draw and to all of my clients for having faith in the power of design.

Thank you to my mentors: Peter Busby, John Ferguson, Peter Ferguson, Mark Franklin, Fabio Frontini, Rick Haldenby, Martin Liefhebber, Nolan Natale, John Schnier, Tim Scott, and Dimitri Simos. Thank you to Brad Golden and John Potter for believing in me and connecting me to the right people and opportunities.

Thanks to the following people who read drafts and offered the constructive criticism that shaped this book, including Ian Chodikoff, Rita Listner, Lia Maston, Dan McTavish, and many others whose names appear above and below. Special thanks to Thalia Ilechukwu for her design talent and critical input in shaping the first complete working draft of the book. Thanks to Grace Sample, George Tsivikas, and Cindy He for preparing all of the orthographic drawings.

Thanks to my collaborators Michael Aberman, Adam Michaels, and Shannon Harvey at IN-FO.CO for design and collaboration on the final book concept, and to my editor Ned Cramer for helping me shape the story and pull all the threads together. Thank you to Federica Ewing, Gordon Goff, and the team at ORO Editions for publishing, distributing, and "learning me up" to get it all across the finish line.

And lastly a very special thanks to anyone I might have forgotten: You know who you are and how indebted I am.

Author
Andrew Frontini, OAA, FRAIC, LEED BC&C, grew up in Kingston, Ontario, where, as a youngster, he developed a passion for art, music, and messing around in boats. Andrew was drawn to architecture through the sage advice of his uncle Fabio, a Milanese architect who convinced him that "all of the other arts happen inside architecture." Andrew studied at the University of Waterloo and through its architecture co-op program lived and worked in Montreal and Rome before settling in Toronto in the early '90s.

Since 2010, Andrew has served as the design director of Perkins&Will's Toronto and Ottawa Studios. Andrew's approach to design is driven by a strong social agenda, and he uses bold material expressions and considered responses to context to create spaces around which communities form. By maintaining a design philosophy that is open and collaborative, Andrew never stops learning, producing, and evolving. His award-winning designs for universities, municipalities, library systems, and federal and commercial clients have been published internationally.

Andrew has taught at the University of Toronto, Toronto Metropolitan University, and the University of Waterloo, where he remains a visiting critic. He shares his passion for design through exhibitions, published articles, and speaking engagements. Andrew is a member of Perkins&Will's board of directors and design board, through which he contributes to the firm's commitment to design excellence and overall strategic direction.

Essayist
Ian Chodikoff is a licensed architect with over 25 years of experience influencing how we see, discuss, and shape the built environment. He has led advocacy and strategic planning initiatives for municipalities, real estate developers, design firms, and cultural organizations. Ian has created and participated in numerous research projects, exhibitions, publications, marketing campaigns, and events related to architecture and placemaking. He has served as the executive director of the Royal Architectural Institute of Canada, editor-in-chief of *Canadian Architect* magazine, and director of educational programming for international design conferences. He serves on numerous boards, has taught at several universities, and has spoken at conferences and academic institutions worldwide. Ian is deeply committed to fostering inclusive community partnerships, bridging gaps relating to design innovation and promoting regenerative strategies. He holds graduate degrees in architecture and urban design from the University of British Columbia and Harvard University.

Editor
Ned Cramer is a partner in Cramer|Kroloff, an architecture, art, and design consultancy. From 2020 to 2022 he served as co-curator of the American Institute of Architects Conference on Architecture, and from 2006 to 2020 he served as editor-in-chief of *Architect*, the journal of the AIA. He was also vice president, editorial, for *Architect*'s publisher, Hanley Wood, helping oversee some 30 building-industry media brands.

Before launching *Architect*, Ned was the first full-time curator of the Chicago Architecture Foundation and executive editor of *Architecture* magazine. He co-curated the U.S. Pavilion at the 2012 Venice Architecture Biennale, "Spontaneous Interventions: Design Actions for the Common Good." He is the recipient of an arts administration fellowship from the National Endowment for the Arts, and in that capacity worked in the endowment's design program and at the National Building Museum.

Ned has been a trustee of the alternative design school Archeworks and a member of the U.S. General Services Administration's Design Excellence National Peer Registry, the selection committee for the National Building Museum's Scully Prize, and the Cranbrook Academy of Art National Advisory Committee. He received a bachelor's degree from the Rice University School of Architecture, where he also did graduate work in art and architecture history. Ned was born and raised in St. Louis and now lives outside Washington, D.C.

Designer
IN-FO.CO (Inventory Form & Content) is an independent design and editorial studio. Their work encompasses graphic design, spatial design, strategy, and content development–frequently in tandem, and always with an exceptionally high level of attention to detail.

Founded in Los Angeles by Adam Michaels and Shannon Harvey, IN-FO.CO extends the National Design Award-winning practice Project Projects (New York City, 2004-2017). In addition, the firm publishes books on topics in art, architecture, design, and music through their imprint Inventory Press.

The studio's work has been collected by the Museum of Modern Art Library, Design Museum London, the Vassar College Art Library, and New York University Fales Library, amongst others, and an extensive set of Adam Michaels's Project Projects work was acquired by the Art Institute of Chicago for its permanent collection.

The author

Brooklin Community Centre and Library, Whitby, Ontario

ORILLIA PUBLIC

Orillia Public Library and Farmers' Market Square, Orillia, Ontario

Highland Hall, University of Toronto Scarborough, Scarborough, Ontario

Centre for Innovation, Technology and Entrepreneurship, Seneca Polytechnic, Toronto, Ontario

Western University, Ronald D. Schmeichel Entrepreneurship and Innovation Complex

BISTRO MIMMO

Federal Justice Complex, Montreal

Daphne Cockwell Health Sciences Complex